D1526997

Ethnic Groups
and Social Change
in a Chinese Market Town

The Market Town of Sai Kung

Asian Studies at Hawaii, No. 27

Ethnic Groups
and Social Change
in a Chinese Market Town

C. Fred Blake

Asian Studies Program
UNIVERSITY OF HAWAII
THE UNIVERSITY PRESS OF HAWAII

Copyright © 1981 by C. Fred Blake
Manufactured in the United States of America

Library of Congress Cataloging in Publication Data

Blake, C Fred, 1942–
    Ethnic groups and social change in a Chinese market town.

    (Asian studies at Hawaii; no. 27)
    Bibliography: p.
    Includes index.
    1. New Territories, Hongkong—Social conditions.
2. Ethnicity—Case studies. 3. Hakkas.
I. Title. II. Series.
DS3.A2A82 no. 27 [HN754.N48]   950s [305.8'00951'25]
ISBN 0–8248–0720–0   80–16978

to Linda,
Lisa,
Carl,
and to my mother and father

Contents

PLATES — viii

MAPS, FIGURES, AND TABLE — ix

PREFACE — xi

ACKNOWLEDGMENTS — xvii

WEIGHTS, MEASURES, AND MONETARY EXCHANGE RATES — xix

CHAPTER 1   INTRODUCTION — 1

CHAPTER 2   DIMENSIONS OF ETHNICITY IN SOUTH CHINA — 7

CHAPTER 3   DEVELOPMENT OF SAI KUNG SOCIETY: 1842–1972 — 19

CHAPTER 4   ETHNIC GROUPS AND ETHNIC RHETORICS — 49

CHAPTER 5   ETHNIC GROUP CULTURE — 91

CHAPTER 6   FORMATION OF THE LOCAL HAKKA ESTABLISHMENT — 118

CHAPTER 7   THE CHAOCHOW RENEGOTIATE SAI KUNG SOCIAL ORGANIZATION — 133

CHAPTER 8   CONCLUSION: ETHNICITY AS A SOCIOCULTURAL PROCESS — 148

GLOSSARY OF CHINESE WORDS — 159

REFERENCES CITED — 161

INDEX — 173

Plates

FRONTISPIECE	The Market Town of Sai Kung	ii
PLATE 1	A Cantonese Boat Woman Making a Purchase from a Hakka Vegetable Vendor	40
PLATE 2	A Hakka Village Woman Hawking Her Cakes to a Boat Woman	52
PLATE 3	Hakka Village Women Preparing a Wedding Feast	53
PLATE 4	Hakka Women Working on a Construction Site	56
PLATE 5	The Sai Kung Hokkien Boat Community	73
PLATE 6	Hokkien Boat Children Playing in the Refuse-Strewn Tide Pools	74
PLATE 7	A Motorized Cantonese Boat	75
PLATE 8	A Hokkien Boat	76
PLATE 9	Mrs. Shek's Offering to the Deities on the Household's Altar	81
PLATE 10	Hakka Ancestral Hall	92
PLATE 11	Cantonese Boat People's Ancestral Icons	94
PLATE 12	The Floral Shrines of Various Firecracker Associations	97
PLATE 13	The Chaochow Spirit Place	101

Maps

MAP 1	Southeastern Coastal China	6
MAP 2	The Kwangchow-Waichow Region of Kwangtung	9
MAP 3	Sai Kung and Eastern Paoan County, 1866	20
MAP 4	Sai Kung Market Town, 1971	27

Figures

FIGURE 1	Development and Alignment of Associations in Sai Kung Market, 1971	33
FIGURE 2	Organization of Fish Marketing in Sai Kung, 1971	37
FIGURE 3	Marriage Network of a Cantonese Lineage	64
FIGURE 4	Marriage Network of a Hakka Lineage	65
FIGURE 5	The Chan Lineage Commercial Expansion	123

Table

TABLE 1	Sai Kung Tin Hau Temple Firecracker Associations of 1972	95

Preface

Since 1950 the anthropological study of South China has been squeezed into the territorial hinterlands controlled by the Crown Colony of Hong Kong. This area of several hundred square kilometers has sustained such a disproportionate amount of field research that by the time I was ready to embark upon my doctoral dissertation study of Chinese ethnic groups there was hardly a district that had not been the site of major anthropological research. My proposal aimed to study the nature of ethnic grouping by observing how Hakka, Cantonese, Hokkien, and boat people group themselves in a particular local setting. The Sai Kung market area seemed to offer the most appropriate site for conducting such a study.

The Sai Kung area was represented in the anthropological literature by Professor Barbara Ward's study of the Kau Sai boat people and by Professor Göran Aijmer's study of a Hakka village on the north slope of the Sai Kung penninsula. Their studies, in addition to their personal advice, further spurred my own interest in the area because of its particular weave of ethnic minorities. Indeed, the weave of ethnic groups turned out to be far more complex than I anticipated. By 1971 the area had become a very complex patchwork of boat people, land people, Hakka, Cantonese, and Hokkien-speaking local and immigrant groups. In addition to being a variegated patchwork of ethnic groups, Sai Kung was also circumscribed by hills and sea which made it somewhat remote from the concrete jungle of Kowloon and among the least developed areas of the Hong Kong hinterland. In 1971, the market town was still a tight little cluster of shops and houses surrounded by village rice paddies and immigrant vegetables plots, a scene that one might have expected to encounter in a Chinese storybook more readily than in Hong Kong. Aside from gratifying my own romantic sensibility, this situation facilitated the theoretical description of ethnicity as a function of a local social system.

On an August evening in 1971, my wife, Linda Chock, daughter, Elisabeth (Lisa), and I arrived in Sai Kung where a mutual friend introduced us to a local landlord, Tsang Yung-Loi, who agreed to rent us several rooms in one of his new stone houses on the outskirts of the market. Mr. Tsang, together with his wife, two sons, and two daughters were most gracious hosts. They introduced us to shopkeepers, taught us the rudiments of buying and cooking local food, and they introduced us to a medical worker with the Basel Mission, Elisabeth Hammer, who provided us with her German hospitality and facilities for learning Hakka. The eldest son, Tsang Tat-Keung, was of special help in tutoring us in his native Hakka. Throughout the fall and winter of 1971, he sat up with us every evening after supper, drilling us in Hakka. His mother and sisters often looked after our three-year-old daughter who soon became fluent in Cantonese. Why my wife and I learned Hakka and my daughter learned Cantonese is explained in part by the changing structure of ethnic group relations in Sai Kung, the subject of this monograph.

After we settled into our house, our first order of business was to purchase our daily supply of food. This became our main avenue of entree into the lives of the townspeople. Our first encounter with the early morning market where crowds hustle for the freshest vegetables and choicest cuts of freshly slaughtered pigs was a bit jarring to our middle-class sensibilities. (I found it to be even more jarring than having to learn the norms of gift exchange in Micronesia where my wife and I had served as Peace Corps Volunteers.) At first we understood neither the verbal language nor the many hand signals used to bargain prices and make relations, although we soon understood enough to know when we were shouted and laughed at and called "useless." Slowly we learned to employ the more obvious rules of communication and ultimately became competent bargainers. While we began to impress people with our Hakka speech, I cannot claim that I ever mastered all the subtle cues of local conversation or that I "participated" in the lives of these people beyond the superficial level of interaction which the market provided. All I can claim is that I became less awkward culturally, less threatening as an outside agent, and more of a benign curiosity who could be an irritant at one time with persistent questions and useful at another time as a source of credit or a link to the English-speaking levels of administration and charity.

While we learned how in Hong Kong "money talks," we also learned how interpersonal trust is spun in webs of local relationships. Living in this small town not only revealed these webs to us but engaged us in them to some degree. From an outside point of view many of the political and economic strands which tie these people together could be construed in a negative light, whereas the people whose livelihoods depend on those strands see them in a different light. It is important to describe this web of local relationships in order to comprehend the way people take and perform ethnic roles. However, it is also important that my description not do harm to the web of local relations. At the risk of emasculating my description and weakening my analysis while trying to preserve a degree of reality, I have changed most names, deleted or veiled most controversial materials even where such knowledge is common information. Protection of informants is now the paramount responsibility of anthropologists as set forth in Article One of the American Anthropological Association's "Principles of Professional Responsibility." I have attempted to uphold these principles in my work.

Soon we became accustomed to awakening before dawn to the squeal of pigs being butchered in the abbattoir on Main Street and to the chugging boat engines and squeaking tackle hoisting barrels of fish from the boats onto Wharf Street. During the predawn hours most doors are still bolted and protected by fierce door gods pasted on their outer sides. Soon a stick of incense is lit and placed outside the door, providing the narrow streets with an early morning fragrance. With the coming of the light, the fragrance of incense gives way to the sugary smells of freshly baked pastries in the bakeries and tea houses; and as the morning wears on, these mix with the rank odors of the open gutters into which all manner of refuse and residue is swept. By 7 A.M. the streets are crowded with children on their way to school and by villagers on their way to breakfast in the tea houses, to purchase their daily supply of fresh food, and to collect the latest letter from Europe in the shop of a relative or friend. The itinerants are out early to claim a space in the temple square or in the nook of a narrow street where they can hawk jewelry, cloth, herbs, fruits, home-baked pastries, fruits, flowers, fowl, monkey bones, snakes, dried fish, and ten thousand other things depending on the season.

I used the morning market to shop and to strike up conversations with all kinds of persons. Much of my data comes from these casual conversations held in tea shops or more frequently in the front-room parlors and store fronts. Often I spent an hour or two sitting in one store observing and conversing with the proprietor and his or her regular customers from the surrounding villages. I did not attempt to manage these conversations with any obvious or rigorous intent. Most of my substantive questions were simple and naive, for example, "What kind of person is that over there?'' ''How can you tell?'' Other questions I asked about details of local history and custom were not construed as so simple and naive. I also used many of these conversations to cross-check information gathered elsewhere with the purpose of increasing the accuracy of my generalizations. And of course, from the vantage point of my seat in the shop I observed much of the interaction which took place in the shop or in the street just outside.

I spent the most time in places where I was made to feel welcome. Such feelings were usually conveyed with a steaming glass of tea which felt as good on a cold wintry morning as it felt on a hot sultry day—one thing I soon learned from my Chinese friends was the way a sip of hot tea breaks the hardest thirst which no amount of iced water seems to slake. Occasionally the proprietor would send an order down the street for some pastries and glasses of an extremely bitter brew of tea laced with milk and sugar, a most peculiar concoction known, I suspect, only to Hong Kong and perhaps in some ways symbolic of Hong Kong itself.

During the course of the morning I visited several stores or residences in the market. Sometimes I walked around the backside of the town where the mesh of baking goods, fresh and dried fish, and open gutters gives way to stronger odors of decayed wood and refuse strewn along the shoreline and across the tidal flats. Here the boat people live in boats and in shacks built on stilts over the water. Many of these families were especially gracious in receiving me, especially after I demonstrated my usefulness to them as a conduit of information and charity between themselves and administrative and welfare agencies.

After a morning of mixing with the market crowds, purchasing our daily fare, and talking with people I went home to eat lunch and to write my notes on the morning's observations and conversations. I did not take extensive notes in the presence of persons with whom I spoke unless it was a formal interview for the simple reason that I was not accepted on the basis of my claim as an anthropologist but rather as a "foreign friend."

On some afternoons I returned to the market for another round of visiting. In the afternoon the market is much quieter; at least there are no crowds. But another distinctive sound shatters the otherwise placid streets, the clack and shuffle of mahjong tiles. Along every street are several shops where the local residents congregate for games of chance, mostly mahjong, but some play a variety of Chinese and Western card games. These sounds continue far into the night, and they sometimes disturb young people who are trying to memorize their lessons for the next day. Working-class youths use the afterhours to practice martial arts and lion dancing; and hardly an evening goes by that the little town does not resound with the beat of drums and the clang of cymbals and gongs to mark the step of the lion.

On other days we trekked the mountain paths or hired a junk to visit the outlying villages where we occasionally spent the night in the house of friends or their relatives whom we knew from the town. Most of the people we knew in our neighborhood hailed from one of the remote villages and had moved closer to the market to obtain educational opportunities for their children. During our short visits, we attempted to see every village in the Sai Kung market area and to note as much about each village as we could. Most villages were inhabited by old men, women, children, and ferocious dogs—most of the young men were working in Europe. However, by making our connections known and by speaking Hakka we were generally welcomed and invited to have a glass of "tea" which was usually a glass of hot water.

A secondary source of data comes from a series of loosely standardized interviews with local leaders and with non–Hakka-speaking persons. In these interviews I secured life histories, family backgrounds, business activities, facts and figures about local associations, and the like. To facilitate the interviews I hired the services of several students from urban Hong Kong who could speak Cantonese.

Valuable quantitative data were obtained by several procedures. One was a formal survey of all the shops around the town. This Kaifong Survey was accomplished piecemeal over a long period of time by my wife and me, since we did not want to arouse unnecessary suspicions or animosities by confronting every proprietor with a formal questionnaire. These data consist mainly of the kinds of products sold in each store, the proprietor's social background, and so forth. Another extremely useful source of data is the contribution and membership lists which are displayed for public scrutiny on long rolls of red paper during festivals. Most of these lists were obtained by photographing them. These lists are also recorded in books kept by the sponsoring associations, and they provide a serial time record for describing changes in the social registry of the local social system. Because these books deteriorate over a decade or so, they will be lost. However, the most important lists may be preserved for posterity. For example, the 1915 stone tablet in the Tin Hau Temple is etched with the names of 694 contributors to the temple's reconstruction. The tablet is literally the social registry of Sai Kung society during the early part of the century. Mr. Li Tai-Pang, whose uncles' names appear at the head of this list, kindly helped me to identify many of the names on that stone.

Finally, I would like to describe my use of words in this monograph. Since this study deals with ethnic group relations, the terms used to identify certain groups involve inherently ambiguous or downright insulting references to people. For general descriptive purposes I do not use colloquial terms which are presently tinged with ambiguity or are especially insulting even though a number of these terms are found in official and scholarly publications elsewhere. However, understanding the terms that people do use in different contexts, no matter how reprehensible, is crucial to our understanding of ethnic group relations in Sai Kung. Where ambiguous or derogatory terms such as "Tanka" or "Hoklo" are cited, they are placed in quotation marks; and for purposes of general reference other more neutral terms or self-ascribed terms, though a bit awkward for the general reader, are employed, for example, Cantonese boat people instead of "Tanka."

In romanizing Chinese words, I use the following conventions: (1) Personal names and Chinese words that occur in Hong Kong English publications are rendered accordingly (for example, Kaifong, Szeyap). (2) Hong Kong place names follow the conventions of *A Gazetteer of Place Names* (HKG, 1969; for example, Sai Kung). (3) Place names outside Hong Kong jurisdiction follow the international post office spellings in *The Random House Dictionary of the English Language,* unabridged, 1967 edition (for example, Waichow, instead of Huichou, Kwangchow, and so on). (4) All remaining place names are in Wade-Giles, hyphenated and italicized (for example, *Paoan*). (5) Other Chinese words are in Wade-Giles and italicized (for example, *feng shui*). (6) Words that do not exist in standard Chinese or that need ethnic effect are romanized in Hakka (H) or Cantonese (C) following the conventions of MacIver (1926) and Huang (1970) respectively.

Acknowledgments

A number of persons and institutions have been helpful to me at various stages of my study. The fieldwork phase was financed by a predoctoral grant from the National Institute of Mental Health. In Hong Kong the Sai Kung District Officer, Mr. Eason, his Assistant, Mr. Yung, and especially his Liaison, Mr. Lau Ting-Cheung, kindly allowed me to peruse published materials and unclassified records relating to the landholdings and organization of various groups in Sai Kung. Mr. Lau also helped to set up interviews with local leaders, and he took the time to discuss with me matters of local society and custom. Another government official who helped me in these ways was Dr. James Hayes, whose recent book (1977), which bears on matters that concern my own study, was not available to me until after I completed this manuscript.

I obtained documentary data from several other government agencies including the Department of Statistics and Census and the Colonial Secretariat Library. The American-sponsored Universities Service Centre provided valuable library and duplicating services at low cost. Even more important for me and my wife was the intellectual and moral ferment generated among scholars gathered there from around the world to discuss China and to debate America's role in Vietnam.

I owe a very special debt to my teachers at the University of Illinois who saw me through the preparation and completion of my dissertation research. I would like to mention my graduate advisor, Dr. Lawrence W. Crissman and my graduate committee chairman, Dr. David W. Plath. Here at the University of Hawaii other persons were helpful in the revision of my dissertation into the present work. Dr. Harry Lamley of the

History Department, Dr. Richard Lieban, Dr. Richard Gould, Dr. William Lebra, and Dr. Bion Griffin of the Anthropology Department each offered valuable suggestions and much needed encouragement. And the anthropology departmental secretarial staff was most helpful in typing the final draft.

It is my family, my parents, my wife, and my two children to whom I owe the most, for they sustained me and bore the brunt of my frustrations the longest. My wife and daughter participated in the fieldwork phase of my study. As might be expected, my daughter was the icebreaker: Her presence seemed to legitimize and guarantee the goodwill of her parents. She provided a medium through which conversations could be initiated and maintained. Sometimes she even acted as a translator because of her excellent command of conversational Cantonese. Although my wife was destined to become a computer technician by profession, she enthusiastically engaged in my research, and her field notes together with her discussions and photographic records aided my work immensely. I owe her an immeasurable debt of gratitude for going along with me so far in the pursuit of my own professional goals.

Weights and Measures

1. All monetary figures are given in Hong Kong dollars. In 1971 the exchange rate was one U.S. dollar to five Hong Kong dollars.

2. In 1971 a minimal daily subsistence of one catty (0.6 kilograms) of rice cost about one HK dollar.

3. In rural Hong Kong, rice paddy is reckoned by the amount of land that can be planted *(chung)* by one dipper *(tou)* of seed. There are approximately 6 *tou chung* in one acre, or about 15 in one hectare.

CHAPTER 1
Introduction

When the Japanese military ravaged China's east coast in 1937, the Chinese government, factories, and universities were dislodged from the populous centers of their ancient civilization and deluged the vast frontiers of west and southwest China. Among the Chinese seeking refuge were such young anthropologists as Francis Hsu, who in the Malinowskian tradition of exile, seized the opportunity to conduct ethnographic investigation of the native people. Hsu's study of a Minchia-speaking community in a place called West Town appeared in his monograph, *Under the Ancestor's Shadow*. Hsu observed that "West Towners are jealous of their claim to Chinese origin, and become annoyed when suggestions to the contrary are made" (1967:18). Other scholars have identified the Minchia as among "the most civilized of the non-Chinese tribes of Yunnan" (Fitzgerald 1941:1), or as "the original inhabitants of the Nam Chao Kingdom" (Rock 1947:plate 7), or, in the most recent summary, as "Tibeto-Burman" (Lebar 1964:9), even though the Chineseness of their language is attested to by Greenberg (1953) and Forrest (1965). However, Hsu leaves his readers with no doubt that "West Towners not only are Chinese in culture but also tend to insist that they are *more Chinese* in some respects than the Chinese in other parts of China" (1967:19, italics mine).

Similar problems of ethnic identity occur among other groups in southeast China, namely, Cantonese, Hakka, Hokkien, and variations within these groups. Each claims to be "more Chinese" than the other,[1] and each relegates the other to some variety of "barbarian."

Hakka hail from the mountains of eastern Kwangtung where they have been associated with non-Sinitic hill people in a niche which "civilized" lowlanders shunned. Even missionaries joined the debate over the Chineseness of the "Hakka race" as in the exchange between Dr. E. J. Eitel and Dr. Charles Piton (1873:225): "All that Dr. E. has said in his article does not in the least shake my opinion that the Hakkas are Chinese *de pure sang*. . . ."

Hakka think of themselves as refugees from the invasions of northern barbarians and as descendants of Sung-dynasty officials. Hence, they view themselves as patriotic and learned despite their poverty and indelicate manners. Hakka, in turn, view the Cantonese and Hokkien, who inhabit the low fertile lands of Kwangtung, as descendants of aboriginal barbarians.

Cantonese in central and western Kwangtung and eastern Kwangsi, and Hokkien speakers in Fukien, Taiwan, and eastern Kwangtung pride themselves as Tang-dynasty pioneers of these southern provinces. As the pendulum of civilization swung through the south after the Tang dynasty (618–907 A.D.), the Cantonese and Hokkien each established international emporiums and places of learning in the rich alluvial basins. While their orientation toward the sea facilitated international trade, it also provided a marginal livelihood for several million Cantonese and Hokkien living aboard boats. Even though they speak dialects of the same languages as do the land people, boat people lack some of the esteemed attributes associated with an agrarian lifestyle and are therefore despised as local aborigines. Land people commonly call boat people "Tanka" ("egg folk"), which is a derogatory reference to their alleged barbarism. The aboriginal origin of boat people is alleged in imperial Chinese edicts (see chapter 2, note 6) as well as in modern scholarly and popular works (Wiens 1967:54; Lo 1955:209; Huang 1957:37; Burkhardt 1955,2:183; Barnett 1957:261). However, boat people see themselves as Chinese. As in the case of Francis Hsu's Minchia, anthropologists who have lived among boat people tend to substantiate boat people's insistence on a Chinese origin despite a culture radically modified to fit a marine environment (see Ward 1965; Anderson 1972).

Differences in language, native place, and surname have been used by urban and overseas Chinese to organize their communities (Crissman 1967). Here Chinese minorities have generally occupied a common mercantile niche between native majorities and European imperialists. In these contexts the boundaries between Chinese sojourners, indigenous natives, and European rulers are marked by radical differences in technologies, social structures, cultural values, and phenotypes which overshadow the "ethnic" character of alignments within the Chinese communities. The extent of cultural differences among various Chinese vernacular groups is comparable to the differences among the Roman vernaculars of Europe. The rise of an urban Chinese polity in the past century began to veil the ethnic cleavages in Chinese communities.[2] However, the rise of urbanism, republicanism, and communism has not completely cut across old ethnic differences. Traditional ethnic alignments still animate Chinese communities overseas (Tobias 1977: 312), on Taiwan (Mendel 1970), in communist China (Myrdal 1966:59; Vogel 1969: 52, 93), and in Hong Kong (Anderson 1967; Sparks 1976).

The basic proposition underlying my study is that to understand the meaning of ethnicity and in particular differences among groups along the South China coast, we must study them in a particular social setting. The focus is on a market area in the Hong Kong New Territories known as Sai Kung. Over the past century the area has developed marketing facilities in response to the rise of Hong Kong. It has been the host for such immigrant groups as Hakka, Cantonese, Hokkien, and the boat people. In the process of the market town's development these groups have organized their differences in a variety of ways which I describe and analyze in the following chapters.

The idea that ethnic groups are part of a social system is not altogether new in anthropology. Anthropologists have viewed ethnicity as roles people take in complex political systems (Leach 1965; Lehman 1967), or as the social organization of cultural differences in which social boundaries are maintained (Barth 1969). According to Barth, groups recognize and maintain their differences through interaction. Although interaction may include acculturation and intermarriage, it does not necessarily erode ethnic boundaries so much as maintain boundaries. Barth contends that "the critical focus of investigation . . . becomes the ethnic *boundary* that defines the group, not the cultural stuff that it encloses" (1969:15).

Barth's point of view seems to lend itself to an understanding of Chinese ethnic groups since there is little or no cleavage in basic values, or social structures among them. However, Barth's separation of the "cultural stuff" from the "group boundary" goes too far in relegating the symbolic factor to a dependent variable or in dismissing it altogether as an epiphenomenon. I hold to the idea that the ethnic character of a group stems from its "cultural stuff," and in the Chinese case, cultural differences, however superficial, inform the rhetoric that one is "more Chinese" or "more civilized" than the other. Superficial cultural differences still constitute a primary component in the process of ethnic grouping. In fact, when we define our problem to be a study of group *process* rather than group maintenance, the relationship between behavioral and symbolic components assumes greater theoretical significance.

A more dynamic approach has been developed by scholars of urban ethnicity. Abner Cohen (1974; 1976) suggests that ethnicity emerges out of the interplay between political utility and cultural expression. Ethnic identity is an emergent phenomenon in that people may choose to use their traditional cultures in a variety of ways to mobilize collective sentiment and action. When the object is the interplay between culture and behavior, it follows that ethnic identity is only one among many roles that a person plays in society. This is most apparent in fluid urban settings such as the Indian city which Gerald Berreman studied. Berreman (1972) shows how ethnicity is one of many social identities people use to cope with urban life, and it is brought into play on opportune occasions.

This more atomized view of ethnicity brings two questions to mind. The first is what constitutes an ethnic group. At the conclusion of this monograph I discuss this question more fully. Some readers may find it useful to read this part of my analysis before proceeding with the descriptive materials in the pages which follow. Suffice for now that my general approach is to treat ethnic grouping as a matter of *degree*. There are different degrees of ethnic group organization. They range from named categories, which have only occasional relevance to behavior, through community networks based on a higher degree of interaction, sociocultural distinction, and public apprehension, to ethnic associations in which membership is corporate and the group has specific political and economic goals. Given this more dynamic framework, we see how people group themselves, how communities emerge, incorporate, dissolve, or shift their positions in forging or coping with political and economic changes.

The second question is what constitutes ethnicity. Although this question animates my entire study, I answer the empirical part of this question in chapter 2 by considering how Chinese themselves structure the ultimate "We-They" dichotomy. As I have already indicated, Chinese structure ultimate differences in terms of the "civilized" versus the "barbarian." This dichotomy glosses distinctions among different languages, occupying different geographical places and engaging in different livelihoods. These distinctions are used to generate, in various combinations and permutations, the ethnic categories by which people group themselves in Sai Kung society.

Both my theoretical approach and the setting in which I conducted fieldwork impel me to view ethnicity as a phenomenon of sociocultural change. The overwhelming fact about Sai Kung is that it is a changing society. The town developed from a village on the western periphery of the Hakka-dominated Waichow Prefecture into a market town rapidly submerging into the urban sprawl of the Hong Kong–Canton orbit. The burden of chapter 3 is to describe the parameters of these changes in terms of the succession of groups into Sai Kung and the development of Sai Kung in the context of evolving relations between colonial Hong Kong and socialist China.

Chapter 4 focuses on the changing roles of ethnic groups in Sai Kung. Here I examine the relationship between ethnic group organization, the group's sociocultural role in local society, and the nomenclature (or what I call "ethnic rhetoric") which gives the group identity and character in the public domain. Here I am interested in how shifts in rhetoric help to alter group consciousness and characterize changes in intergroup relations. Names, images, and reputations are properties of ethnic groups; they are as much the object of political struggle as are economic goods because they reflect the motivational level of claims to positions in the social order.

Chapter 5 focuses more attention on some of the cultural differences among the groups in Sai Kung. I demonstrate how differences are, by and large, manifestations of an underlying Chinese culture. The underlying culture forms a common pool out of which groups draw food-getting techniques and expressive symbols in creating certain niches, enhancing group survival and affiliation, and structuring interaction with other groups.

In chapters 6 and 7 I examine the changing organization of ethnic groups in Sai Kung. Chapter 6 describes the organizational processes by which the Hakka established and maintained their dominance in Sai Kung town. Immigrants adapted by acculturating to the dominant Hakka, while Hakka adapted to the dominant Cantonese outside the market area. After 1960, the massive influx of immigrants, including many Cantonese and Hokkien speakers, brought about new arrangements in Sai Kung society as local Hakka and Cantonese combined to cope with their rapidly changing environment. Chapter 7 analyzes this process from the point of view of the Hokkien-speaking immigrants and explores the nature of corporate ethnicity. I suggest that as an ethnic group attains corporate status along with greater economic autonomy, the ethnic group must define on a jural basis the criteria for access to its corporate holdings. Membership in the group seems to have more to do with political and economic competence than mere cultural performance.

My aim in the following chapters is to shed more light on the ethnic groups along China's southeast coast. However, as I already indicated, we cannot understand these ethnic groups in the cultural abstract. We must observe these cultures in action, that is, within a particular social system. We must examine the ways in which Chinese use their cultural identities to group themselves in Sai Kung market. Ethnic groups are a component of a social system, and, therefore, they are subject to change as the social system changes.

NOTES

1.   The terms by which Chinese have identified themselves denote the "civilized" in opposition to the "barbarian." (For further discussion of the earliest terms for Chinese, see Creel 1970:196.) Hence, the idea that one can be "more or less Chinese" is a reasonable point of view in the context of traditional Chinese social structure. The criteria which distinguish the "civilized" from the "barbarian" are parallel to those which distinguish the scholar-officials from the common people. Those criteria are simply patterns of learned behavior. Given this context, each localized ethnic group attempts to articulate a set of claims on proximity to a civilized origin by citing original native places in North China, genealogical connections to renowned scholar-officials in the service of particular dynasties, and/or by demonstrating their regard for the hallmarks of civilization, namely, propriety and charity.

2.   China's cultural heterogeneity is comparable to Europe's Holy Roman Empire. However, while the Holy Roman Empire tended to disintegrate into its constituent regional nationalities under the forces of capitalism and Protestantism (Weber 1958), the Celestial Empire tended to hold together under the more compromising sway of Confucian imperialism (Weber 1968). And in its most recent phase, China has actually begun to amalgamate its "regionalities" under the forces of a Confucianized socialism.

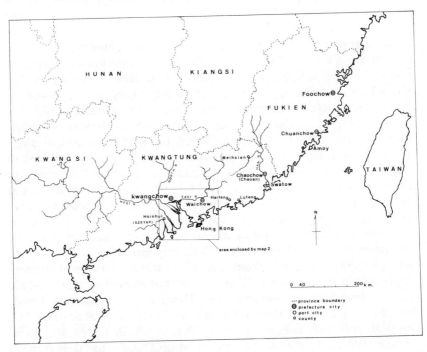

Map 1. Southeastern Coastal China

CHAPTER 2

Dimensions of Ethnicity
in South China

If "ethnicity" is defined as the organization of claims to a cultural tradition, no single criterion differentiates the array of organized claims in such areas of South China as Sai Kung. In fact there are at least three criteria which distinguish ethnic groups: language, native place, and the way people make a living. Each of these criteria delineate fundamental cultural cleavages, which, in Chinese eyes, separate the "civilized" from the "barbarian."

LANGUAGE OR SPEECH GROUP

The speech group is one of the most salient dimensions of ethnicity in South China. Cantonese, Hakka, and Hokkien (Fukienese) with their common root in ancient Chinese are as diverse from one another as are French, Italian, and Spanish with their Latin taproot. Western observers have erroneously viewed the Chinese speech groups as different "tribes," "nations," even "races," although more contemporary scholars think of them as "cultural" variations on a Chinese theme. The spoken words are different in sound and intonation, but the majority of them can be written with standard Chinese ideographs. However, among the traditionally illiterate speakers of these languages, that is, the majority of Chinese, there is a subjective attitude that one's own language is derived from the true civilized tongue of northern official speech (Mandarin), or at least that one's own language is more "civilized" than other "bastardized" versions. This attitude has not been altogether muted by increasing literacy and national consciousness. However, before we get embroiled in the folklore of these claims in Sai Kung, it is useful to consider some of the culture-historical facts by which these speech groups have been differentiated.

Cantonese

Five percent of the Chinese speak a dialect of Cantonese. These people are descendants of northern soldiers, refugees, and exiles who fought and mingled with indigenous peoples of the Yüeh kingdom along the southern coast between fifteen and twenty centuries ago.[1] Their speech preserved many ancient Chinese sounds mixed with aboriginal (Thai) elements and thus became distinct from the changing speech of the north (see Egerod 1967; Hashimoto 1972:1–20).

The Cantonese are concentrated along the original riverine routes which their ancestors followed down the southern slope of the central Nan Ling Mountains and into the most fertile areas. Here, the North and West rivers converge into a great flood plain of six-thousand-square kilometers. The thousand kilometers of waterway form a veinous system of channels navigable by ocean-going ships. These are interconnected with a capillary system of irrigation ditches and fishponds.

The rich soil and water of the delta support high annual rice yields (Yang 1965; II, 27). In such flat areas as Shunte county, 82 percent of the land is cultivated. Here population density averages over five hundred persons per square kilometer. At the head of the delta is the provincial capital, Kwangchow (Canton). From the Tang dynasty, it has been a commercial city linking China to the trade of the maritime world.

The agrarian and commercial richness, the long-term stability and the density of the population are all coextensive with the tradition of large lineage organizations, which have been the subject of intensive anthropological study (Freedman 1966; Potter 1968; Baker 1968; Watson 1975). The long-term stability of settlement has also led to a diversity of Cantonese dialects. Each district is characterized by its particular form of Cantonese to such an extent that the speech of neighboring districts is sometimes mutually unintelligible. The standard Cantonese is spoken in urban Canton and in Hong Kong.

Hakka

Four percent of the Chinese speak Hakka. Their ancestors moved under the pressure of Tartar onslaughts from southern Kiangsi and western Fukien into the narrow valleys and uplands of eastern Kwangtung over eight hundred years ago.[2] In Meihsien, the traditional center of Hakka concentration, no more than 8 percent of the land is cultivated. The average population density is only 154 persons per square kilometer. Rice yields are smaller than in the deltas, and they are supplemented by

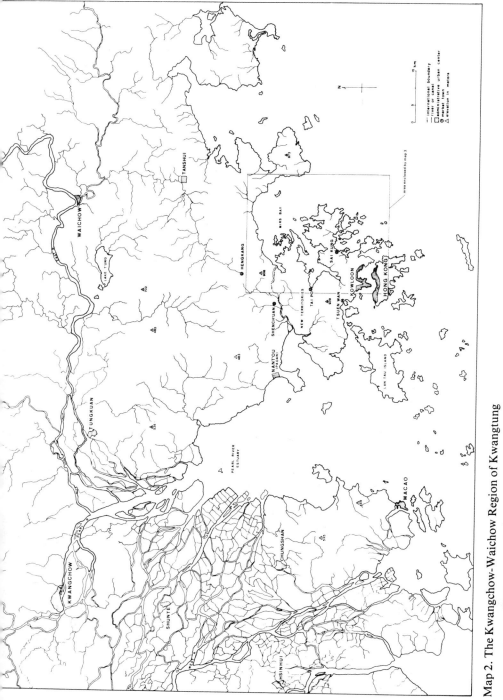

Map 2. The Kwangchow-Waichow Region of Kwangtung

cultivation of potatoes, which were introduced by the Portuguese around 1500.

During the past several centuries the Hakka expanded westward along the East River and southward following the Han River through the hills and valleys of Kwangtung and Kwangsi, and further to Taiwan. Meyners D'Estrey wrote of this expansion:

> The incessant wave of migrations of the Hakka has never stopped, it appears, they continue today in the same manner as before, i.e. by innumerable little branches which spread little by little through Kwangtung (1890:31).

In the nineteenth century, Hakka expansion into Cantonese and Hokkien areas erupted into large-scale feuds over the control of land and water (Lo 1965; Cohen 1968; Lamley 1977). In the end the Hakka retreated into their traditional marginal niches which by then included the foreign controlled treaty port areas (such as Sai Kung).

Hakka tend to emphasize their speech group identity over native place identities. Their sense of native place is comparatively weak, perhaps because they never had a great agricultural or commercial homeland as did other speech groups. The Hakka's uncanny speech group cohesiveness correlates with the unusual homogeneity of their language. According to Mantaro Hashimoto:

> Despite the wide geographical distribution and variety of localities, the Hakka dialects show a surprising homogeneity in their phonological systems, vocabularies, and grammatical structures. . . . The Hakka dialects do not strictly represent a group of regional dialects but constitute a group of "ethnic dialects"; in addition, the extraordinary firm ethnic tie and consciousness among the Hakkas must have been constantly contributing to the unity among the dialects (1973:410).

Their linguistic homogeneity and ethnic consciousness is due partly to the Hakka experience of discrimination and segregation,[3] the recency of the Hakka diaspora, and the migratory nature of their economic adaptation.

Hokkien

Four percent of Chinese speak a Hokkien dialect. This is the speech of southern Fukien province. Like Cantonese, Hokkien is the result of ancient intermingling of northern Chinese immigrants with Min aborigines (see note 1, herein), possibly remnants of Austronesian groups, whose cultures were oriented toward the South Seas. As the area came under northern Chinese influence, the seafaring orientation of the Hokkien people remained characteristic:

More than the Hakka, the Min-Hoklo (Hokkien) are audacious sailors and have shown in the past centuries that they are not adverse to piracy. The disposition and situation of their native country gave them their taste for adventure on the sea. The arid coast which they inhabited forced them to seek their livelihood on the ocean (Meyners D'Estrey 1890:33).

The Hokkien hail from the ancient entrepôt of Chuanchow Prefecture, and in more recent times, the great port city of Amoy. From early times Hokkien speakers sailed along the coasts of Taiwan and Kwangtung, pushing inland here and there. Along the eastern coast of Kwangtung they settled the entire Chaochow Prefecture and the coastal counties of Waichow Prefecture, Haifeng and Lufeng.

The nine counties in the rich Han River delta, which make up Chaochow Prefecture (in their language, "Teochiu") and in modern times centered on the port of Swatow, has been inhabited by persons speaking a dialect that is perhaps 75 percent intelligible to Amoy Hokkien. However, even the dialects of Chaochow have distinct cultural flavors:

Although the language is largely the same among the various counties which make up Chaochow, nevertheless, the various peoples, in adapting to their environments, are not the same. Each people has developed its own disposition (Han 1971:2).

For example, people who inhabit Chaoan county, the ancient prefectural seat at the head of the Han delta, are considered more refined in contrast to harsher sounding and less polished people in surrounding counties.

The Han River delta, though smaller, is comparable to the Canton delta in soil fertility and commercial wealth. In Chaoan county, 50 percent of the land is cultivated, and the rural population density is over four hundred per square kilometer. The people from Chaochow form an important new ethnic category in Sai Kung where they are extremely conscious of their dialect and native place affinity.

The prefecture of Waichow is similiar to the hilly land and low population density of Meihsien. Waichow is inhabited by both the Hakka, who are oriented toward the East River, and the Hokkien, who inhabit the coastal county seats of Haifeng and Lufeng. Unfortunately we have no linguistic studies of the Hokkien dialects spoken in this area. However, it is known that they retain a very close linguistic affinity to the Chaochow. Presently in Sai Kung society there are Hokkien groups which hail from the counties of Hai-Lufeng.

NATIVE PLACE

The Chinese attach great value to the identity of their own or their ancestral birthplace. The relevance of native place for ethnic group organization occurs in the context where one group moves into the native domain of another group, or where two local systems share a common border and where there is a tendency toward mutual encroachment upon or exchange across borders.

When Chinese sojourn or immigrate to a new place, they are viewed by the natives as "outsiders" or "immigrants." In most places interaction is organized around this distinction; and in Chinese thinking this distinction assumes an essential cultural character. As a basis for social organization, the distinction is drawn between the landowning natives who are considered "passive" and "civilized" and the immigrant squatters or tenants who, as outsiders, are considered "rootless," often "threadbare," "aggressive" and "barbarous" in their interpersonal manners and speech. The de facto use which Chinese make of this distinction between natives and outsiders is reported by Fei Hsiao-Tung in his study of K'aihsienkung village in eastern China:

> This is not a legal distinction; from the legal point of view those who reside in a district for more than three years become members of the local community. But this does not constitute, in the people's eyes, real membership of the village. . . . The distinction of natives and outsiders is significant because it has been translated into social relations. The fact that outsiders are engaged in special professions and possess no land is alone sufficient to indicate that the distinction has far-reaching economic consequences (1947:23–24).

Fei also notes that the outsiders have a slight dialectical difference from the natives, and their women dress differently from the natives.

The organization of locals and outsiders is not due simply to the discriminatory attitudes of locals but is also due to the desire of Chinese immigrants to retain their native identities. The boundary between natives and immigrants takes a variety of forms depending on a number of demographic, economic, political, and cultural factors. Immigrants may attempt to retain their native identities covertly while overtly acculturating and integrating into the local society as many did in Sai Kung before 1950 (see chapter 4). In other circumstances, as in post-1950 Sai Kung, immigrants may try to articulate and organize their native identity vis-à-vis local people. (This process is described in chapter 7.)

WAYS IN WHICH PEOPLE MAKE A LIVING

Modern ethnologists might assume that language distinctions are the more salient cultural categories; however, the imperial Chinese view makes little reference to the vernaculars such as Hakka, Hokkien (or Min), and Cantonese (or Yüeh). In keeping with the official view that common people have little to say which is worth hearing, the vernaculars are barely distinguishable from non-Sinitic languages nor indeed from "the chatter of birds." Nevertheless, the common people do contribute to the support of officialdom through their labor. Hence, the imperialists give recognition to the different ways that people make a living in the system of the "four classes." These are, in order of *political* status (not economic power): literati, peasant, artisan, and merchant.[4]

A further distinction is drawn between these four classes and those which are not classed. The "classified people" are controllable. They are settled on the land, therefore they can be counted, and subjected to corvée labor. They are employed in "productive" occupations, hence taxable. Among the unclassified folk are several million people who until recently lived their entire lives aboard boats along the South China coast. Boat people are difficult to control because they are able to move from place to place. Their nonagrarian mode of subsistence is difficult to exploit by imperial authorities. The liminal role of boat people is rationalized in the cosmic framework: Boat people are not subject to the natural forces of *feng shui* ("wind and water") in the way that people living on land in fixed abodes are.[5] Rather as "floating people" they are in constant motion with wind and tide; they are more a part of nature than apart from nature, that is, "floating," "atomized," "uncivilized," "barbarian," and therefore impossible to classify. As unclassified people, they were often denied such basic privileges available to Chinese of all classes, such as access to an official career through the civil service examination (Ch'u 1965:132).

Despite official discrimination there were times when the imperial authorities attempted to settle and classify boat people in order to control the southern seashore against threats from antiimperial forces. (The present efforts by the People's Republic of China to settle boat people is also motivated, in part, from the need to control the seashore against anticommunist forces.) For example, in 1729 the Yung Cheng Emperor issued an edict for the settlement and registration of boat people arguing that even though they are barbarian Yao, they are still human and deserve a place in the imperium.[6] Undoubtedly, boat people were able to settle on shore in various places, and at different times. As part of the common folk they were able to take the imperial examinations. But in the process, they completely lost their identity as boat people. At the same time there was a constant trickle of land people onto boats. The movement of persons between land and sea and imperial attempts to control the boundary were analogous to that which occurred across the Great Wall along the northern frontier (see Lattimore 1962).

More pertinent to my study is the attitude of common folk to boat people. At the *local* level, boat people were discriminated against since they were correctly perceived as possible contenders for access to land. In

C. K. Yang's study of Nanching village during the communist land reform:

> One class of people whose demands for land were denied were the migratory farm laborers, the "boat people" who lived on floating homes and worked up and down the Pearl River. Since some of them had worked in Nanching regularly every year at planting and harvesting seasons, they sent several representatives to the village to talk to the cadres about sharing in the confiscated land; but the villagers raised stiff opposition on the grounds that land was already short in the village, and the boat people were not established members of the village (1965:149).

Boat people were thus perceived as transients, uncommitted to the local community. During periods of political upheaval and economic collapse they could sail away with all their worldly possessions. (For example, in Sai Kung the two sharp decreases in the boat population occurred during the Japanese invasion [1941–1945] and the riots of 1967.)

This stereotype of boat people as "transients" is challenged by Barbara Ward's work (1955, 1959, 1963) which shows how dependent boat people are on maintaining personal connections to a particular land community. Traditionally, land people supplied boat people with their most elementary needs (fresh water, agricultural products, credit, boats, and tackle), while boat people offered land people cheap sources of protein (fish), and to a limited extent, labor and transportation. In other words, boat people's survival depended on their ability to maintain access to terrestrial resources through long-standing personal bonds. Such heavy dependence on local patronage tended to commit boat people to a local land community.

On the other hand, this structure of dependency really only qualifies the "transient nature" of boat life since it is precisely that reliance on terrestrial resources which becomes problematic when those resources are in a state of collapse. When such is the case, boats begin to leave an area. The pattern of departure is predictable: newest arrivals are the first to depart, and those who have lived several generations in an area and have developed extensive patronage are in a better position to cope with hard times. They are the last to depart. There is a dynamic relationship between the productive state of terrestrial resources and the flux in size of boat communities.

OTHER RELEVANT OCCUPATIONAL CATEGORIES

In Sai Kung there are several other salient occupational categories which have almost as much cultural significance to the Chinese as the distinction between living on the water and living on the land. Although these other occupations are not thought to be as 'ascriptive', they nevertheless constitute a continuous extension of social cleavages from what is clearly "ethnic" (analytically and descriptively speaking) to what is more simply "occupational." This continuum of social categories also may be seen to double back on itself such that "occupational" roles cut across and ameliorate "ethnic" roles in one case or coextend with and reinforce the consistency and visibility of "ethnic" roles in another case.

Among land people is the distinction between doing business in town and working the earth in villages. Townspeople are described as *tso sheng li* ("making a living by profit") and are highly respected. There is some ambiguity here since "making a living by profit" was ranked in the imperial system as the lowest class. Yet from the common people's view it was the most lucrative way to make a living, and in fact, many among the scholar-official class combined the moral wealth of agrarian economy with the much greater lucre of mercantile economy. With the rise of the Chinese Republic and the Crown Colony of Hong Kong, the legal-political apparatus was geared to the interests of the businessman. To gain a niche in the market economy became, therefore, a traditional goal of many Sai Kung people.

Individuals who identify themselves as townspeople perceive themselves to be more progressive than and superior to "village fellows." Townspeople regard villagers as impoverished and superstitious bumpkins. However, there is little sense that these distinctions are necessarily ascribed by birth. Most townspeople are connected to native villages through collateral kinsmen, and many are absentee village landlords (see case studies in chapter 6). In fact several who became shopkeepers and Kaifong (neighborhood) leaders began as village representatives.

A similar relative status distinction exists between villagers who "cultivate fields" in rice and truck farmers who "plant vegetables." Of course rice cultivators also plant vegetable gardens for home consumption. In Sai Kung the rice farmers are predominantly Hakka women. When they are not working their paddy, they "work with mud," that is, they earn wages laboring on construction sites.

People say that it requires a man's rational and technical competence to manage a truck farm. Yet vegetable farming is held in much lower esteem than rice farming. Part of the difference is, of course, the fact that rice is grown by local Hakka folk while truck farming is the domain of immigrant or refugee families. But why is occupational distinction coupled with ethnic boundary?

Vegetable planting requires constant daily labor (watering, fertilizing, and weeding) in an endless succession of short cycles (planting and picking) without a slack period. There are certain advantages in the higher yield of vegetables over rice and the shorter turnover in the cultivator's investment. Also, gardening is profitable to individuals and small family groups possessing a minimum of capital. It is precisely these advantages that make truck farming an attractive gamble for poor tenants (Yang 1965:29, 62) or immigrant tenants (Topley 1964). The labor is bitter, individualistic, geared completely to fluctuations of the market, and thus inherently insecure compared to growing rice. Rice is a staple, it can be stored, and its planting and harvesting is more sociable, involving neighborhood collectives, and finally rice was traditionally used as a means of gift and pecuniary exchange.

CONCLUSION

The language a person speaks, the place of birth, and the occupation are all important criteria for organizing ethnic groups in South China, and especially in Sai Kung. All of these distinctions involve claims to a cultural tradition of a more or less ascribed nature (see Introduction, note 1). In various permutations and combinations they generate the ethnic names by which people individually and collectively negotiate their positions in the local society.

NOTES

1.   Yüeh (originally, "to go beyond") denotes the aboriginal groups which lived "beyond" or south of the Yangtze River, or later, the Nan Ling Mountains. Over a period of centuries, from earliest historical times to the Tang dynasty, the Paiyüeh ("The One-hundred Yüeh Tribes" as they were usually called) were more or less unified in opposition to the "Central Kingdom(s)" in the north which were establishing their imperial hegemony in East Asia. A Thai-speaking group was probably one of the dominant groups in southern Yüeh, in what became the provinces of Kwangtung-Kwangsi. Another major group was Min in eastern Yüeh, what became Fukien province. It is not yet clear to which modern language group aboriginal Min belonged, although there is some speculation that it was Austronesian (Bayard 1975:77).

2.   According to the Hakka historiographer, Lo Hsiang-Lin (1933), the Hakka originated in North China and were successively pushed to the south by northern barbarian onslaughts. The first move was from Honan to the eastern Yangtze valley. It began in 317 A.D. under pressure from the eastern Tsin. The second move was from the Yangtze into western Fukien during the ravages of the Huang Chao Rebellion in the ninth century. The move into eastern Kwangtung began in the twelfth century as the southern Sung retreated from the Chin Tartars and Mongols. The fourth move occurred with the overthrow of the Ming dynasty by the Manchu in 1644 during which the Hakka dispersed into Szechuan, Kwangsi, and Taiwan. This dispersion continued into Szeyap, Hainan, the treaty ports of

Hong Kong and Swatow and overseas after the disastrous defeat of the Hakka-led Taiping Rebellion in 1865.

3. Another linguist, Paul Yang (1967:320) classifies Hakka into seven dialect groups. Yang calculates the degrees of mutual intelligibility among them based on phonological differences. All the Kwangtung groups are between 85 percent and 95 percent mutually intelligible. Between the Szechuan and Kwangtung groups the range drops to a low of 65 percent. A purely impressionistic interpretation of the linguistic data and my own experiences lead me to accept the general impression of most other scholars that the Hakka vernaculars are more homogeneous than other southern vernaculars for the sociohistorical reasons cited in the text. In her study of Cantonese dialects, Oi-Kan Hashimoto (1972:9) makes no general statement about the homogeneity or heterogeneity of Cantonese dialects. She says only that "there is uncertainty concerning the grouping of dialects. . . ." In keeping with my general thesis it is worth noting that over geographical space, linguistic boundaries tend to be arbitrary, that is, sociological. There are gradients and clines rather than language boundaries; and factors influencing mutual intelligibility, as we shall see, are not purely linguistic but are also sociological in nature.

4. The concept of the "Four Classes" is not to be confused with the analytical concept of class based on objective economic criteria. The "Four Classes" constituted a classificatory system of sociocultural sanctions by which the imperialists maintained their agrarian base.

5. Several boat people told me that *feng shui* was irrelevant to their lives. There may be more than one reason why they felt this to be so. However, one reason must have to do with the concept of *feng shui* itself. *Feng shui* "is the effect which arrangements of land, buildings, trees, graves and other developments on land are believed to have on the destiny and fortune of individuals and groups" (Topley 1964:171). By ordering things in space, people bring cosmic balance and therefore health and prosperity into their lives. When boat people move onto land, *feng shui* becomes more relevant to their lives. No longer are they simply at the mercy of wind and water, but are in a position to stabilize their lives, to distinguish themselves from their surroundings and to manipulate the forces in nature.

6. The official Chinese view of boat people vis-à-vis local level views is illustrated in a 1729 edict of the Yung Cheng Emperor "Granting Imperial Favor to Kwangtung's People of the Tan Registry":

> Be it made known that among the declassed people of eastern Kwangtung are those registered as Tan. They are a type of Yao barbarian who live on boats and catch fish throughout the provincial waterways. They are so numerous that they cannot be counted. Cantonese regard the Tan registry as a mean breed and do not allow them to live ashore. Nor do Tan dare contend with the common people. They patiently suffer their whole lives aboard cramped boats and never know the joy of a secure dwelling. Such a pity, for those of Tan registry are virtuous folk. There is no reason to expel them. Moreover, they pay taxes as fishermen and are one with the masses. How can it be that a local tradition of discrimination forces them to rove about scattering hither and thither? The Governor-General is to instruct his civil authorities everywhere to proclaim among those of Tan registry whosoever among them lacks strength may remain aboard boats; but those of sufficient strength should move ashore

to build houses in villages near the water. Together with the masses they are to arrange themselves in public security units in order that they be easily controlled. Local bullies (village leaders) are not allowed to fabricate pretexts with which to mistreat or expel them. And civil authorities are ordered to persuade those of Tan registry to reclaim barren land, to engage in agriculture, and to thereby afford themselves of the opportunity to be like ordinary local folk and to regard the humanity of Our special decree (*Hsinan hsien chih,* Introductory *chuan;* 21. See Ng, 1961, for a somewhat different translation of this document.).

CHAPTER 3

Development of Sai Kung Society: 1842-1972

Having outlined the regional context of ethnic groups in South China, I will now describe the particular social system in which my study takes place, namely, the Sai Kung market. Sai Kung market is the relevant level of community organization in my study, not only because the local market is the natural unit of social interaction in rural China (Skinner 1964), but in particular, Sai Kung has become a center of interaction and the object of competition for large numbers of persons grouping themselves under ethnic titles.

An insight of the anthropological study of complex society is that local villages and markets are not social isolates. Local level units are not independent from higher levels of sociocultural integration. To comprehend Sai Kung market society, we must study its interrelationships with higher levels of commercial and administrative organization in Hong Kong and South China.[1] In this chapter, I attempt to describe the interaction of various levels and various agencies in the historical development of the Sai Kung market. This description is a prelude to the more detailed study of particular aspects of ethnic grouping within Sai Kung society in the chapters which follow.

LAND AND PEOPLE OF THE TRADITIONAL MARKET AREA

Sai Kung lies along the South China coast about thirty kilometers east of the Pearl River estuary and about ten kilometers northeast of Hong Kong Island. Here the grass covered and sparsely wooded hills rise steeply over narrow valleys that are drained by fast-flowing streams which often run dry in winter. Lack of water puts severe limits on the area's rice

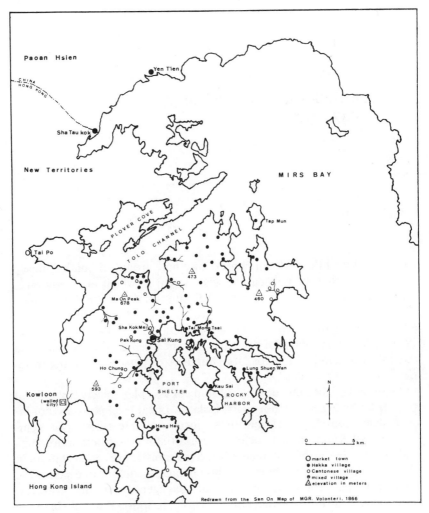

Map 3. Sai Kung and Eastern Paoan County, 1866

paddy production. And in recent years, rampant urbanization in areas adjacent to Kowloon has drained the meager water supply further causing many people to give up rice cultivation altogether.

From Map 3 we see that Sai Kung is a crescent-shaped landform divided into three areas. The western edge is a twelve-square-kilometer barrier of high plateaus separating Sai Kung from eastern Kowloon. The northern part of the area is oriented toward urban Kowloon while the southern part centers around a minor Hakka market named Hang Hau. Hang Hau traditionally transacted goods between Sai Kung and Hong Kong.

In the central section is the Sai Kung market proper and its immediate hinterland, consisting of about twenty square kilometers. A high backbone of slopes divides the series of broad valleys between Kowloon Peak and Ma On Peak. On the north side are mostly Hakka hamlets wedged in narrow valleys. They orient toward the traditional market at Tai Po. On the south side around Sai Kung town are the three largest, most fertile, well-watered, and longest inhabited valleys in the area. From west to east they are Ho Chung, Pak Kong, and Sha Kok Mei. Each valley is dominated by Cantonese villages with smaller Hakka hamlets nestled in the surrounding slopes. However, the Hakka market at Sai Kung has dominated the area during this century.

Clusters of Hakka hamlets dominate the peninsula east of Ma On Peak. Its 33-square kilometers is sliced into narrow valleys by a fine network of ungraded streams. The only flat land is in the estuaries of the larger streams, and it is seldom more than 300 meters wide as compared to the larger Cantonese valleys around Sai Kung town which are over 700 meters wide. According to Davis (1964:75), only 281 hectares, or 2.5 percent, of the peninsula is arable. This may be compared to my estimate for the entire marketing area of an overall 1,141 arable hectares or 6 percent of the land.

Arable land varies from first-class wet land which yields two crops of rice each year to third-class dry land, which may be planted with taro and sweet potato, "the poor man's food." In between is the second-class land that may support one crop of rice in a year, or vegetables.

Cantonese tend to dominate the most productive agricultural land, while the Hakka hold drier, hillier land. For instance, according to the 1905 Block Crown Lease records, members of the leading Cantonese lineage in Sha Kok Mei owned 9.5 hectares, 82 percent of which was first-class paddy yielding about 300 catties per *tou chung*. Under optimal conditions this would support about two hundred persons.

By comparison the members of a leading Hakka lineage in Tai Mong Tsai on the peninsula owned exactly the same number of hectares (9.5), but less than 1 percent of it was first-class paddy, and 72 percent was third-class dry land. The Hakka average between 100 and 200 catties per *tou chung* of rice, depending on the supply of water, and often they are unable to plant more than a single summer crop. Under optimal conditions, the Hakka lineage land in the case just cited could, and by my calculation did in fact, support between fifty to sixty persons.[2]

In 1911 Sai Kung's populations of 2,633 Cantonese and 6,599 Hakka

(SP 1912) seem to have maintained optimal numbers on the land at a low subsistence level. As industrial and commercial opportunities opened to them, they maintained larger populations than the land could support. Göran Aijmer (1967:43) found that a Hakka emigrant village in the area could grow enough rice to maintain its subsistence for only seven months of the year.

South of the market town are five inhabited islands and numerous smaller rocks and islets, which total thirteen square kilometers. The inner recesses are appropriately named Port Shelter and Rocky Harbor. They provide a strategic anchorage for vessels plying the rough seas between Hong Kong and Mirs Bay. The maze of shallow and narrow passages also provided privateers, smugglers, and communist guerrillas protection from imperial authorities (Chinese, British, and Japanese, respectively) during the past hundred years. Nowadays, there is less piracy, although opium smugglers still abound, and the small junks unlicensed to carry weekend picnickers use this labyrinth to elude the Hong Kong marine police.

From the northeast tip of Sai Kung peninsula, a large inlet runs due west to Sai Kung's traditional market at Tai Po. This inlet is called Tolo Channel. It provides a passageway for boats and bypasses the much longer land route between Tai Po market and its Sai Kung hinterland.

CANTONESE SETTLEMENT

The earliest extant settlements in Sai Kung are the Cantonese lineages of Ho Chung, Pak Kong, and Sha Kok Mei. These villagers claim to have come to Sai Kung at the end of the Ming dynasty (circa 1600). For example, the Wan lineage household register of Ho Chung records that by the third generation they were settled in Tungkuan county, from which a member of the eighth generation, named Wai-Pun, moved to Tai Po. However, the Tai Po people discriminated against him. After he and his wife died, his son, Sing-Yu, moved to Cheung Shue Tan, a village south of Tai Po, and opened the land to cultivation. There Sing-Yu died. Sing-Yu had two sons. One moved to the Ma On Peak area; the other moved to Ho Chung and sired four sons. These four constitute the four branch halls; the fourth branch is settled in Tai Po Tsai, two kilometers southwest of Ho Chung.

Oral tradition indicates that the Wan lineage was the third to inhabit Ho Chung. Today there are nine lineages. Ho Chung has always been the largest and agriculturally richest village in the area. It has been eclipsed only by the rise of Sai Kung market in this century. In 1911 Ho Chung had 418 persons compared to Sai Kung's 512 (SP 1912); and in 1970 there were over 800 persons in Ho Chung and over 2,000 in Sai Kung town (HKG 1972).

Although there is very little information in either their written or oral records about how Ho Chung was settled, it is interesting that the immigrant Wai-Pun was discriminated against in Tai Po, a market town dominated by Cantonese, and that his son moved to Cheung Shue Tan, a large Hakka village, two kilometers southeast of Tai Po. It is possible that the Wan lineage, who are adamant in their claim on Cantonese identity, were originally Hakka. Further evidence is deduced from the time when the original ancestors settled in this part of southern Paoan. According to a Paoan county gazetteer, translated by Ng (1961:38), this part of the county was settled exclusively by Hakka after the Ch'ing dynasty lifted its ban on coastal settlement (1662–1669). Counting twenty years per generation, the eighth generation of the Wan lineage immigrated to Tai Po just after the ban was lifted in 1669.[3]

Another original Cantonese lineage is the Lok surname group of Pak Kong. Their records indicate that all trace of the first fifteen generations in North China was lost. Around 1600, one Lok Wei-Shen moved from his native village of K'unkang in Tungkuan county to Paishih village east of the Paoan county seat. Later he moved to a small village near Kowloon called Pak Kong where the environment was good and his posterity flourished. The Lok lineage has four branches, three of which maintain small ancestor halls. Similar to the Wan lineage and all other Cantonese or Hakka lineages in Sai Kung, lineage segments reflect economic equivalences, and there is no overall lineage hall. Pak Kong village had almost 190 persons in 1911 (SP 1912), and by 1960, 234 persons in three main lineages (HKG 1962).

Unfortunately I was unable to copy the written genealogy of the dominant lineage in Sha Kok Mei.

In the remote valleys of Sai Kung peninsula are several Cantonese villages. None of them have ancestral halls or genealogies. (Most of them were converted to Catholicism in the midnineteenth century—see Ryan 1959:44.) Their origins are uncertain. They may be descendants of boat people. In 1663, boat people who were deprived of their livelihood, due to the Ching dynasty's ban on coastal residence, attacked Canton, were defeated, and retreated to Mirs Bay (Balfour 1970:177). It is possible that they found refuge in the remote valleys of Sai Kung, especially on the peninsula jutting into Mirs Bay.

The Cantonese lineages of today probably had diverse origins. Some may have been Hakka; others may have been boat people. In chapter 6, I examine in detail how individuals, families, and lineages in Sai Kung town altered their ethnic affiliations in particular and in general historical contexts.

HAKKA SETTLEMENT

Whatever the actual origins of the first settlers, they identified as Cantonese when additional waves of Hakka settlers arrived during the eighteenth and nineteenth centuries. There is little genealogical or oral tradition which indicates exactly why or how the Hakka came. The meager tradition which does exist suggests that most Hakka immigrated from all three prefectures in eastern Kwangtung in order of their proximity to Sai Kung. Some also came from Cantonese-dominated areas west of Canton. They came in small groups and single families by boat and on foot, and they spread into the hills around the native villages, up narrow ravines and along the seashore. Much of this movement, at least what occurred during the nineteenth century, was in response to the general disorder of South China caused by land hunger, economic depression, foreign incursions, the commercial attraction of Hong Kong, and Hakka retreats from losses suffered at the hands of Cantonese, Hokkien, and imperial troops.

Most Hakka genealogies record a host of local branches in various places around eastern Kwangtung. Only on the last few pages do we glean information about the local Sai Kung branch. For example, the Tsang genealogy of Tai Mong Tsai indicates on its last page that in the seventy-first generation (probably in the 1820s), Tsang Kiet-Chong sired six sons. He is buried in a place outside of Sai Kung. His wife and six sons settled Tai Mong Tsai. His wife's surname was Chu, and her tomb is on High Island, two kilometers south of Tai Mong Tsai.

Orally, the Tsangs claim their ancestors originated in Wuhua county, up river from Meihsien, long before living memory. They built a compound alongside another surname group named Lo who settled Tai Mong Tsai at the same time. Both groups prospered, and each lineage maintained an ancestral hall of equivalent proportions. Although six brothers founded the local Tsang lineage, only five branches remained in Tai Mong Tsai. Another moved to Sha Kok Mei and became more or less Cantonese. (See chapter 5 for further details on the five branches of the Tsang lineage in Tai Mong Tsai.) Until recent times the Tsang lineage paid their annual respects during Ching Ming at the tomb of their founding ancestress.

Another Hakka group named Liu settled two places in the Sai Kung area. One branch is Pak Wai village near Ho Chung. The other branch is Mang Kung Uk village near Hang Hau. Typically, this Liu genealogy records several hundred pages of other Liu branches extending across the generations from North China into Kiangsi, eastern Kwangtung, Szechuan, and overseas. Only in the last few pages does it record which local branches inhabit which of the two villages in the Sai Kung area.

Another Liu lineage claims in its oral tradition to have immigrated to Sai Kung during the latter half of the nineteenth century. One segment settled the little hollow above Pak Kong (C) village, while another segment settled on the side of a steep hill four kilometers to the east. After several generations each branch built a fortresslike compound which housed about fifty persons and which was centered around an ancestor hall.[4] These two localized branches claim to be genealogically related, although I heard of no attempt to maintain permanent political and ritual relationships between them. There are several other genealogically unconnected Liu lineages with histories of expansion and extension through the Sai Kung area (see Aijmer 1967); however, there is no record of permanent amalgamations of these diverse Liu lineages into a Liu surname group.

Agnatic relations have proven useful in organizing groups at the hamlet *(tsuen)* and to some degree the village or valley *(hsiang)* level, but not at the market area level. At the market level, agnatic as well as affinal, matrilateral, and friendly relationships within the Hakka ethnic community prove useful. It is also at these higher levels of political economic integration that public deities are enshrined to sanction networks of interlineage and interpersonal relations. Sai Kung town with its Tin Hau temple has been the center for the Hakka community during the past century.

I have presented evidence to show how many local Cantonese lineages have non-Cantonese origins. The same diversity in origins is undoubtedly true of the local Hakka. Many Hakka lineages are located near the seashore. Hakka families, even whole lineages, have made a livelihood aboard boats, fishing, trading, and in the old days, pirating. Although I lack demonstrable cases, there is plenty of hearsay evidence that some of these Hakka came from, or in other cases merged with, Hokkien or Cantonese boat communities.

BOAT PEOPLE

Unlike land people, boat people do not make grandiose claims on history. They do not keep genealogies. They live their lives in small conjugal and stem families aboard boats. In modern Hong Kong these boats average about ten meters from stem to stern and about four meters abeam. The twenty square meters of living space aft the main beam is usually divided into a main cabin, two tiny cabins, followed by a poop deck containing cooking and bathing facilities. It is an understatement to say that the members of a boat family live and work closely together (see Anderson 1972). In this way, they contrast with village families whose fathers and brothers spend years working in foreign countries.

Boat people contrast with villagers in other ways too.[5] The equivalent of hamlet-level social organization for boat people is the cluster of boats anchored close together in a particular harbor. Often these clusters are formed by several or more boats using the same fishing technique and living at the same socioeconomic level. They are tied by kinship, real and fictive, and friendship. The clusters are not incorporated on the basis of shared agnatic ancestors with historical roots beyond the immediate organization of coresidence and economic cooperation. The cluster of kindred and friendly boat families may be incorporated for short-term economic purposes into firecracker associations, which I describe in chapter 5. Such corporations focus on the worship of a public deity in whose harbor the group maintains residential and economic connection.

Beyond their immediate clusters, the boat family maintains an extensive network of dyadic relations based on kinship (agnatic, affinal, matrilateral) as well as friendship with boat families in other harbors extending from Tap Mun Island to Hong Kong Island. Through such networks marketing and technical information is exchanged, physical security is maintained, and all forms of mutual aid are facilitated. Their networks of kinship and friendship also extend to the shore population upon whom the boat people are ultimately dependent. The older resident boat families tend to have more extensive and intensive relationships with land people in their vicinity than the immigrant boat people, who are the last to come and therefore the first to leave during hard times.

Given their mobility, the changing number of boat people in an area is a fairly accurate barometer of the prosperity and security of the market. Over the past century there has been a general increase of boats anchoring at Sai Kung. While certain periods are marked by sharp increases (during the communist consolidation of the South China coast in 1950 and after the collectivization movement in China in 1960), other periods are marked by sharp decreases (during the terror and starvation caused by the Japanese invasion of Hong Kong in 1941 and during the Hong Kong riots of 1967).

THE EMERGENCE OF SAI KUNG MARKET

The establishment of Hong Kong as a crown colony in 1842 stimulated an increased array of industrial and commercial alternatives to agricultural subsistence in Sai Kung.[6] Some of these exploits included either new

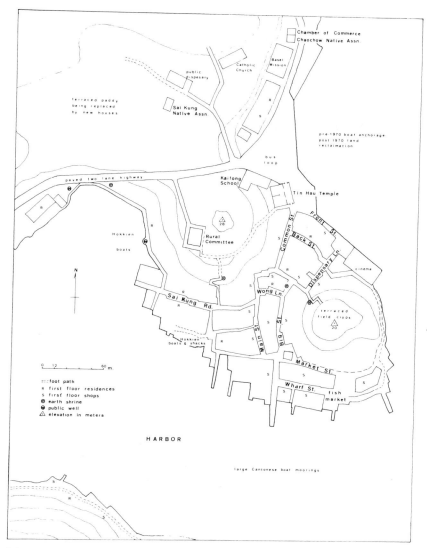

Map 4. Sai Kung Market Town, 1971

or increased crop production (for example, sugarcane), fish-drying, lime-
and charcoal-making, stone quarrying, piracy, smuggling, shopkeeping,
and sojourning abroad. The Hakka village of Sai Kung, located on a little harbor between the large Cantonese villages, became the site for increased trade with Hong Kong and eastern Paoan.

By 1900 Sai Kung was a thriving little center. The 1905 Block Crown

Lease records indicate that around the turn of the century there were over fifty shops and a hundred and fifty houses. Of the landowners there were thirty-two surnames in the population of 512. The town began to eclipse the large rice-growing Cantonese villages in size, wealth, and heterogeneity. According to my analysis of the 1915-commemorative temple tablets, 80 percent of the town's population was Hakka, half of whom were traders from markets in eastern Paoan. Twenty percent were local and immigrant Cantonese merchants. There were also a number of boat people who made Sai Kung harbor their home.

Sai Kung market was linked to the sea from its beginning. There were no roads for mechanized commercial traffic until 1960. Overland trade with Kowloon markets was carried on shoulder poles over mud and stone paths winding through the hills. Therefore, Sai Kung traders took advantage of their proximity to the sea and developed their market as a port town. By 1902 a harbor station was established in Sai Kung to regulate the flow of seaborne trade. In 1905, 459 tons of seaborne cargo were transacted at Sai Kung. This compares to the 603 tons of seaborne cargo handled at Tai Po. However, 63 percent of Sai Kung trade was with China (mostly with markets in southern Waichow) compared to 26 percent for Tai Po, whose China trade was largely overland (SP 1905:208). In both cases, the bulk of the sea trade consisted of exports to urban areas of the colony. Thus, the overall direction of seaborne trade was from the rural hinterland of Paoan and the New Territories into the urban areas, and Sai Kung traders were forging themselves a link in the chain of supply. By 1915, Sai Kung was handling 1,929 tons of cargo, almost four times the amount of the previous decade (SP 1915:T-6).

During these early years Sai Kung had the following enterprises: one bamboo wares shop, two jewelry shops, three bakeries, three brick kilns, three blacksmiths, four boatbuilding yards, five furniture and coffin makers, fifteen lime kilns, and thirty-two distilleries (SP 1914). Although it was the smallest marketing center in the British-controlled New Territories, Sai Kung had the most bakeries, lime kilns, and distilleries. The distilleries were owned by general stores. Altogether, Sai Kung distillers produced 15,219 registered gallons of liquor in 1916, which was over one-third of the total distilled in the New Territories. By 1919 the amount produced in Sai Kung had more than doubled (SP 1917 and 1920:J-2). By the preceding reckoning, there were at least sixty-eight industrial concerns in Sai Kung compared to only thirty-one and thirty-nine in the same list for the area's traditional markets at Tai Po and Kowloon City respectively.

Although Sai Kung was nominally part of the Tai Po market area, Sai

Kung's increasing autonomy does not seem to have been a source of conflict between the two markets. The two markets were quite different. They were more complementary than competitive. Sai Kung's economy was a response to the burgeoning Hong Kong entrepot, and it was not an attempt to take trade away from Tai Po. Sai Kung supplied Hong Kong and Kowloon with various industrial products including preserved fish, wood fuels, sugarcane, liquor, masonry products, and labor. Sai Kung also transacted goods between the urban areas and the network of Sai Kung villages and Hakka markets along the east coast of Paoan. While Sai Kung emerged in relationship to Hong Kong and Kowloon, Tai Po was a traditional market based on agricultural production. In fact, to the extent there was conflict between Sai Kung and Tai Po, it seems to have had little to do with the emergence of a Hakka-controlled market in a traditional Cantonese market area. The conflict, such as it was, seems to have concerned the exercise of control over revenues generated by the production of rice in the large Cantonese valleys. It was a conflict between the Cantonese tillers in Sai Kung and the powerful Cantonese lineage which controlled the Tai Po market and owned the agricultural hinterlands (see note 9).

Sai Kung's market was different from Tai Po's in another way. The Hakka traders at Sai Kung made no attempt to insert their market into a regional schedule in order to articulate trade with the traditional marketing system. In fact, one Hakka businessman says that: "Sai Kung never had a real market place *(hsü ch'ang);* Sai Kung was only an administrative village *(hsiang hsia)*." Although this statement was made in the context of contrasting the small size of the pre-1950 market to the present market, it nevertheless indicates that the emergence of commercial and industrial facilities in Sai Kung was not conceptualized as a traditional periodic market.[7]

Half of the early trade in Sai Kung market was in the hands of immigrants from China, while local people began to travel abroad to earn a living. Although this pattern became even more pronounced after 1960, we can see it already taking shape in the initial organization of the town. With the increased shipping and the extension of the British dominion over the New Territories in 1898, Sai Kung villagers began to seek wage labor on the ships which called at ports in Kowloon. Sai Kung men became involved in various guild, secret society, and trade union activities. Urban and overseas work led to greater opportunities for villagers than what accrued to them as rice or sugarcane farmers, wood or stonecutters, charcoal or lime burners. As these sojourners returned some of their earnings to the village, the local villages experienced increasing prosperity (SP 1910:1–7). By 1915 local commerce and overseas remittances were sufficient to finance the reconstruction and expansion of the town's Tin Hau temple and the building of new village houses with brick rather than pounded earth or adobe.[8]

IMPERIAL ADMINISTRATION AND LOCAL LEADERSHIP

A crucial factor in development of ethnic relationships in Sai Kung is the role of imperial administration. In this section I review the history of the three imperial powers which have ruled Sai Kung during the past century. The Chinese ruled the area until 1898, when the British forced the Peking government to sign a ninety-nine-year lease on the 945-square kilometers of Paoan county surrounding Kowloon. This area became known as the New Territories, and it included Sai Kung. In 1941, the Japanese invaded Hong Kong and occupied the area until their defeat in the Pacific. After 1945 the British resumed their control of the area, and there is every indication that the British will maintain their nominal authority over the New Territories well beyond expiration of the lease date in 1997.

Before 1898 Sai Kung was controlled by a Chinese submagistrate in the Kowloon Walled City. Under his agency, the influential men of the largest villages around Kowloon formed an alliance *(yüeh)* to protect the local populations against pirates, immigrants, and the rapacious power of the Tang lineage which controlled Tai Po market and owned much of its cultivated hinterland (see Freedman 1966:86).[9] The Tang lineage claimed ownership of the paddy land in Sai Kung, and Tang rent collectors made periodic forays into Sai Kung villages. According to an old man in Sha Kok Mei, the Tang rent collectors chased the local men from their homes and spent the night with the local women. The local men exacted revenge by watering down the rice which the collectors carried back to Tai Po. However, in at least one instance the villagers managed to scare off the collectors with threats of organized violence.

When the British attempted to take control of the New Territories in 1899, they encountered violent resistance from the Tang lineage at Tai Po. Sai Kung people did not resist the British takeover. The Kowloon City submagistrate probably counseled restraint through the old *yüeh* network of village headmen. The British quickly secured support from the people of Sai Kung by recording the tenure of the land in the name of the local tiller, giving little regard to previous claims. This wiped out Tang lineage claims on the land farmed by the Sai Kung Cantonese. Hakka traders also benefited as British succession brought greater security and legitimacy to their fledgling market.

With subjugation of the Tang lineage, the British established their

New Territories administration at Tai Po. A British magistrate administered Sai Kung in the same way as his Chinese predecessor. He maintained personal liaisons with the big men of the old established lineages. In Sai Kung, the most prominent men included the Hakka townsmen and the Cantonese landlords of Ho Chung. Most were self-made men. Most had a rudimentary education from a village tutor, and many were engaged in rough-and-tumble trade along the China coast or in wage labor of Hong Kong ports.

These early decades of the twentieth century were the heady years of Chinese nationalism. Sai Kung men, as China coast traders or as wage laborers, became involved in nationalist-inspired secret societies. One of these societies was the Chung Wo Tong, organized to support Sun Yat-Sen's revolutionary efforts in Hong Kong (see Morgan 1960). According to several men whose fathers and grandfathers were leaders, the center of the Chung Wo Tong organization was Sai Kung. Sai Kung was strategically located for such activities. Its location in remote hills bordering a lucrative foreign enclave coupled with deprived socioeconomic conditions of its inhabitants helped to create Sai Kung's tradition of radical nationalism which continued to spur resistance to the Japanese occupation.

In 1941 the Japanese invaded Hong Kong and imprisoned the British colonialists. At Sai Kung, the Japanese garrisoned troops. The Japanese conscripted villagers to build a military road between Kowloon and Sai Kung town. As the Japanese attempted to extend their control over the area, they were contested by communist-led Hakka-speaking guerrillas of the East River Anti-Japanese Brigade. A hundred guerrillas from southern Waichow infiltrated the remote mountain villages in Sai Kung. The contest between the Japanese and the guerrillas revolved around which side was able to supply the starving population with rice. The conflict was violent at times. Japanese summarily executed "bandits," and guerrillas assassinated collaborators.

To increase their control the Japanese established a Sai Kung Self-Administration Association. What this title actually meant was that the head of each hamlet was liable to the Japanese commandant for the conduct of his fellow villagers. This placed each village leader in a precarious position, since each also served the interests of guerrillas who lived and governed among them. Most wily young men who volunteered as headmen became experts at supporting each of the protagonists in order to preserve the middle.

Upon the defeat of Japan in 1945, the East River Brigade took outright control of Sai Kung town until they were ordered to relinquish control of the area to British forces and to withdraw to Waichow as part of the Communist party's overall strategy against the Kuomintang.

The British instituted a system of rural representation similar to that organized by the Japanese. Sai Kung leaders were wary of British motives. At a public meeting in Sai Kung in 1947, the new district officer informed the people that this new system of rural representation was "the first step toward self-government." However, the unspoken motive which proved more enduring was the need to *increase* imperial control in face of communist influence in the area.

Under their new system, which the British dubbed "Rural Affairs Committee," each of the ninety-one hamlets centered around Sai Kung market sent a representative to sit in the general assembly. Larger, mostly Cantonese, villages were allotted several representatives in proportion to their populations. And Sai Kung town was allotted twenty-one representatives in proportion to its population. The town representatives organized their mercantile interests into a Kaifong ("neighborhood") association.

In 1960, eight Rural Committee positions were created for representatives of the boat community.

Village representatives were selected in traditional style by villagers from among village notables. However, the town was socioculturally heterogeneous; it included many immigrant shopkeepers. Therefore Kaifong elections were formalized. Each family which resided on a street for three or more years cast one secret ballot for any candidate who resided on that street for ten or more years.

Together, village, Kaifong, and boat representatives elected an executive committee every two years. This all powerful committee was soon dominated by Kaifong representatives. Their disproportionate power in the Rural Committee stemmed from their mercantile wealth and from their willingness to utilize that wealth to mobilize political support in ways that villagers were unwilling to or could not afford. Kaifong representatives lived at the hub of day-to-day decision-making while many of the politically influential villagers were overseas and not in immediate touch with market-town politics. Thus, through the political apparatus of the Kaifong, immigrants seized opportunities for exercising their influence in Sai Kung. As we shall see, the expansion of immigrant opportunities continued to animate factional and ethnic politics in Sai Kung.[10]

During the formative years of the Rural Committee (1947–1953) two rival Hakka- and Cantonese-led village factions vied for the executive positions. The Hakka leader owned a shop in town and enjoyed Kaifong support. By 1953 he was able to consolidate his position at the head of the Rural Committee. The Cantonese village leader accused his Hakka

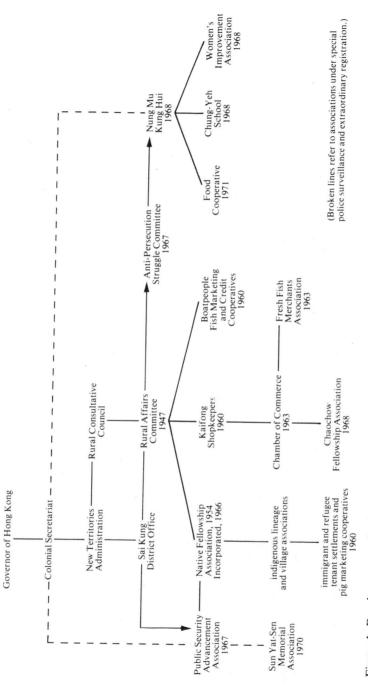

Figure 1. Development and Alignment of Associations in the Sai Kung Market, 1971

Governor of Hong Kong

Colonial Secretariat

New Territories Administration

Rural Consultative Council

Sai Kung District Office

Rural Affairs Committee 1947

Native Fellowship Association, 1954 Incorporated, 1966

indigenous lineage and village associations

immigrant and refugee tenant settlements and pig marketing cooperatives 1960

Public Security Advancement Association 1967

Sun Yat-Sen Memorial Association 1970

Kaifong Shopkeepers 1960

Chamber of Commerce 1963

Chaochow Fellowship Association 1968

Boatpeople Fish Marketing and Credit Cooperatives 1960

Fresh Fish Merchants Association 1963

Anti-Persecution Struggle Committee 1967

Nung Mu Kung Hui 1968

Food Cooperative 1971

Chung-Yeh School 1968

Women's Improvement Association 1968

(Broken lines refer to associations under special police surveillance and extraordinary registration.)

rival of being the secret agent for immigrant interests. The Cantonese leader attempted to organize the Sai Kung Native Fellowship Association. The district officer refused to register the new association on the grounds that it rivaled the Rural Committee. But after protracted negotiations, the district officer registered it as a "social club," and thereafter refused to deal with it. The Native Fellowship Association remained politically inert until 1960 and politically unsuccessful until 1967.

By 1963, Sai Kung was tied to daily markets in Kowloon. To control expanding numbers of shopkeepers, the Kaifong leaders organized a chamber of commerce. The Chamber of Commerce incorporated both local and immigrant commercial interests. As immigrants began numerically to dominate marketing in Sai Kung, the chamber fell increasingly under their influence. As such, it was structurally opposed to the landed village interests of the Native Fellowship Association.

In 1960 the Hakka chairman of the Rural Committee resigned under pressure from the government. The vice-chairman was a popular Cantonese merchant named Chan Yat-Kuan. He became the new chairman. At this juncture, the (Hakka) nephew of the original chairman openly mobilized opposition to Chan's leadership of the Kaifong, the Chamber of Commerce, and the Rural Committee. The Hakka-village-led faction joined the Native Fellowship Association and took over its executive offices from the Cantonese village founder. For seven years the two factions sparred for control of the Rural Committee. The Hakka Native Fellowship faction accused the Chan (Kaifong) faction of being comprised mostly of immigrants opposed to local interests and customs. This pattern of factional struggle whereby those in power must accommodate immigrant interests while those out of power mobilize support on the basis of opposing all such accommodations soon came to characterize ethnic politics in Sai Kung.

In 1967, Chan Yat-Kuan, the Cantonese Kaifong leader, joined the patriotic movement to oppose British colonial authority. His move was part of the radical hightide of the Cultural Revolution in Canton. The radicals transformed their Rural Committee into the Sai Kung Struggle Committee, which was the first substantive assertion of local level "independence" from imperialist controls in Sai Kung history (see note 9). The district officer deposed Chan and shifted his support to the Hakka-village-led Native Fellowship Association in an attempt to organize a new Rural Committee. In chapters 6 and 7, I examine these factional struggles in greater detail. Suffice it for now to say that once in power the new Hakka faction was forced to accommodate immigrant political demands to such an extent that by 1971 a new faction formed to oppose accommodation of immigrants.

The New Road, New Technology, and New People

In 1960 the Japanese-built military road between Kowloon and Sai Kung was widened and paved. No single innovation brought more fundamental a change to social relationships in Sai Kung. Following completion of the road, the fertile fields of Ho Chung, Pak Kong, and Sha Kok Mei began to attract commercial truck farmers. Some came from China during the hunger following the Great Leap Forward (1958-1960). Others came from overcrowded tenements of Kowloon to seek a niche in the Sai Kung market. Some were successful in opening shops right in the market town. Others set up little general stores, sundries shops, and mahjong parlors in newly settled areas around Ho Chung, Pak Sha Wan, and a labyrinth of houses, shacks, and shops on the hill between the market town and Pak Kong. If we exclude the boat people, by 1970 these immigrants (Hakka, Hokkien, and Cantonese) outnumbered the local people (Hakka and Cantonese) 7,722 to 6,921.

Another radical alteration brought about by the new road linked the marine resources of Sai Kung with the demand for fresh fish in eastern Kowloon. Formerly there were several hundred boat people anchored in Sai Kung harbor. After 1960 they increased to 4,755, outnumbering the land people in the immediate vicinity. As we shall see shortly, this migration of populations facilitated by the new road brought a profound reorganization of ethnic group identities and relationships.

With the road came electrical lighting, piped water, and bottled gas for stoves. By 1970 most large shops had telephones, and a number of families around town owned television sets. However, villagers still burned grass for cooking, and only recently have they installed plumbing and electricity for lighting and refrigeration.

Market Organization

In 1945 when the British reestablished authority in Hong Kong, they immediately instituted controls in the local markets aimed at increasing the self-sufficiency of the colony's food supply. The need was spurred by the rising tide of Chinese nationalism and the attempt on the part of the communist government to feed its own population without considering the needs of a British colony. The colonial government helped the local producers of fresh foods (fish, pork, vegetables)—rice was more easily imported from Southeast Asia—to reorganize their operations into efficient enterprises. The Department of Agriculture and Fisheries established marketing organizations to provide marketing facilities for primary producers which greatly restricted the power of traditional middlemen (see Topley 1964:180-181). The organizations aided producers in forming credit cooperatives to stimulate capital development of food production; it provided transport of foods to market at reasonable costs; and for fishermen it instituted a daily auction to guarantee a fair price from the fish dealers.

In Sai Kung the vegetable and swine cooperatives began marketing their products in 1954. The 197 members in the four cooperatives were mainly local village women. After 1960, immigrant farmers began renting fields and organizing swine and vegetable production around the large Cantonese villages. The local women moved into other newly opened niches for reasons that will be discussed later. At the time of my study, Chinese production brigades north of the border were exporting pork to Hong Kong at prices with which even the most efficient immigrant producers found difficult to compete.

In 1953 the Sai Kung Fishermen's Credit Cooperative Society was established with the aid of the government-controlled Fish Marketing Organization. By 1960 five additional credit cooperatives were formed and incorporated within the Sai Kung District Federation of Fishermen's Cooperative Societies. They represented 110 vessels and 152 families in the harbors of Sai Kung, Kau Sai, and Lung Shuen Wan. Each of the five cooperatives was organized on the basis of native residence and/or fishing technique. Today, the directorship of the federation is controlled by five individuals from four of the old-time resident boat families.

The credit cooperatives enabled the boat people to motorize their propulsion and their net winches and to install onboard refrigeration. These capital investments not only made life and work afloat easier, they also facilitated greater range over, and much more intensive exploitation of, the fishing grounds. They facilitated longer storage and greatly increased the productive capacity of fresh rather than dried and salted fish. Building on these successes, recently, a seventh Better Living Cooperative was added to the federation. It builds houses across the harbor from Sai Kung town, thus enabling boat families to live ashore; and it provides a special school for boat children.

Traditionally, boat people depended on their patron fishmonger to market their hauls of fish. Boat people were stuck in a position which was naturally exploited by the fishmongers. However the Fish Marketing Organization required fishermen who land hauls in excess of one picule (60 kilograms) to auction them to the fish dealers. The auction brought a profound shift in power between fishermen and fishmongers. The auction forced fishmongers to compete with each other for the wholesale market. Partly to stem this increased competition, the fishmongers organized themselves into the Sai Kung Fresh Fish Dealers' Association in 1963. Today, both sides are formally organized. Although their trans-

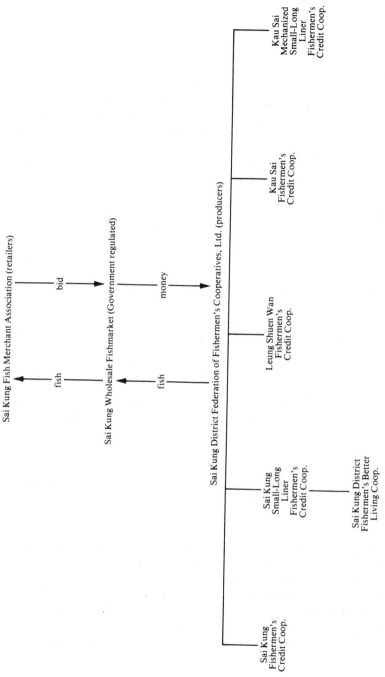

Figure 2. Organization of Fish Marketing in Sai Kung, 1971

Sai Kung Fish Merchant Association (retailers)

bid →

Sai Kung Wholesale Fishmarket (Government regulated)

money →

Sai Kung District Federation of Fishermen's Cooperatives, Ltd. (producers)

← fish

← fish

Sai Kung Fishermen's Credit Coop.

Sai Kung Small-Long Liner Fishermen's Credit Coop.

Sai Kung District Fishermen's Better Living Coop.

Leung Shuen Wan Fishermen's Credit Coop.

Kau Sai Fishermen's Credit Coop.

Kau Sai Mechanized Small-Long Liner Fishermen's Credit Coop.

actions tend to become personalized in ways that circumvent government controls, the organized fishermen now receive equal benefits in the marketplace.

The government was successful in turning fish production into a prosperous trade with glimmerings of a modern business enterprise. Consequently, the boat community stratified (see Ward 1967). A small percentage of successful fishermen enjoy unparalleled prosperity. They own large motorized junks, and many possess residences ashore. A sizeable group of poor boat people huddle together in dilapidated boats which wallow in the tidal mud at the back of the harbor. Their young people hire out as crewmen or seek jobs in factories. In between the prosperous and the poor is still a majority of people who live and work as family units aboard their mechanized boats.

The Hong Kong government is not the only outside influence on the Sai Kung boat people. Many are also connected to the People's Republic of China. Large-scale fishing operations depend on access to Chinese waters. Sai Kung boat people who fish Chinese waters are required to obtain licenses from the Yent'ien commune, twenty-five kilometers north of Sai Kung. Here boat people renew their licenses every New Year. They also maintain bank accounts, attend political meetings, purchase some of their staples, and since 1958, have been required to sell a percentage of their hauls to the commune. The boat people also help the Chinese government to secure its borders against illegal passage of foreign agents and refugees. Boat people prove instrumental in the control of this traffic.[11]

Contrary to the opinion of some Hong Kong anticommunists, boat people are not communist agents. In fact, they are what I would call "agents of the border." They protect Hong Kong interests as quickly as those of China, for in a very palpable sense, boat people enjoy the benefits of both worlds. On the one hand, they enjoy the esteem of being part of the People's Republic of China, while on the other hand, they thrive in the freedom to prosper which is available in Hong Kong for those with a lot of luck and cunning.

THE NEW MARKETPLACE

According to the survey of Kaifong storefronts which my wife and I conducted in 1973, the ethnic composition of Sai Kung shopkeepers is altered from the traditional makeup. The largest grouping is thirty-seven Cantonese immigrants from counties around the Canton delta. The second largest group of thirty-five local Hakka is the traditional majority. Many Hakka who work in Europe rent their shop spaces for about $500 a month to immigrants. A new group of Hakka immigrants totals twenty-nine. They are followed by twenty-five Chaochow immigrants, ten Waichow (Hokkien) immigrants, nine local Cantonese, and several former boat people selling sodas and snacks in little shops located across the harbor or selling fish in the government-owned stalls along the Sai Kung pier. It is clear that Hakka no longer dominate marketing in Sai Kung, although they still retain dominion over the political end of the economic equation.

According to our Kaifong survey, there are about 150 first-floor shops in Sai Kung market town. This is three times the number of shops that existed during the early part of the century. About half the proprietors and their families live behind or above their shops, while others live on a second floor elsewhere in town.

Most shops fall in the category of the general store. These twenty-five stores carry staples including rice, oil, sugar, and salt in addition to packaged and tinned foods from China. They carry other household items from soap to kerosene.

There are twenty-two soda and cracker shops in town, and numerous ones cropping up in the emerging centers frequented by vacationers from Kowloon. These small shops sell chilled soda, beer, fruit, crackers, cookies, and bread. They also sell the all-important daily newspapers from Hong Kong. Most of these little stores provide a table or two where neighbors congregate to play mahjong for a small fee.

There are fifteen restaurants and tea houses. Three of them are multi-storied establishments. The other twelve include ground-floor establishments and open-air stalls.

Eleven sundries shops sell modern stationery, sewing materials, cosmetics, and nicknacks.

Seven tailor shops make work clothes and Chinese- and Western-style suits. Eight dry goods stores sell cheaper factory-made clothes. Some also carry cheap plastic footwear made in Taiwan. A number of these stores are owned by local Hakka who quit tailoring in the face of immigrant competition.

Each of seven hardware stores specializes in fishing supplies, general household tools and fixtures, or electrical supplies and repairs. One sells modern appliances including Japanese-made refrigerators and televisions.

Six building supplies stores sell lumber, plumbing fixtures, and sheet metal.

Four traditional "mountain products stores" specialize in forged iron farm implements, plowshares, sickles, hoes, rakes, and such bamboo wares as baskets, hats, mops, and brooms, and crockery also. Most

Plate 1. A Cantonese boat woman purchasing a melon from a Hakka vegetable vendor along Wharf Street

mountain products are imported from China. Nowadays the stores also sell Hong-Kong–made plastic pails and pans, and a variety of factory-made utensils.

During festivities, the five traditional paper stores thrive on sales of ritual paraphernalia (gold and silver paper bullion, hell bank notes, candles, incense, talismans) for the dead. They also do a daily trade in toilet paper for the mundane rituals of the living.

Four bakeries sell Chinese cakes and a few Western-style pastries. One shop specializes in making noodles. Notably all bakeshops are owned by Chaochow people. This is the only marketing niche that is visibly monopolized by a particular ethnic group.

There are four barbershops, one of which specializes in permanents for women.

Each of four large apothecaries employs one or more pulse doctors. There is another small herb shop, a Chinese bone-doctor clinic, and a professional spirit medium who happens to be paraplegic. There is one Western-style private physician's clinic and a fair-sized government clinic and pharmacy just outside the main market.

There are five dry docks, boat repair and building yards along with two motor and machine works for fishing boats.

Five cottage industries are located in town and a dozen more are strung along the road leading to town. In addition, there are two carpenter shops turning out custom furniture and coffins, a couple of metal welding works, two chicken hatcheries, two rice mills, and two jewelry shops. The largest ground-floor establishment in town is the China Products Emporium. A number of other shops can be found nestled in the labyrinth of narrow lanes: a cobbler shop, a steam laundry, a seamstress, a bean curd maker, a slaughter house, a Caltex bottled gas distributor, a bike shop, a photo studio, a cinema, two Kowloon bank branches, a communist bookstore, and a candlestick maker just outside town.

Fresh foods are marketed in permanent government-owned stalls along Market Street. However, in the past two decades, many makeshift stalls have sprung up along Wharf Street and other streets in town. Altogether there are well over two dozen vegetable and fruit stalls. There are altogether also about two dozen fish, pork, and beef stalls. Each day 1,600 kilograms of fresh fish are sold in Sai Kung market by twelve men and women. (Another 4,500 kilograms are sold to Kowloon dealers at the predawn auction.) During the predawn hours an average of fifteen hogs and two cows are slaughtered in the abattoir on Main Street. The animals are butchered and sold by ten men. Finally, there is one woman who sells frozen chicken parts and one who sells sausages.

Not included in our survey of shops are a number of second-story and backroom businesses. Second-story hostels provide beds for itinerant hawkers and such transient professionals as injection doctors, pulse doctors, dentists, and gamblers. The biggest businesses in town are also upstairs. These include the two travel agencies and several construction companies owned by local Hakka and Cantonese leaders. The two travel agencies are each owned by a Hakka and a Cantonese leader (see chapter 6, A Local Hakka Merchant Family). The Hakka-owned construction and real estate firms compete for government and private contracts. Given the economic importance of overseas jobs and investments and of land ownership in Sai Kung, we can understand why local people, especially Hakka, have monopolized these businesses. The owners of these businesses also constitute the economic nuclei of Sai Kung's political factions.

The tight network of syndicate-owned gambling casinos and opium dens are secluded from the main streets. They are controlled by a Kowloon City–based syndicate whose members are veterans of such various triad societies as the 14-K. The Kowloon bosses are in league with some local leaders who manage directly and indirectly the town's gambling casinos and opium dens (see chapter 4, The Backbone of the Hakka

Community). I estimate that on an average day, the syndicate drains Sai Kung of several thousand dollars in gambling revenues alone. During public festivities, the syndicate sets up gambling stalls along Wharf Street or around the matshed housing the opera. On these occasions, its take is so large that I had no means by which to estimate the amount.

Our inventory of shops needs to be qualified in four ways:

1. Smaller shops are not stable. Every few months one goes out of business and another replaces it. For instance when the local activists opened a communist bookstore, many townspeople thought the venture would fail because few people have the time or money to read more than a daily newspaper. Many people did come to browse, but few came to buy. The young proprietor, an unemployed schoolteacher, was heavily in debt and was not sure he could last even several months.

2. Most stores sell anything they can, therefore it is sometimes difficult to classify the store. For example, one cloth shop also sells foods. The sheet-metal shop sells comics and plastic toys in front. A number of storeowners sell or allow friends to hawk vegetables or fruit out front.

3. Some stores alter their products by the season. One chicken hatchery converts to a special restaurant serving dog meat stew during the winter, and by spring it is again a hatchery.

4. During the post-1970 building boom, Market and Wharf streets were being extended into a landfill area, and new shops were going up. The Sai Kung described in these pages has already passed into history.

COTTAGE INDUSTRY AND FEMALE LABOR

Since the last century, the main source of employment for Sai Kung village men has been urban and overseas wage labor followed by commercial investment. Before 1941 many men worked as sailors and stevedores. After 1950 Hong Kong changed from a great shipping center serving South China to a more self-contained industrialized city-state. Few villagers, other than some young women, responded to the demand for unskilled, unorganized labor upon which Hong Kong's industry began to thrive. Opportunities for advancing one's fortunes beyond the horizons of a poorly paid life of labor were, and still are, considered extremely limited compared to what could be accomplished overseas. Therefore as shipping diminished, many village men left to work in phosphate mines of the western Pacific.

After 1960 Sai Kung men reoriented their labor and investments to the rapidly expanding Chinese restaurant business in western Europe. According to the records held by the Sai Kung Post Office in 1971 Sai Kung families received a total of $4,459,130 from their menfolk working abroad. If we divide this total remittance by 12 (the number of months) and again by 1,500 (the approximate number of families with members working abroad), we can see that an average remittance comes to only $250. Bearing in mind that money may be remitted by other means, for example, it may be hand carried by returning sojourners, $250 amounts to a subsistence income. Until the 1950s, village women supplemented the meager remittance of their menfolk by growing rice and sweet potatoes.

As I have already noted, 1960 was the year the road was built linking Kowloon with Sai Kung. The road became a conduit for immigrants looking for space to farm vegetables and for outside industrialists looking for cheap land and labor for their mills. Farmers and mill managers were able to rent the Cantonese village fields through which the road was built. The substantial rents which the Cantonese villagers extracted from the commercial farmers and industrialists supplemented the remittances from Europe.

Today Ho Chung has several cloth bleaching and dyeing factories and several preserved seeds factories. The drying seeds give the area its distinct aroma, and the toxic dye infuses the stream and bay with an unnatural shade of indigo blue. Along the road leading into Sai Kung town are several small factories for stamping plastic toys, cutting canvas gloves, and processing medicinal herbs. Around town are about five factory outlets where women sew gloves and shoes, assemble plastic flowers and toys. The pool of female labor includes immigrant, boat, and some village women. Adolescent and teenage girls sit at rows of sewing machines where each can earn $15 a day. In one large room in a remote corner of the market I observed fifteen young teenage boat-girls operating heavy press machines, a job usually done by men. Older women and their children assemble plastic flowers and toys at home. Many poor boat women carry this work home to their boats. Even Hakka village women who are too old or too ill, or during a rainy spell, may spend their days and evenings with their children assembling plastic flowers. All female employment is diurnal, and remuneration is on a piecework basis.

Hakka village women generally own land that is too remote to facilitate commercial use by immigrant farmers or industrialists. Hakka women also seem to consider cottage labor their least rewarding option. When possible they continue to plant rice and/or to seek employment with several locally owned construction companies. Local Hakka contractors prefer to hire Hakka women for the heavy labor of digging foundations and carrying mud, stone, and sand. Each woman receives a daily wage of $15 to $20 including breaks for tea and bread supplied by their boss. Many of these women work with their village cohort, and they know their bosses personally, in many cases as kinsmen. In the next chapter I shall examine the role of Hakka women in much greater detail.

CONCLUSION

Sai Kung society constitutes a market area which has become closely tied with outside governmental, technical, economic, and demographic forces and is undergoing rapid change in the process. We cannot comprehend the process of ethnic grouping outside these changes in the local and regional contexts.

The original Cantonese settled the most fertile valleys in the seventeenth century. They were followed in the next two centuries by the Hakka who settled the marginal agrarian niches. Traditional interethnic violence over land and water was obviated by an internal alliance of Sai Kung Hakka and Cantonese against outside landlords and by the opening of nonagrarian opportunities in the rise of Hong Kong commerce and industry. During the latter half of the nineteenth century, Hakka traders developed the market at Sai Kung. Local Hakka and Cantonese men also began to sojourn to urban jobs in Hong Kong, Kowloon, and overseas, while Hakka women worked the ancestral fields.

Major changes came about after the end of Japanese occupation with the establishment of the People's Republic of China, with intervention of the Hong Kong government in the production and sales of fresh foods, with development of an industrial economy in Hong Kong, and with construction of a road between Kowloon and Sai Kung. Sai Kung became an important supplier of fresh fish, while waves of immigrants reworked desiccating paddy fields into vegetable patches and pig pens. Less productive, hilly land was turned into residential and small industrial sites. Land along the new road and around town became commercially valuable. Many Sai Kung natives in this area became landlords to immigrant tenants. Both native and immigrant women filled the demand for cheap cottage-type industrial labor. Other immigrant women, worked alongside husbands growing vegetables or staffing shops, while women in remote villages, especially Hakka women, continued to plant paddy and to fill the demand for unskilled construction labor.

While local menfolk continued to sojourn and to invest overseas, immigrants gained influence in the local market economy as farmers and merchants. Immigrants are always ready to take over niches locals abandon. The local Hakka are rapidly becoming a numerical minority in the market. However, they retain political control. Some boat people and immigrant groups, especially Hokkien-speaking groups, have organized in a variety of ways and have begun to exert political influence on local Hakka leaders.

NOTES

1.   While anthropologists have stressed the integrity of tribal and village units, historians stress the overarching power of government on society. Thus in his new book, James Hayes offers fellow historians a new point of view—local Chinese villages were organized without the "managerial" skills of the "gentry." However, as an anthropologist I prefer to point out how local society was plugged into the imperial circuit of official "controls." Part of the difference between Hayes' understanding and mine of the relationship between traditional Chinese government and society is probably directional and semantic, rather than conceptual. In this regard I follow the distinction which Franz Schurman draws between "managerial" functions and "control" functions:

> Management means operational leadership through organization, and constant directive efforts over men to achieve goals. Control means the exercise of restraint over and the checking on human beings to make sure they are doing what is expected or are not hurting the interests of those in power. The weight of evidence from China's long history indicates that the state was far more oriented toward control than toward management of society (1973:406).

2.   The 1911 census gives 138 persons for Tai Mong Tsai village. However, there were three lineages in the village. The Tsang and Lo groups were equally dominant, while the newer Wong group constituted only a few families. It seems likely therefore that each of the main lineages had fifty or sixty members, which was the optimal carrying load of their paddy. My calculation of rice consumption is based on C. K. Yang's (1965, II:54) estimate of one pound of rice for an average peasant's daily consumption. However, not included in my estimate of production and consumption is the sweet potato crop upon which Hakka villagers also relied.

3.   Some of the largest Cantonese lineages in the New Territories were originally part of this Hakka resettlement. In certain contexts the Liao of Sheung Shui claim a Hakka ancestry (Baker 1968:39). According to one of my informants, the well-known Cantonese leader of the New Territories Congress of Rural Committee Chairmen joined the Hakka Tsung Tsin Association based on his claim of Hakka ancestry. Additional cases are beginning to emerge (Hayes 1977:207). We may find in the end that the Tang lineage is the only original Cantonese lineage in the entire area. According to Lo Hsiang-Lin (public address), the Tang were the only ones exempted from the Ching dynasty's ban on coastal settlement.

4.   Both Cantonese and Hakka villages were constructed for self-defense. The Cantonese villages which are larger and have more lineages are arranged in rows of houses (somewhat like modern American townhouses) separated by narrow alleys. The largest village, Ho Chung, had a wall around it. The Hakka hamlets are smaller, single lineage compounds. The classic style in Sai Kung consists of two rows of four three-room apartments dug into a hollow on the side of a hill. Each apartment opens onto a narrow corridor extending from one end of the compound to the other. In the center, the passageway opens into the ancestral hall. From the outside, the compound looks impregnable. However, in the past few decades, these compounds have begun to break down. With increased police security, increased commercial prosperity and widening disparity in wealth between compound members seeking fortunes outside agriculture, new houses are built outside the compound or even replacing old houses within the compound,

and each reflects a different level of family prosperity from its neighbor. The Hakka say, "life is no longer compound centered, now it is family centered!"

5.   The 1970 census indicates that the average size of Sai Kung boat families is seven persons compared to five for land families. The boat population is generally younger with 47 percent under the age of fifteen years compared to 45 percent for the land population. Also, the longevity of the Sai Kung boat people is much less than land people. Only 8 percent of boat people are over fifty-five years old in contrast to 22 percent of land people (HKG 1972).

The educational level of Sai Kung boat people is far below that of land people.

Educational level	Boat People (in percent)	Land People (in percent)
No formal education	73	33
Primary	26	56
Secondary	1	10
Postsecondary	0	1

It is also notable that among boat people twice as many males are educated than females, whereas among land people the ratio only slightly favors males (HKG 1972).

6.   James Hayes (1977:35) stresses the opinion that not all economic activity in the Hong Kong region during the nineteenth century was stimulated by the rise of the British colony. I concur with this well-informed opinion. However, it is also clear that the development of the Sai Kung market beyond a minor node in the exchange of local goods was almost a direct response to the rise of Hong Kong.

7.   Hayes designates Sai Kung a "coastal market" to distinguish it from G. William Skinner's "standard" periodic market. According to Hayes, the coastal market has a daily street market that sells fresh foods, and its shops are always open to transact business between the fishing and farming populations. Hayes (1977:38) explains the daily market as a response to the constant demand by large populations for a wide range of locally available goods. Although "coastal market" is a useful geographical expression, I am not convinced of its analytical usefulness. It seems to me that the characteristics of the coastal market, which Hayes mentions, are characteristics of a modernizing market system in general and of the Sai Kung market in relationship to Hong Kong in particular (see Skinner 1965:195–228).

8.   The building or repair of a public temple (a shrine dedicated to one of the patron deities in the Chinese pantheon) is the sine qua non of a community's social heterogeneity, economic prosperity, and cultural solidarity. In the annals of Sai Kung town, there are three such benchmarks. The first, 1842, dates the building of the Tin Hau temple in Sai Kung village (Hayes 1967:96). During this time, Sai Kung village obtained substantial central place functions probably in response to British colonization of Hong Kong Island in that same year. At the same time Sai Kung distinguished itself as a center for Hakka immigrant activity from the much older Cantonese center in Ho Chung village with its seventeenth-century Che Kung temple. Sai Kung also distinguished itself with its eighteenth-century Tin Hau temple from Lung Shuen Wan island. Lung Shuen Wan was a traditional outpost for the Chinese imperial navy's regulation of eastern approaches to the Pearl River. I wonder if perhaps Lung Shuen Wan was the original "coastal market center" in this area? It is notable that the Cantonese-dominated

villages of Pak Kong and Sha Kok Mei never completely switched their patronage of Tin Hau from Lung Shuen Wan (over four kilometers by sea) to Sai Kung town (half a kilometer on foot). These temple affiliations may express the traditional antagonism between the Cantonese villagers on either side of the Hakka townsmen over tenure of surrounding rice fields.

In 1878, Pak Kong did establish its own Tin Hau temple (Hayes 1967:88). Other temples were built in the area also. The most prominent of these I discuss in chapter 5.

In 1915 the Sai Kung Tin Hau temple was rebuilt and an adjoining temple for Kuan Kung was built. Tin Hau is the patroness of primary producers (fishermen, farmers, and women), while Kuan Kung is the male patron of soldiers, police-men, and merchants. If the establishment and juxtaposition of these deities has any social significance, I would think that before 1900, Sai Kung was an adminis-trative village with a "minor market" where fishermen, farmers, and traditional industrialists produced and transacted goods. After 1900, Sai Kung began to prosper as a more widely recognized commercial center.

The third date, 1965, marks the third building boom when Sai Kung's Tin Hau and Kuan Kung temples were again rebuilt along with new village houses with the flow of remittances from western Europe.

9. Maurice Freedman argued that:

> At least in coastal Kwangtung, *yüeh* were looked upon by the people who engaged in them as instruments of local control independent of state supervi-sion. They might be used for treating with the state, as seems especially to have been the case with the three *yüeh*-complexes oriented to Kowloon City, and might have allied themselves with officialdom in the face of banditry or attack by rebels and foreigners, but they were far removed from being mere tools in the hands of the government (1966:88).

As I read the meager data, the Sai Kung Liu Yüeh (Six-way alliance) probably consisted of leaders from the string of large villages extending east from Kowloon City, Nga Tsin Wai (C), Tseng Kuan Au (C), Tseng Lan Shue (H), Nam Wai (H), Ho Chung (C), and Sai Kung (H). (I wonder if the equal represen-tation of Cantonese and Hakka was purely fortuitous or was an attempt to balance ethnic group influence?) The *yüeh*'s main function, as that of the Rural Committee in later years, was to order intervillage relations and to maintain local hegemony against disorderly elements. I suspect that from the Kowloon sub-magistrate's point of view, the *yüeh* was useful in maintaining the integrity of the China coast against the incursions brought on by the British colony at Hong Kong (immigration, smuggling, piracy) and also toward countering the revenue-generating power of the Tang lineage which collected rent on paddy in Sai Kung and elsewhere in the Kowloon jurisdiction. Supposedly having collected rents, the Tang lineage paid the land taxes to the county magistrate in Nant'ou. However, great and powerful landowners were known to pay little or no tax and to be able to resist compliance with imperial decrees. Recall the Tang lineage was able to exempt itself from the imperial decree evacuating this region in 1662. I think the county magistrate, not to mention his Kowloon assistant, exercised very little authority over the Tang lineage. The Kowloon subofficial probably used the Sai Kung *yüeh* to orient trade if not revenues away from Tang-controlled Tai Po and toward Kowloon.

In emphasizing the interrelationship (rather than the "independence") of the *yüeh* with imperial officials, I would point out that the *yüeh* were often coterminus with other imperialist control mechanisms such as *pao chia* (a system of neighborhood surveillance) and *ti fang* (officially appointed local policeman). Sai Kung was a *pao chia;* and one of the local Hakka landowners was the *ti fang* appointed by the Kowloon official to police the area.

While Freedman emphasizes the "independence" of *yüeh* and James Hayes (1977) stresses the organizational autonomy of local society, I see no contradiction between the nature of imperialist control mechanisms such as *yüeh, pao chia,* or *ti fang* and the high degree of self-control which these very institutions allowed for or imposed upon local leaders. So long as order was maintained, and revenue was generated, the imperial officials took little interest in local society. The *yüeh* was part of an overall imperialist social structure which emphasized agrarian economy, taxation, and self-control, but not local organizational "independence."

10.   In his study of Tsuen Wan, a small Hakka enclave, which after 1950 became a highly industrialized and densely populated part of Kowloon, Graham Johnson (1971) emphasizes the gulf in political power between local people and immigrants. He argues that this situation is largely the result of the Hong Kong government's system of Rural Committees, which places power in the hands of local village landlords. My study takes a somewhat different tack from Johnson's in that I emphasize the ways that immigrant groups exercise political influence by their organizational finesse of local factions and colonial officials through cultural displays, and financial and moral support. It is not clear if the difference in Johnson's presentations and mine is an artifact of the data (two townships at different stages of development) or if it is an artifact of our different methodologies. I suspect it is both. In the first place, the proportion of immigrants to local (Hakka) power holders is much greater in Tsuen Wan than in Sai Kung; therefore the contradictions are undoubtedly more severe in Tsuen Wan. In the second place, Johnson focuses on the formal structures of power, while I focus on the factional struggles for power.

11.   In one incident, where I witnessed the most dramatic part, a group of Haifeng fishermen commandeered the commune trawler, locked up their coworkers who refused to mutiny, and sailed for several days along the Kwangtung coast. When they entered Hong Kong waters, they were being pursued by three Chinese militia boats. The refugees begged the boat people who dwell on the island to allow them respite until they could sneak into Hong Kong. The island boat people refused their requests and advised them to go back to China.

CHAPTER 4

Ethnic Groups and Ethnic Rhetorics

In this chapter I examine in more detail various ethnic communities in Sai Kung. I focus on the relationship between what people say about certain groups and the role that these groups play in the local society.

People may refer to more than one group with the same term, or they may use a variety of names to refer to one group in different contexts. The ethnic names reflect varying dimensions and images of the group's character and position in society. People usually stereotype outgroups with negative attributes, while people tend to attribute positive images to their own group. Depending on a group's position in society, its self-image may be more or less acknowledged in the public domain. Moreover, the ethnic rhetoric, pro and con, which surrounds a particular group shades the underlying sociocultural reality. And that reality is largely a product of the political-economic position that the group occupies in society. The rhetoric of ethnicity symbolizes and rationalizes a group's position in society, and as such people use it in the process of social change.

ORIGIN OF THE HAKKA MYSTIQUE

To have a better grasp on what "Hakka" means to people in Sai Kung, we need to review briefly its origins in the turbulent history of South China. Hakka literally designates "guest people." In general, it is a polite reference to immigrants. But in particular historical contexts, the name "Hakka" expressed contempt for people from northeastern Kwangtung. In nineteenth-century feuds with the Cantonese and the Hokkien, the Hakka were stigmatized as "rootless vagabonds" and "rabble-rousing hillbillies." Specifically, Cantonese and Hokkien referred to Hakka as "guest bandits" (Cohen 1968:275), "surly foreigners" (Kulp 1966:88), and "wild aborigines" (Hurlbut 1939). Well into the twentieth century, groups who were customarily identified as "Hakka" on the basis of their speech renounced the name as degrading to their dignity (Hsieh 1929:202). In fact modern scholars still find it difficult to understand "why the Hakkas should be without a name with which to describe themselves other than the one which means foreigners" (Forrest 1965:219).

Although many local communities surrounded by non-Hakka majorities rejected the "Hakka" label, others, mostly urban bourgeois elements, organized Hakka associations and articulated their Hakka origins in the ferment of Chinese nationalism. In 1921, the international Ch'ung Cheng Association was organized in Canton to unify the many local Hakka associations in South China and overseas. Its first order of business was to protest perennial references to Hakka as "non-Chinese" and "wild barbarian tribes" in the Chinese and Western presses. However, instead of rejecting their "Hakka" label, they expressed the positive implications in being "guest people." Hsieh T'ing-Yu, a young Hakka scholar, discovered references to "Hakka" in Tang and Sung dynasty census reports. These reports indicated that "locals" (by implication Cantonese) were aborigines and the "Hakka" were immigrant Chinese from North China.

Another Hakka scholar, Lo Hsiang-Lin (1933:2), went on to argue that "Hakka" refers to a people who have no relationship with people in China's southern parts. In 1965 Lo published his volume of Hakka genealogies to validate Hakka claims on a North China (by implication "civilized") origin (see chapter 2, note 2). In 1971, the Ch'ung Cheng Association published a golden anniversary yearbook in which the editors embellished Lo's solution to the mystery of Hakka origins.

> Our people's distant ancestors migrated from the fertile (northern) plains into the barren hills (of the south) where they forged a character of resistance and nonappeasement. Here our people have steadfastly served the ancestors by multiplying and carving out a niche in which to survive. By developing independently, our customs have remained distinct from the local people's, and we have not mixed as easily as does water with milk (Ch'ung Cheng Editorial Staff 1971:1).

Today in Sai Kung, the name "Hakka" designates the local political majority who are cognizant of this mystique. The name is always uttered with pride by those who identify with it. But the name still evokes the earlier stigmata by persons who are not familiar with or who reject Hakka mystiques. Toward such persons, Hakka may capitalize on their stigmata in various ways, or they may conceal their identity by speaking Cantonese. Depending on how one intones or modifies the word "Hakka" one may convey either contempt or respect. As most ethnic labels, "Hakka" is ambiguous in the abstract but meaningful in concrete situations.

THE BACKBONE OF THE HAKKA COMMUNITY

The most salient and perhaps universal stereotype of Hakka is their "gall." It is expressed in both positive and negative idioms. In Sai Kung Hakka sometimes say of themselves: "Hakka no longer feel their gall." The reference is to the Hakka establishment and to the fact that Hakka constitute the majority of landowners and leaders of the local community and that as leaders they must accommodate immigrant interests and comply with colonial policies. Ironically, the only local politician in recent times to feel his "Hakka gall" was Chan Yat-Kuan who was actually Cantonese. This case is described and analyzed in chapter 6.

The image that Hakka no longer feel their gall does not quite apply to Hakka village women. Contrary to the male politicians in the market town the village women "have great gall." The Hakka women maintain a more traditional role in village society which includes responsibility for cultivating and protecting the ancestral lands while their menfolk sojourn abroad. This traditional role of Hakka women in the subsistence economy and in the defense of their villages, their ability to withstand the stress of poverty and oppression have been observed widely in South China (Piton 1873:224; Campbell 1912:473; Oehler 1922:352; Han 1972:21; Wolf 1975:134). Most of these reports point out that Hakka women never practiced footbinding, were more self-reliant than other Chinese women, and enjoyed more or less equal status with their menfolk. This legacy is preserved in collections of earthy Hakka love songs (see, for example, Li 1970).

Comparative data from more recent village studies lend support to a general difference between the role of Hakka and non-Hakka women. In his description of a large Cantonese village on the outskirts of Canton, C. K. Yang (1965, II:91) observed that the women participate in many types of farm work except the heaviest work, such as plowing. In southern Taiwan, Burton Pasternak (1972:131) found that the Hokkien reluctance to put women into the fields exacerbates labor shortages at critical points in the agricultural cycle. In these ways the role of Cantonese and Hokkien women are distinct from Hakka women who are often responsible for the entire cycle of agricultural tasks from plowing to harvesting. For instance, before their fields were sold in the process of Kowloon's ur-

Plate 2. A Hakka village woman hawking her homemade cakes to a boat woman on the Sai Kung pier

ban expansion into Tsuen Wan, "the younger (Hakka) women worked the fields, growing rice and vegetables . . . raised pigs and chickens and cut grass in the mountains as fuel for their cooking stoves, carrying it down to the village in enormous loads on carrying poles." "They often cut in large groups organized . . . by age and marital status" (Johnson 1975:218). Young Hakka women may also market some of the fruits of their labor. The beginning of a typical day is described by Jean Pratt (1960:150) for a Hakka village north of Tolo Channel.

> The day begins about 5:30 or even earlier if vegetables have to be taken to market. By 9 o'clock the children are at school, the men have left for work or a day's gossip at the tea-shops, and the women are working in the fields or returning from market with the fish, pork, fruit or paraffin they have bought with the money from the sale of the vegetables.

The scenes described by Johnson and Pratt were common everyday occurrences during my stay in Sai Kung. Young village girls are sent up the mountain to cut grass and herd cows. Where roads are not yet built the journey to market requires fortitude and self-sufficiency on the part of women. One woman recalled that before she was married in the 1930s she carried firewood from Tai Mong Tsai to sell in urban Kowloon. The journey lasted two days. And she was expected to fend for herself while traveling beyond the village gates. The ability of such women to ward off assaults is celebrated in Hakka stories, some of which are legendary.

Plate 3. Hakka village women preparing a wedding feast (photo by Linda Blake)

In another study of a large and powerful Cantonese lineage in the New Territories, James Watson (1975:169–171) describes how the San Tin village men left their rice paddies for better-paying restaurant jobs in Europe after 1960. The men's absence created security problems for the women left behind in the village. In Sai Kung, the task of protecting the village is one which Hakka women are expected to perform. Although police protection is now more reliable than ever before, the Hakka women still do not shrink from their traditional duties to resist any encroachments on village lands, even if it means taking the law into their own hands. During my stay, a team of government surveyors was sighting a new road across the ancestral lands of one village when they were attacked and beaten by several Hakka women. The women were arrested and jailed until embarrassed male elders negotiated their release.

Any attempt to discern differences between Hakka and Cantonese village women within Sai Kung itself would have to measure far more subtle traits than I have discussed thus far. My own attempts were, by and large, fruitless. I came to realize, however, that in Sai Kung, Cantonese and Hakka patterns of economic adaptation are similar even while the two groups maintain distinct identities. Unlike well-to-do San Tin Cantonese whom Watson studied, the Cantonese men of Sai Kung have a long tradition of working in the urban and overseas sectors. As we shall see in the next section, Sai Kung Cantonese solve the problems of insecurity and subsistence in their native villages by taking Hakka women for wives. Aş a result Hakka feminist culture pervades both Hakka and Cantonese village life in Sai Kung.

With the rise of the People's Republic of China after 1950, the Hong Kong economy shifted from its entrepôt base to a light and medium industrial base. The demands for cheap, unorganized labor enticed some Sai Kung village women away from their paddy fields into the urban wage economy. At the same time, the urban and industrial demand for water, which the government accommodated by tapping village supplies, also forced village women out of their wet rice paddy. After 1960, newly-wed village women began to accompany their husbands to seek restaurant jobs in Europe. The women's sojourn was facilitated by the increased ease of air travel.

At the same time, however, many older Hakka women remained steadfast in their regard for rice cultivation. According to their way of thinking, village paddy provides greater long-term stability whereas wage labor and cheap imported rice is vulnerable to the flux of international and colonial economies. This conservative agrarian rhetoric found more precise articulation among local, mostly youthful, Maoists who added to the list of benefits the ideals of village self-sufficiency and nonparticipation in a colonial economy. Throughout the 1960s Hakka village women organized protests against government attempts to tap village water supplies for urban users. The desiccation of their peasant economy was one grievance which fueled the anti-British riots in Sai Kung in 1967.

Continued interest in growing rice on the part of village Hakka is motivated also by the fact that there is no competition in this niche with other groups. The villagers own the land; the terraced paddy represents considerable capital investment; the villagers possess the expertise to grow rice, and their sociocultural existence is geared to the seasonal cycles of rice cultivation. Finally, it is a task which allows women to stay near the village, and this is necessary for women caring for children. When a woman working in the urban or overseas economy has a child, she usually returns to the village. For these reasons, many Hakka women cling tenaciously to their rice paddies.

In the 1950s, some village women attempted to raise pigs and vegetables for the market. However, they were soon displaced from this niche by tough competitive immigrant families who quite literally "out-Hakka-ed" the Hakka. Truck gardening is considered a male-managed occupation, because it is geared completely to the daily demands of the Kowloon wholesale market, which increasingly supplies Sai Kung market with produce. Truck farming also requires the continuous, unstinting daily labor of the entire family. As noted previously, this pattern of food production does not appeal to landowning paddy cultivators. Finally, truck farming is based on short-term capital investment, which immigrants readily obtain from government-sponsored credit cooperatives and from immigrant native place associations. The associations also provide immigrants with the necessary connections in the urban economy.

A niche which attracted village women after 1960 was construction labor (digging and carrying mud, sand, gravel). The Hakka women soon monopolized this occupation. "Working mud," as it is called, is not very different from the grueling drudgery of working wet paddy. Furthermore, carrying mud is considered a day-to-day or, at most, a month-to-month commitment, which complements the long rest seasons in the Hakka single-crop rice agriculture. Thus during the dry winter fallow and the summer growing season, women can earn a daily wage carrying mud while commuting only as far as the market town.

The Hakka women think of themselves, and are considered by others, to be predisposed toward physical labor. People point out that "Hakka women have strong backs." A medical missionary who ministers to Hakka women says that one of the most frequent complaints of Hakka women is chronic backache! Strong, weak, or merely worn out, Hakka women have little competition for their jobs for which they are paid women's wages, $15 to $20 per day. (Men allegedly shovel more mud, therefore earn $25 to $30.)

Among the potential competitors for the women's construction jobs are poor boat people. However, the consensus among land and boat people is that boat people, especially boat women, are not fit to perform heavy labor on land: "They lose their vitality too quickly."

A remarkable test of this rhetoric occurred while my Hakka friend accompanied me around the harbor one day. On the shore we encountered a couple of boat women carrying rock and cement along with two boat men carrying a bag of cement slung between them. My Hakka friend quipped: "Not enough Hakka women are available for hire these days, so we must hire these Tanka women." (Later I learned that the man building the house was a boat man who hired his own kin to give them work.) Then on the same site, a single Hakka woman came along with two baskets of mud on each end of her carrying pole. "See!" my Hakka friend pointed out, "One Hakka woman can carry two loads, while it takes two Tanka to carry one load!" However, when two Hakka women followed carrying one bag of cement between them, we walked on without further comment.

At least one function of these images of ethnic predisposition is to ra-

Plate 4. Hakka women working for wages on a construction site

tionalize the Hakka monopoly on construction jobs. These images and attendant hiring practices are strongest among local Hakka contractors, although I suspect that they will erode as the demand for manual labor exceeds the supply of Hakka women. During my stay in Sai Kung, an Italian contractor hired a large number of unskilled laborers to begin work on a government reservoir. A number of poor boat men I knew obtained jobs as hod carriers and ditchdiggers.

This special role of Hakka women with regard to the social and political implications of their labor power has been given some theoretical scrutiny in recent studies. A number of scholars assume a direct correlation between the Hakka women's agrarian productivity and their influence on family and community affairs. For example, Dorothy Bracey (1967:80–84) suggests that the women of Chung Pui, a Hakka village north of Tolo Channel, "get authority when men are gone and power since, though men own the land, women have the skill and experience to work it." However, Elizabeth Johnson (1975:219) found that Tsuen Wan Hakka women feel no loss of status as a result of their change from rice cultivating to rent collecting in the context of industrial and urban development. Based on Johnson's work, Wolf and Witke (1975:8–9) question the hypothesis that productive labor on the part of women increases their social and political power in the community.[1]

Based on my observations in Sai Kung, I would say that to the extent that the village women make day-to-day decisions in earning money, marketing, depositing wages or overseas money orders in their own bank accounts, they exercise that degree of de facto power. However, there is little evidence that Hakka women exercise greater jural influence in family or village affairs than other Chinese women. I agree with Jean Pratt (1960:148) who studied a Hakka village north of Tolo Channel that "status in the village . . . is expressed solely in terms of the men. . . ." Hakka women are still economic and political dependents.

In the first place, the agricultural work of Hakka women is not clearly "productive labor" as Wolf and Witke, although questioning the productive labor hypothesis, seem to assume. The women's agricultural work is subsistence oriented more than market or profit oriented. Indeed, there is little evidence that the Hakka in Sai Kung ever paid any patrimony (tax or rent) to the Tai Po lineage which extracted agrarian revenues from Sai Kung Cantonese villagers. Also, the Sai Kung market developed on the basis of precapitalist industrial and commercial activities rather than on the basis of agrarianism. In one sense, Hakka redefined agricultural work as subsistence labor and therefore merged it with the women's domestic routine, which is by definition "nonproductive" in complex stratified societies.

Secondly, no matter how much time and effort women spend working their desiccated fields, men are viewed as the mainstays of family economy even if they live most of their productive lives abroad. Village women live in dread of any sign or threat by their menfolk to stop remittances. The economic exploits of their menfolk is a topic of constant conversation and gossip. In these conversations, men are evaluated as "good" or "bad" according to the amount of money they remit rather than according to their sexual loyalty. Rose Hum Lee (1960:208) writing in the context of male emigration says that: "the wifes' emotional reactions to their husbands were correlated with these tangible possessions (remittance) rather than to the latters' physical presence or emotional ties to them." In fact when a village woman is abandoned by her husband or son abroad, there is even less scope for her exercise of personal power in family much less village affairs. Consider the case of Ah-Fong who is one among many remarkable Hakka women we knew.

Ah-Fong was in her late sixties when we met her. In the early 1950s her husband abandoned her and their young daughter. Ah-Fong stayed in the village and planted rice and potatoes upon which she and her daughter subsisted. When the daughter was old enough she sought employment in Kowloon. While Ah-Fong continued to cultivate her fields her daughter supplemented Ah-Fong's subsistence with wages earned as a servant. When Ah-Fong grew too old to plant and harvest all her fields, she moved to the market town where her husband's younger brother owns a small shop. There Ah-Fong began cooking and caring for her brother-in-law's grandson while her brother-in-law's wife earned a daily wage carrying mud for a construction company. Until recently, Ah-Fong returned to the village, a walk of some five hours over rugged terrain, to plant and harvest a few fields. When I think about Ah-Fong's life of labor it seems almost ludicrous to suggest that she ever enjoyed any social or political influence comparable to that which menfolk enjoy as owners of the means of production. While working in the fields or even earning wages on a construction site does not automatically increase women's power in the organization of the local community, there are other obvious social rewards such as freedom from the drudgery and especially the isolation of the domestic routine. In spite of the debilitating labor women seem to find a great deal of satisfaction in working and associating with other women in the fields or especially on the construction site.

Finally, a third factor which mitigates the labor value of Hakka women is that the family and village decision-making structure does not disintegrate with the absence of the male decision-makers. Positions of village leadership are filled by older retired male sojourners. Important decisions are made through letters and periodic visits from abroad (for an example, see Aijmer 1967:66–69). Furthermore, political authority in the village is tied directly to higher levels in the market town and in the district office which are managed exclusively by men. However, it is worth noting that in my survey of local leaders one question which I asked each was how he would feel about a woman being selected as a village or neighborhood leader. The vast majority of respondents hardly batted an eye; none objected strenuously; most felt it altogether acceptable, at least in theory. Although there are no actual cases of women in positions of public authority, not all the political power is exercised by men. There are the arenas of indirect, informal and illegitimate power which women occupy and in which they excel. The exercise of informal feminine power in family, village, and market affairs is, and always has been, considerable.

In Sai Kung town there are several women's cliques which are formally organized, although they do not engage in overt political activities as do the male-dominated associations. The leader of the Elder and Younger Sister Association is important in the informal power structure of the market. She is an attractive widow who is the head cashier in one of the large restaurants. In the evenings she and her "sisters" play mahjong with the man who owns the restaurant and who is also a local leader. This woman has similar liaisons with other male leaders in town; and it is common knowledge that through her invisible position as a power broker she wields considerable influence on local affairs.

Another Hakka woman from a local village heads the town's gambling syndicate, while her son, a local leader, manages the other vices. During the major celebrations such as the Tin Hau Festival this woman and her henchmen can be seen organizing the voluntary labor needed to arrange the hundreds of chairs for the opera. Although this woman wields considerable influence in Sai Kung market, her powers are veiled by the rules of secrecy.

A Hakka woman heads the Sai Kung Village Women's Improvement Association which was organized by young activist women in the wake of the 1967 riots. However, even within the network of patriotic associations the women's association does not exercise overt authority. It is aimed mostly at disseminating birth-control information and at holding tea parties on patriotic holidays. Many of the members participate individually in the town's traditional religious festivities which the young feminists who head the association regard as wasteful and superstitious. Unlike other women's groups, this association actively recruits women from all segments of the society including many boat women. However, the boat women tend to swell the nominal ranks of the association and tend not to occupy leadership positions.

Finally, there is Mrs. Ho who happens to be a Cantonese immigrant and who together with her immigrant husband owns one of the jewelry shops in town. Mrs. Ho is one of the biggest moneylenders in Sai Kung, and many of her clients are women. In fact she sponsors a large firecracker association for her circle of clients which I will describe in detail in chapter 5.

The unique role alleged to Hakka women is rooted in the group's subsistent adaptation to marginal agrarian resources. Although they are the backbone of the local community, Hakka women do not enjoy a social status higher than other Chinese women in their respective communities. Nor is their traditional agricultural work necessarily "productive" in the subjective cultural sense even though it is "productive" from an objective, analytical, or feminist point of view. On the other hand, the subjective definition of women's labor as "nonproductive" is more difficult to maintain when women work for wages on construction sites. However, women seem to prefer to work on construction sites for purely social rewards and not only the paltry wages that supposedly measure their productive labor value in a capitalist society. These are at best tentative conclusions. Further research on this problem should specify more precisely what is meant by "productive labor." And the collection of field data should aim toward more comparative analyses. In this section I have dealt with the Hakka women of Sai Kung. In chapter 5 I describe several Hakka men and their families.

PUNTI ATTRIBUTES

"Cantonese" is an English transliteration for people who live within the jurisdiction of Kwangtung province. From outside the province, this includes Hakka- and Hokkien-speaking people.[2] Within the province, "Cantonese" generally refers to the people living in Kwangchow Prefecture (Canton), the capital city of Kwangtung. These people refer to themselves as "Punti" to distinguish themselves from Hakka.

The term "Punti" compounds the ideograph for "root" with the ideograph for "cultivated land" or "place." "Punti" literally means "rooted in the place," or "local folk" in contrast to Hakka as "guest folk." The Punti title implies that the people have lived long in the place, they peacefully cultivate the land, pay property tax, and enjoy the protection of the government. It therefore implies that they own the means of production in the area. In a broad historical framework, this describes people who speak a dialect related to the speech of Kwangchow. However, the native place and speech group criteria may not correlate in other particular historical contexts, and the different criteria for being Punti may facilitate claims by diverse groups for Punti status.

In Sai Kung, those with undisputed claim to the title Punti are local villagers who speak a rustic dialect of Cantonese and inhabit the most fertile lands. They claim to be descended from the original inhabitants of Sai Kung who emigrated from Tungkuan county during the seventeenth century, a century before the ancestors of the present-day Hakka arrived. As I noted earlier (chapter 3, Land and People of the Traditional Marketing Area) the Cantonese in Sai Kung tend to occupy the most fertile land. However, their overall ecological adaptation, when compared to those elsewhere in the Canton delta, is more similar to that of their Hakka neighbors in Sai Kung.

OTHER CLAIMS ON PUNTI STATUS

In certain contexts the Hakka may claim to be Punti, that is, apart from attempts to pass as Punti. For instance, when I asked a man if he was Punti, he replied, "Yes, I'm Punti." Then I asked, "You mean that you are not Hakka?" "Of course I'm Hakka," he replied: "I'm *Punti* Hakka." By stressing the "Punti" he meant that he is a local Hakka rather than one whose parents are mixed. Another Hakka, a recent immigrant, boasted : "The Hakka in Sai Kung are *Punti* Hakka, but I am Meihsien Hakka."

The Hakka claim on Punti status is based on the fact that their ancestors were the original settlers of their particular villages, and that they were the original owners of the land. Their claims are substantiated by the 1905 Block Crown Lease records, in which the tillers of the land were made the owners of the land. As we saw in chapter 3, the British land reform at the turn of the century also established the Punti (or local) credentials of Sai Kung Cantonese vis-à-vis their erstwhile Cantonese landlords in Tai Po market.

The Hakka claim to "Punti" is sanctioned by local Cantonese for purposes of political alliance against the new wave of immigrants since 1960. The Hakka-Cantonese alliance is incorporated in the Sai Kung Native Place Association. In this unusual case, a native fellowship association is composed of two different speech groups. Within the association, the cleavage in speech group identity is a keen source, but by no means the only source, of factional rivalry. The Hakka have, by and large, maintained their control of the association due to their numbers; and within their cliques they speak Hakka. However, the language spoken at association functions is standard Cantonese. This reflects the overall purpose of the association to deal with outsiders along with the fact that Cantonese dominates the outside world.

The incorporation of the two speech groups under the rubric of "Sai Kung born" expresses their collective claim to control of local resources against immigrants. Unlike its constituent identities of "Hakka" and "Punti" (in its narrow sense), the native place identity is incorporated. Any person born in Sai Kung may apply for membership. However, a native who owns little or no land has little or no interest in such a membership. On the other hand, several immigrants who have purchased land in recent years have been accorded "honorary membership." While this and other such associations are ostensibly "ethnic" groupings, they are, from a more analytical point of view, socioeconomic strata or "class" groupings. The nature of corporate ethnic identity in relationship to socioeconomic strata is examined in greater detail in later chapters.

Boat people may also claim to be Punti by virtue of their speech group affiliation, and in a few cases, residential status. In the Basel Mission clinic, which traditionally caters to Hakka, I inquired of a man if he was "Punti?" He hesitated then affirmed: "Yes, I'm Punti." A Cantonese village woman piped up: "No he isn't; he's a water-borne person." The Cantonese villager defined the context as a boat man among villagers rather than as he had, a Cantonese speaker among Hakka.

There are other purely legal definitions pertaining to a person's local identity which may be used as a basis for claiming Punti status. For example, anyone born in Hong Kong has the right to Commonwealth membership and a British passport. Anyone who has resided in Sai Kung for three or more years has the right to vote in the Kaifong elections; and after a residence of ten years one may hold office in the Rural Committee. However important these legal identities are for practical purposes, they are not recognized by Sai Kung folk as a normative basis for Punti status.

DEROGATORY TERMS FOR LOCAL CANTONESE

"Punti" is a general, inclusive, neutral reference. It is similiar to our use of "American" for people who are able to claim a Western European background, while those without a European background are "hyphenated Americans." To dub the political majority with an ethnic character, minority groups devise names which give the white majority a more specific and derogatory character; hence, "W.A.S.P.," "honky," "cracker," "haole," and so forth.

Chinese groups have the same facility for dubbing outgroups with derogatory names. Chinese caricaturize "southern barbarians" as reptiles (Schafer 1967:13). In Chinese lore, the reptile is timid, lazy, and treacherous. Hakka employ this rhetoric when referring to the original Cantonese villagers as *sa* (H) ("snakes"). Specifically, Cantonese males are dubbed *sa-lao* (H) ("snake fellows"), and females are called *sa-ma* (H). (The *ma* means "maid" or "mistress," and may imply a promiscuous character depending on ideograph and/or tone of voice.) The local Cantonese speech, which is barely intelligible to urban Cantonese, is called *sa-va* (H) ("snake talk"). Hakka describe *sa-va* as an "unwritten patois."

The same suffixes are used to vulgarize Hakka as Hakka-*lao* and Hakka-*ma;* and to insult a member of the outgroup one need but alter the tone of voice or use the feminine gender in reference to an outgroup male.

The Hakka emphasize the aboriginal connotations in the Punti claim to Sai Kung. One elderly Hakka explained:

> Those *sa-lao* were the original people living in South China. When the first Chinese emperor marched south to oppress them, these aborigines escaped into the remote areas of the region. That is why they are named *sa*. They are like snakes. When they see a stronger adversary, they slither away into the bushes.

The name *sa* is employed in many contexts, even in casual speech. I suspect that its use parallels the more or less casual manner in which American blacks employ "honky" in reference to whites, while the white's use of "nigger" for blacks is considered a reprehensible racial slur (see Blake n.d.).

However, in other contexts where Hakka natives need to express their unity with Cantonese natives against immigrants, the Hakka cite affinal and matrilateral connections with the erstwhile "snake folk." The tradition of Cantonese and Hakka intermarriage gives rise to a view among outgroups that the local Cantonese are half-Hakka. One influential Cantonese boat man stated this view in earthy terms: "Those people in Sha Kok Mei village are not really Punti." "They are simply half-breed Hakka, whereas local Hakka are pedigree Hakka."

ETHNIC INTERMARRIAGE

In the abstract, Sai Kung people insist that they marry within their own ethnic groups. However, my data on actual marriages indicate a definite pattern of interethnic and hypergamous marriage. Figures 3 and 4 illustrate the marriage networks of five generations of wives of a Cantonese lineage segment in Sha Kok Mei and a Hakka lineage segment in Tai Mong Tsai. (As shown in chapter 3, Land and People in the Traditional Marketing Area, the Cantonese lineage was much wealthier in land ownership than was the Hakka lineage.)

In the Cantonese settlement, I recorded thirty-seven marriages of which five were from outside the market area (and are excluded from Figure 3). In the Hakka segment, I recorded forty-five marriages of which eleven were from outside the market area, including one boat woman from Hong Kong Island (excluded from Figure 4). Most marriages were contracted between 1920 and 1950. Those marriages excluded from analysis because they are outside the area are not, however, with neighboring market areas, but rather from urban Hong Kong, Kowloon and China. Most of the Hakka men who contracted urban (usually Cantonese) brides moved from the village to the urban areas.

The overall marriage distance for the wives of the two segments is about the same. In the Cantonese segment, four are from within the large and heterogeneous village of Sha Kok Mei. The overall mean marriage distance is 3.6 kilometers in a straight line. The mean marriage distance for the Hakka segment's wives is 3.8 kilometers. Due to the rugged terrain, this distance is considerably greater on the ground. It accords with the average marriage distance reported by Pratt (1960:151) for a Hakka village north of Tolo Channel, and it conforms to the standard marketing area as a natural system of marriage alliances described by Skinner (1964:36). We can also see that each segment maintains a network of affinal connections in almost equally large proportion of villages in the four directions. This pattern further confirms Freedman's "guess" (1966:103) that poor and humble lineages tend to maintain a broad set of alliances within a limited geographical range.

However, there is a significant contrast in the number of interethnic wives in each segment. The Cantonese segment has at least twice as many

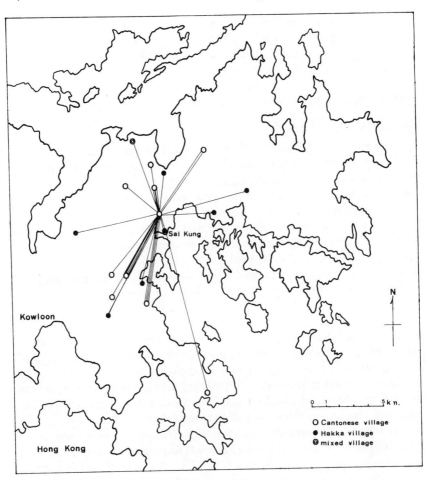

Figure 3. Marriage Network of a Cantonese Lineage

Hakka wives as the Hakka segment has Cantonese wives, that is, eight to four. In other words, at least one-fourth of the Cantonese segment's wives are Hakka; but less than one-eighth of the Hakka segment's wives are Cantonese. This pattern holds in other villages too. In a Ho Chung Cantonese segment, out of eleven wives in the past four generations, four are Hakka, and seven are Cantonese (three from the village of Ho Chung and two from outside the market area). Of the seven women given away in marriage, all are married to Cantonese (four within the village). Only in the fifth, most recent, generation is there one woman married to a Hakka and one married to a Waichow Hokkien tenant. In yet another

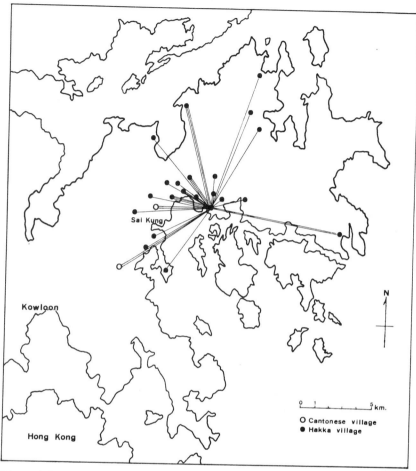

Figure 4. Marriage Network of a Hakka Lineage

village survey of a small single lineage Cantonese hamlet above Ho Chung, I found that almost half, that is, eight out of seventeen, market area women presently married into the lineage are Hakka. Most Hakka hamlets of comparable size have no Cantonese wives. Thus there is a distinct pattern of interethnic exchange between Cantonese men and Hakka village women in the Sai Kung market area.

The only factor which clearly tends to encourage the choice of a Hakka bride by a Cantonese household is her ability to manage the household subsistence in the absence of the sojourning menfolk. She is expected to perform the agricultural tasks as well as the marketing in the

Hakka-controlled town. Conversely, the Cantonese are reluctant to give
their women in marriage to Hakka villagers since Cantonese do not relish
the thought of their daughters doing the heavy work expected of Hakka
women. There is a local Cantonese proverb (cited by Bracey 1967:5) to
the effect that a person who misbehaves in this life is punished by being
reincarnated as a Hakka woman. (The fact that Chinese brides ritually
experience the mysteries of death and rebirth [Blake 1978; 1979] only
gives such words a ring of reality in the ears of a misbehaving child or of
a young girl about to be wed to a Hakka villager.) Indeed, Hakka villagers say they cannot depend on a woman reared in a Cantonese village to
maintain the same level of endurance as do their own Hakka women.
The Hakka villager who marries a Cantonese woman may be considered
somewhat of a maverick by his fellow villagers. The initiation of his Cantonese bride into village life may be comparatively severe because the
villagers may display some contempt for the Cantonese-speaking bride
brought into their midst. However, these difficulties are lessening as
Hakka give up their agricultural subsistence and are increasingly forced
to learn Cantonese in the government schools which have now penetrated
every village.

Nevertheless, some Hakka men have taken Cantonese brides. In fact a
very substantial number of Hakka shopkeepers have Cantonese wives.
The Cantonese wife facilitates her Hakka husband's contacts with the
larger networks of Cantonese commerce. I have already described how
the Sai Kung market, though a Hakka enclave, is part of the larger commercial networks controlled by the Cantonese. Thus, at the village level it
is useful for Cantonese and Hakka alike to have Hakka wives. At the
level of the market town it is useful for Hakka to have Cantonese wives
and, as we shall see in chapter 6, for the early Cantonese immigrants to
have local Hakka wives.

Extensive interethnic marriage between local Hakka and Cantonese
creates a network of social alliances which support the formal political
alliance of the "local born" against the postwar immigrants. In expressing this higher order identity, many Hakka say they are *Ch'in ch'i,* "related by marriage," to the Cantonese. While interethnic marriage is
adaptive and leads to a certain amount of acculturation and assimilation,
especially on the part of Cantonese villagers regarding their division of
labor, the rhetoric of ethnic endogamy tends to maintain speech group
consciousness.

THE TRADITIONAL IMAGE OF CANTONESE BOAT PEOPLE

The name by which Cantonese-speaking boat people are widely known is
"Tanka." It compounds the word for egg *(tan)* with the occupational

classifier *(ka)*. (A strict translation of "Tanka" would be "egger" as Hakka would be "guester.") Additional suffixes *(-lao* and *-ma)* may be added in the same way they may be added to Hakka and *sa*. More commonly one hears *-tsai* ("small one") suffixed to "Tanka." In reference to adult males or the class of boat people, "Tanka-tsai" denotes their lack of humanity, and is equivalent to the American word "nigger boy" for the black community.

The egg symbolizes the state of nature in which boat people are alleged to exist. It symbolizes their lack of genealogy and native place. Land people say, for instance, "if you ask a Tanka where he is from, he doesn't know." As "egg people," they are ascribed with biological attributes of physical prowess, sexual promiscuity, and fertility.

In ancient Yüeh (as in many other cultures) the egg symbolizes fertility (Eberhard 1968:420). This symbolism underlies the land people's stereotype of boat people as extremely prolific and promiscuous. These stereotypes are conveyed through such slurs as: "Tanka have such big feet," and "Tanka like loose shoes." These are innuendo for the alleged sexual appetite of boat people.[3] So entrenched is the stereotype of "Tanka promiscuity" that a Cantonese woman who was born and reared in rural Hawaii and who never saw a boat person recalls how her mother scolded her when she sat with her knees apart: "Don't sit like a Tanka-ma!"

It is important to the thesis of my study to reiterate the point that such stereotypes are not based simply on the cultural background of the boat people so much as on the role they are constrained to play in this particular social system. Where the Hakka are a minority as in Honolulu, they are similarly stereotyped; and I have heard of mothers warning their daughters not to sit like a "Hakka-ma." (In fact many Cantonese from Honolulu erroneously assume that the boat people they see on their trips to Hong Kong are Hakka.)

The biological reality in phenotypic stereotypes such as big feet is also a function of the social organization. Boat people (and villagers) do have large feet because they do not wear shoes. In the old days the only boat people allowed ashore were those who had personal sponsors in the community; and even then, the boat man did not dare to wear shoes. People still recall the local custom which prohibited boat people from wearing shoes on shore. This is similar to caste mechanisms found in India where the mark of the dark-skinned untouchables is maintained by local laws prohibiting them from wearing shirts while working in the sun (Srinivas 1971:16). The boat man's bare feet symbolize his attachment to nature, his natural prowess and, obversely, his separation from civilized society, his social vulnerability to land people, and perhaps in a deeper sense, his inability to possess land women.

Intermarriage Between Land and Boat People

Between boat people and land people, ethnic endogamy is insisted upon verbally; hypergamy is, in fact, allowed; while hypogamy of land women to boat men is rare. The only cases of hypogamy I know about occurred recently when the young couple were privy to the contract and where the newlyweds lived ashore. In a typical case, the bride and groom were factory coworkers. The marriage ritual required that the bride traverse a long wobbly plank from the shore to the groom's parent's boat where the couple bowed before his ancestors, served his parents tea, and ate a feast before returning permanently to the shore.

Boat women are allowable as wives and mistresses for land men. A land man takes a boat woman to gratify his desire for an exotic woman, more children, and/or to expand his clientele in a certain boat community. Many Hakka and Cantonese villages have one or more boat women to facilitate the exchange of foodstuffs. Among shopkeepers who solicit the fisherman's business there are many wives from the boats. In chapter 5, I describe several cases. The popularity of boat wives among shopkeepers seems to correlate with the increasing buying power of the fishing community.

Development of the Boat Community and Its Self-Image

Today, there are two contradictory stereotypes of Sai Kung boat people. One is that "Boat people have no business" which refers to their traditional poverty. The more recent and often heard phrase is: "Boat people are rich." The newer image applies to the organized stratum of boat people which emerged after 1960. The changing stereotype from rags to riches is rooted in the development of Sai Kung as a fish market.

As the Sai Kung market developed during the first half of this century, it attracted increasing numbers of boat people. The earliest record of their presence is found on the list of contributors to the 1915 reconstruction of the town's Tin Hau temple, which is carved in stone. The largest contribution from a boat man is $25, and he is listed twelfth of 694 contributors. The first hundred contributors gave a total of $1,367. Twenty-eight of these are positively identified as boat men whose contributions total $285. (There are a number of unidentified persons among the first hundred.) Most boat people gave less, according to what they could afford. I would guess that of the 443 one-dollar subscriptions, half came from boat people. This list provides a fairly accurate social registry of the local society in 1915.

In 1915 there were several hundred boat people actively involved in the Sai Kung market. By 1931, according to a government census, there were

738 boat people anchored in the market area. My informants estimate that of these, about 175 persons (approximately twenty-five boats) resided in Sai Kung harbor. These boat families maintained patron-client, and in some cases, affinal ties with the shopkeepers by supplying fresh and dried fish, the land people's main source of protein. The boat people were a factor, if not yet the key factor, in the local economy.

Where a land person maintains a personal relationship with a boat person, the land person tends to use names for the boat person that are more polite than "Tanka." Before the Japanese occupation, for example, the Hakka called the boat people in Sai Kung *"ka-siu-lao"* (H) which means "house-floating fellows." This name identifies boat people by their domicile, and it endows their identity with social rather than biological attributes. While the name removes the stigma of the "Tanka" paraiah, it still lacks the attributes of a positive self-image. *Ka-siu lao* is the semantic equivalent of "Negro" in America. Both names reflect an attitude of "benign neglect" toward a traditionally deprived minority. Today, only the older generation of Hakka use this name for boat people.

The name upon which boat people insist is *"seui-seuhng-yahn"* (C) ("water-borne persons"). I do not know the historical origin of this term. Burkhardt (1955:II:183) reports boat people insisting on its use in the early 1950s. Its social symbolic origin may be found in its semantic contrast to *gaai-seuhng-yahn* (C) ("Street-borne persons" or "townsfolk"). In other words, boat people prefer to see themselves as opposite and yet equal with townspeople. This self-appellation also implies a sense of origins: Boat people see themselves as Chinese who live aboard boats and trade in the market. They insist on a distinct *occupational* identity coupled with a claim on majority status as Chinese. This is comparable to the demand on the part of American blacks for a distinct racial identity coupled with the political and economic rights of American citizens. There is a remarkable parallel in the change of ethnic roles (and terms) in America from "nigger" to "Negro" to "black" and the change of ethnic roles in Sai Kung from "Tanka" to *"ka-siu-lao"* to *"seui-seuhng-yahn."* It is also worth noting that in both of these societies, the respective corpora of terms are still used in particular contexts.

Nonetheless, while I lived in Sai Kung I noted a concerted effort on the part of many land people to comply with boat people's desire to be known as *seui-seuhng-yahn*. I even witnessed a few cases in which school children corrected their parents' use of "Tanka." Most Sai Kung people accord the boat people the attributes of humanity. For example, one day I told my working-class Hakka neighbor that there are "well-educated Cantonese" in urban Hong Kong who say boat people have six toes on each foot (see Ward 1965:118). My Hakka neighbor shot back:

> The *seui-seuhng-yahn* are people just like you and me. Long ago they had no fields to till and were forced off the land. They did well fishing and developed their own customs which were passed down from father to son.

The land people's compliance with boat people's symbolic demands seems to be coupled with the boat people's rapidly rising economic power in the market.

Categorically, boat people are more prosperous than land people. This fact is made more significant by the fact that by every other measure of social and economic scale, boat people rank lower than land people (see chapter 3, note 5). The 1970 Census for Sai Kung shows that the mean land family income is $578 per month (median $500) compared to the mean boat family income of $1,035 (median $700). Twelve percent of land families are in the lowest income bracket (less than $200) compared to 11 percent of boat families—and this bottom stratum includes most of the Hokkien boat people. Less than 1 percent of the land families are in the highest income bracket (over $4,500) compared to 5 percent of the boat families. About one-sixth of the boat community are members of the Federation of Fishermen's Cooperative Societies (that is 110 vessels, or 152 families). This organized stratum of the boat community has an annual catch worth $4,720,000, or about $2,588 per family each month. These families, which represent 4 percent of the Sai Kung population, control about 14 percent of Sai Kung's gross annual income.

The stereotype of "the rich boat people" is based on the boat people's flamboyant spending in the market and during community festivals and weddings which I shall describe in the next chapter. Sai Kung merchants find themselves competing for this patronage not only among themselves, but with other urban market centers on Hong Kong Island, which Sai Kung boat people also patronize. The economic importance of the boat people to Sai Kung is best stated by a Cantonese merchant whose mistress and clientele are boat people:

> Sai Kung business depends on the boat people. No boat people, no business. Take myself for example. If I wait for the Hakka villagers to buy batteries, they will buy only two at a time. The boat people buy at least two dozen. Most of my merchandise is purchased by the boat people; they buy without dickering about the cost. They have the money to buy electrical appliances when they move onto the land. They are not tight with their money.

This view is popular among merchants whose trade is dependent on the boat people. All business across the harbor, along Wharf Street and the lower ends of Main and Big streets, that is, about half of Sai Kung's shops, cater to boat people.

By 1962, their economic impact was so profound that the Rural Committee revised its constitution to incorporate eight representatives from the boat community. Three boat men were immediately elected to the powerful twenty-one member Executive Committee. Until this time, boat people's interests were represented by their Hakka patrons in the market town. In the words of Mr. Lai, a boat representative who owns a soda store across the harbor, "Formerly the Hakka called us Tanka-tsai, but now that we have political power in the Rural Committee, they don't dare to insult us with these words!"

IMMIGRANT GROUPS

In Sai Kung, 7,722 *wai-lai-jen* (immigrants) form a residual group of many subcategories.

There are over four thousand Cantonese from the delta counties of Tungkuan, Nanhai, Chungshan, Shunte, P'unyu, and Paoan. There are over four hundred from "Szeyap" (mostly Hsinhui county), almost two hundred from places along the West and North rivers and forty-five from elsewhere in South China. Many are refugees from the Great Leap Forward. Many still retain connections in urban Hong Kong and villages in China. None have organized their native place identities beyond casual interpersonal relationships. Most feel no compulsion to speak Hakka, especially now that Hakka feel compelled to speak Cantonese in their own market town. The immigrant Cantonese may claim to be Punti, taking as their point of reference Hong Kong into which Sai Kung is rapidly integrating. They are scattered throughout the Sai Kung occupational structure. There are truck gardeners, small factory owners, shopkeepers, professionals, and skilled laborers.

About two thousand immigrant Hakka have been attracted to Sai Kung where they patronize local Hakka on the basis of common speech. They are not engaged in truck farming to the extent of other immigrants. The more prominent ones fled from Meihsien when the communists took over. Among the most visible Hakka immigrants are the Catholic school principal, the pastor of the Basel Mission Church, several tailors, a steam launderer and dry cleaner, a glove factory owner, and a large restaurant owner. The Meihsien restaurateur rents the garret over his restaurant to the Sun Yat-Sen Memorial Association, a Kuomintang Club composed of Hakka refugees from Waichow. Their leader is a pulse doctor who works in the herb shop owned by a leader of the local Hakka community. This local leader, Chin Fuk-Loi, in turn uses the Hakka restaurant as the meeting place for his local faction. These are the kinds of informal arrangements by which immigrant Meihsien and Waichow Hakka have adapted successfully while keeping a low profile as immigrants.

The only immigrants to formally organize their ethnic identities are the several thousand Hokkien speakers. Three groups have become differentiated over the past decade. There are several hundred "Hoklo" boat people, a thousand or more Waichow "Hoklo" from Hai-Lufeng counties and a larger group of Chaochow "Hoklo." Their exact numbers are problematic for several reasons. First, they tend to be transient, especially the boat people. Second, the government census uses categories that are different from the way Hokkien identities are organized in Sai Kung. Finally, the leaders of these groups claim larger numbers than can be derived from the census and from my own observations.[4]

NAMES FOR HOKKIEN SPEAKERS

The local folk generally regard Hokkien speakers as "dirty, superstitious, and unreasonable Hoklo." "Hoklo" is the Cantonese and Hakka vernacular for persons who speak a Hokkien (South Fukien) dialect and who reside in Kwangtung province. The word compounds *hok,* the Hokkien pronunciation for *fuk* in Fukien with *lo* (C) or *lao* (H). "Hoklo" means "Fukien fellow" and "Hoklo-*ma*" means "Fukien mistress."

Many Hokkien speakers recognize a linguistic affinity with Fukien. But the Hokkien in Sai Kung cite only native places along the Kwangtung coast: Chaochow and Waichow prefectures, or the lower level county administrations. While the boat people name the smaller ports of P'inghai and Chiehshih along the coast of Hai-Lufeng, or Tai Po market in the New Territories.

There are strong correlations between the status of each group's native place in Kwangtung and its status in Sai Kung society, and between the structure and scale of its organization in Sai Kung society and its tendency to reject the appellation "Hoklo." The boat people do not object to being called "Hoklo." Of all the ethnic communities in Sai Kung, they are the smallest, the most culturally conservative, the most impoverished, and have the least claim on a prestigious native place. One of them explained:

> We don't know where we were born, but somewhere on the water. . . . We supposedly originated in P'inghai, but no one really knows.

Instead of native place, their community is organized on the basis of surname affiliation (see note 4). They are similar to Hakka insofar as their ethnic identity is rooted in language more than in native place.

The Hokkien-speaking land people from Hai-Lufeng are less satisfied with the name "Hoklo." They usually insist on being known by their Waichow prefectural affiliation to distinguish themselves from Chaochow, which for reasons we shall examine later, they dislike. They may

Plate 5. The Sai Kung Hokkien boat community comprising small boats and stilt shacks along the shore

subscribe to the appellation "Waichow Hoklo" to distinguish themselves from the Waichow Hakka.

The Chaochow leaders are most averse to being identified as "Hoklo." Speaking Cantonese they remind you that: "We are not Hoklo, we are Chaochow!" In other words, they are adamant about their native-place identity in Kwangtung, and they deny the implication that they are foreign-tongued immigrants. Among the Hokkien speakers, the Chaochow constitute the largest group, appear the most acculturated, maintain the tightest organization and enjoy enormous success in Sai Kung's commercial niches and status positions.

HOKKIEN BOAT PEOPLE

Several hundred Hokkien fishermen live in a conglomeration of small boats and stilt shacks along the shoreline of Sai Kung Road. Occupants of the newer boats moored just offshore are more transient. The permanent residents are those whose boats are dilapidated and have sunk in the tidal mud or have been rebuilt into shacks over the water. The Hokkien abodes blend with the general seascape of Cantonese boats moored in the deeper water. Many land people do not distinguish Cantonese from Hokkien when referring to any boat person as "Tanka" or "seui-seuhng-yahn." Occasionally one hears all boat people referred to as "Hoklo." Hokkien boat people regard themselves either as "Hoklo" or as "seui-

Plate 6. Hokkien boat children playing in the refuse-strewn tide pools near their boats

seuhng-yahn," depending on the situation. When distinguishing them-selves from Cantonese boat people, they usually say: "We are Hoklo *seui-seuhng*—they are Punti." Occasionally they refer to Cantonese boat people as "Tanka."

As one becomes familiar with the sociocultural details of the Sai Kung waterfront, one notices that Hokkien boats are low slung, rakish look-ing, and in Sai Kung they tend to be smaller than the higher-pitched, jaunty looking Cantonese junks that reflect a higher and wider range of the economic strata.

The Hokkien boat people are very conscious of their low economic status. Even when I begin a discussion in terms of "ethnicity," they tend to switch into an occupational frame of reference. For example, a Hok-kien fisherman was cleaning his small boat which was dry docked next to

Plate 7. A motorized Cantonese boat

a larger Cantonese vessel. I asked the Hokkien man if the neighboring boat family was "Hoklo." He replied: "No, they are 'purse seiners.' " By referring to their fishing technique, he indicated their greater productive power. The man's brother then lapsed into a description of their own (Hokkien) gill-netting technique, which involves setting small nets near the shore and beating on the boat floorboards to drive the small fish from their rocks into the nets.[5] He added that this is a poor means of subsistence, and often, the "Hoklo" men must resort to "working mud" to make ends meet.

Another Hokkien fisherman I knew offered a class analysis of the boat community. According to him, there are three classes of boat people. Members of the first class make the most money because their boats are mechanized, and they are organized into cooperatives. Members of the second class own the same type of boat but their engines are in disrepair, so they use different fishing techniques, such as lamp fishing around the shore at night. They break even each day, and they are not much better off than the third class. According to my friend the first two classes are "Punti." The third and poorest class is "Hoklo," most of whom spend half their time ashore earning wages.

Plate 8. A Hokkien boat

At other times my friend collapses the three classes into two—rich Punti and poor "Hoklo":

> The Punti have more money to invest in their business, so when they get 300 to 500 catties of fish, they can't even pay for the petrol expended. But for us, 20 to 30 catties of fish give us cause to celebrate.

Within the Hokkien speech group, boat people feel despised by the Waichow and Chaochow land people. Sometimes the boat people try to identify their "Hoklo" speech group with the Waichow or Chaochow. The latter groups publicly reject such claims, although they may acknowledge them for specific purposes on an informal political or interpersonal basis.

For example, during the Chaochow auction on the last night of the Tin Hau Festival, a Hokkien boat man was explaining in heavily accented Cantonese various aspects of the auction to me. When the daughter of a Chaochow leader appeared dressed in modern Hong Kong clothes, the Hokkien boat man, somewhat unsure of himself, asked the young lady if she was not "Hoklo?" She assured us in impeccable Cantonese that she was not "Hoklo," that she is Chaochow and that the two are not the same. One of the factors underlying her choice of rhetoric was her presumption that successful interaction with the "prestigious foreigner" required that she put as much sociocultural distance between herself and the boat man as words would allow.

However, in another case, a poor boat woman returned home from market on the morning of the Mid-Autumn Festival. She gleefully proclaimed to her husband that she went to the Together Achieving Store to buy twenty catties of rice, but the proprietor refused: "No," he said, "I'll sell you thirty catties of rice." She protested that her sack only holds twenty catties. He insisted on selling thirty, but she only had money for twenty! Finally he said: "Oh, that's okay, take thirty catties and pay for twenty!" So he wrapped an extra package of ten catties along with the twenty in her sack. The poor woman identified the proprietor to me as a fellow "Hoklo." But her neighbor who was standing in the doorway said, "No he isn't; he's Chaochow. Those Chaochow are really generous with us."

According to Ma Fat-Li, the representative for the Hokkien boat community,

> the Chaochow are all rich. They own big farms and employ local people to work for them while they themselves do not have to work. Some Chaochow have big stores. They are so rich that one of them can contribute $5,000 to their fellowship association, and ten will total $50,000. But the Waichow Fellowship is poor. Its members grow vegetables, dig the land, or raise pigs from which they reap very little profit. They can barely support their families. The most that one of them can contribute to their association is $100. The majority can give only $50. That can't even amount to $5,000, can it?

The boat people feel closer to the Waichow than to the Chaochow in speech, native place, and socioeconomic status. Ma Fat-Li maintains a close *informal* political liaison with the Waichow leaders. The liaison is bolstered by right-wing sentiments. As we shall see, the Waichow are closely aligned with their Cantonese village landlords in the distribution of refugee relief. Ma Fat-Li's position on the Rural Committee facilitates his standing among the Waichow cohort and his claim on a share of the refugee aid. However, as a group, the boat people have no standing among the Waichow clansmen. Boat people point out that, "even though we are Hoklo, we cannot join the Waichow Fellowship Association because we have different occupations. They won't help us (for example, lend money) because we work on the water."

The Hokkien boat people feel most alienated from the local Hakka establishment. They even relish the thought that their Chaochow speech cousins have begun to dominate certain sectors of the political economy. According to one outspoken boatman:

> In the old days the Hakka held power in Sai Kung. But now the Chaochow are rising because the Hakka are ignorant of how to do things. They don't mind their manners. They don't know how to make relationships with outsiders.

This boat man went on to describe how the Hakka village elders opposed immigrant and government attempts to develop the Sai Kung society:

> Before 1967 when the Hakka under Chan Yat-Kuan established a Chamber of Commerce, the Hakka used it to oppose outside investments and urban development. They felt anxious lest their young be corrupted by gambling casinos and abandon farming the fields; they feared that their land would be bought at very low prices and there would be none to pass to future generations. They organized protests against government inspired improvements using the pretext of *feng shui*.

This informant related how when he argued for the government's proposals, the Hakka attacked him saying, "You boat people know nothing —you have no land." My informant claims to have retorted:

> You Hakka are afraid that your children will gamble. But now, when they go to the market to sell the pigs and vegetables, they go to gamble, and they don't return with the money their parents expect. So what? Your children will do what they please. Gambling is an individual decision. It depends on one's self control, not on the environment. . . . Are you so sure that your children will take care of you in your old age? You must enjoy life now because your children will simply divide your property no sooner than you have drawn your last breath of air! Without even taking care to bury your body, they will be staking out their claims on your land!

THE POLITICS OF DEPENDENCY

The strategy of Hokkien boat people can be described as the politics of dependency. Shek Lok, who is fairly typical, receives unsolicited benevolence from the Chaochow rice merchant. He occasionally receives a share of refugee aid (food, blankets, and so on) via Ma Fat-Li's patronage system. He owes money to his Hakka fishmonger, who loaned him money on his boat before it broke apart in the June rainstorm of 1972. Shek Lok even owes the interest on the $1,000 that he borrowed in the Tai Po market to get married eighteen years ago. He says the debt will be cleared even if it takes three generations! Not the least of his troubles stems from his squatting on Crown land where the shack he built from the wreck of his boat is periodically threatened with demolishment by government inspectors. The Shek family depends on other people's mercy and charity.

As indicated, the Hokkien boat community as a whole exists at the bottom end of the aid funnel funded by the United States and its client government on Taiwan. Some of this aid is funneled through the right-wing network of Cantonese village leaders and the Waichow cohort. Another portion of this wealth is funneled through the local Catholic church, also a bastion of anticommunism in Sai Kung. Just as Ma Fat-Li maintains liaison with the Waichow cohort, he also controls the funnel between the church and the Hokkien boat community. Since the early 1950s, Ma Fat-Li has been a member of the church, and it is through his grace that free rice and blankets are distributed to his Hokkien clients (see note 3). It is significant that no other Hokkien boat family has joined the church. Nor has Ma Fat-Li ever encouraged any family to do so. For their part, the fishermen insist that to join the church would violate their religious traditions. (As we shall see, the Hokkien boat people cling more tenaciously to their religious traditions than any other group in Sai Kung.) Yet, Ma Fat-Li's membership in the church has never dampened his enthusiastic leadership of the community's traditional rites.

The church possesses other assets in its mission to convert poor boat people. It sponsors the resettlement of poor boat people on the hill across the harbor. Most of the resettled boat people are Cantonese and members of the church. They have a representative on the Rural Committee who is a Catholic and who is Ma Fat-Li's closest confidant in the market town. The two men, one Cantonese, the other Hokkien, can be found often drinking tea together in a restaurant on Wharf Street. In contrast to the poor boat people's dependency on the church, the organized stratum of boat people (all Cantonese) recently established their own Better Living Credit Cooperative which is aimed at building its own resettlement housing on the hill across the harbor.

The politics of dependency is most palpable on Double Ten (October 10) when the little Hokkien shanty town is strung from head to foot with Republican flags and pennants. Many of the Hokkien fishermen, especially those who left China after 1950, remain convinced of the anticommunist rhetoric which their display implies. Others fall silent when the subject is broached. It seems ironical at first encounter that the poorest and potentially most "class conscious" group in Sai Kung lends public support to the anticommunists, while the wealthiest boat people (that is, the Cantonese) give their support to the communists on October first when the harbor of Cantonese junks is a veritable sea of red flags (see chapter 3, Market Organization).

THE RITES OF DEPENDENCY

The extent of their dependency on other people is reflected in the Hokkien boat people's feelings of indebtedness to their spiritual others. According to Shek Lok:

> We boat people lead an unknown fate from day to day. We will worship whenever or whatever there is, a heaven or a god. We see the sky, and we worship it. We worship as many gods as we know in order to protect our lives from unsuspecting storms. Whatever god gives us mercy, we keep the faith.

Other people, such as immigrant shopkeepers, say similar words: "I'll worship anything that provides food to eat." But the Hokkien rhetoric seems more sincerely spoken, and it is substantiated by their attention to the domestic rites. The Hokkien seem to have more patron saints on their home altars than do other groups. Even more distinctive is their demonstrated *devotion* to their patron saints. All of this earns them the stereotype of being "superstitious."

For example, Shek Lok's illegally constructed shack, measuring thirty square meters, houses seven persons, not including the three infant daughters that his wife "gave away" to Cantonese boat people. The family lives on an income from Shek Lok's daily construction wage of $35 and his daughter's $300 monthly wage from a Kowloon textile mill. All the family possessions, clothes, fishing gear, kerosene stove, pots, a cot, cotton quilts, and a wooden box containing identification cards, letters, and contracts are kept in this room. However, the family's most valued possession which adds much warmth and color to the room is the long row of altars extending from the standard sky shrines and door shrines to the ancestral shrine at the opposite end of the room. In the center is an earth deity nailed to the main pole stuck in the harbor mud, which supports the shack. Worship of the earth deity is supposed to distinguish land people from boat people. However the Shek's home rests on a pole sunk in the floor of the harbor. Therefore, Shek Lok's devotion to the earth god is all the more crucial.

Fastened to this center pole is a long shelf holding three prominent homemade shrines. Shek Lok and his wife find great satisfaction in telling about each shrine. The first is a Japanese Buddhist shrine of the Nichiren sect. Mrs. Shek joined the sect after seeing how her friend was healed by the power of faith. Mrs. Shek and several Cantonese boat women occasionally attend meetings in the sect's splendid Kowloon headquarters. Every morning and evening Mrs. Shek repeats two short chants before the altar in her shack.

Plate 9. Mrs. Shek's offering to deities on the household's altar. To the right of the altars in the photo was a Nichiren shrine.

Shek Lok comments that when his wife joined the sect, he thought she was going to learn something worthwhile. "But it is nothing more than a social club . . . like a mountain climbing club . . . just play."

The Nichiren shrine, a dark stained cabinet, has no part whatsoever in the Chinese ritual cycles or styles of worship. It is distinctly separate from the other two that are cruder and gaudier shrines of red-painted cratewood.

The two Chinese altars hold five shrines. Proceeding from stage left, the first honors Tin Hau, or more popularly, "Our Mother of Mercy." Tin Hau is the patron host of Sai Kung for the boat people. No people are more devoted to Tin Hau's local dominion than the Hokkien boat women. Twice a month, on the first and fifteenth day of the moon, the women lay offerings at the Tin Hau temple before attending the daily market. Other women also attend to these twice-monthly rites, but the Hokkien boat women are distinguished by their lavish offerings, the way they come in small groups, cleaned from head to foot, wearing ornate coiffures and traditional hand-stitched clothes (see chapter 5, Women's Ethnic Adornments).

Next to Tin Hau is the vegetarian Buddha. Shek Lok explains:

> It is an inheritance from my father who worshipped at its huge temple in Chiehshih along the coast of Lufeng. The stones of the temple were so large that even four men could not lift one. When the communists came they tried to get the people to topple the temple. Seven times the communists tried but failed because the villagers believed in it. Finally, one night the temple destroyed itself. The villagers didn't know why, but the Buddha probably felt it was an opportune time to escape the communists.

Shek Lok went on to describe the necessity for ritual purity, which I observed the women attending to with such diligence in their interaction with the local Tin Hau (see chapter 5, Women's Ethnic Adornments and Hairdressing):

> Anyone going to worship that Buddha had to clean every inch of his boat with fresh water. The pilgrim had to bathe and eat only vegetables for several days. Men and women had to be serious in attitude with absolutely no joking or swearing. Clothes had to be tidy and clean. And if everything were not clean, one would never return from the temple.

In the next altar there are three incense pots. The first is an unmarked pot for the "mother and child spirit." It protects mother and infant from illness during and after parturition.

The second unmarked incense pot is for the kitchen god, which all Chinese households have. To the right of the kitchen god is the ancestor tablet. It consists of a red strip of paper pasted over the incense pot with the simple, crudely written phrase, "Shek's ancestors." The ancestral rites are purely domestic. These people have little or no access to extended kin groups. The Sheks emphasize that they live and work in small family units, and there is really little cooperation between brothers. Each brother has his own shrine. Shek Lok for instance has eight brothers. Four of them live in the colony. The third brother lives in an urban resettlement block. The fourth brother lives on a boat moored off the two adjoining shacks of the sixth (himself) and seventh brothers. The third and seventh brothers each have their own ancestral shrines while Shek Lok shares his with the fourth brother on the boat. Speaking of the fourth brother, Shek Lok says:

> There is a good relationship between us. We therefore share one tablet. But if elder brother decided to work in Tai Po, he would come here and invite the ancestors to go along with him and then set up his own shrine aboard his boat. The seventh brother has his own shrine because he often went fishing

in Tai Po. Now he is a road worker and goes fishing in his work boat only during the fishing season.

BOAT PEOPLE'S RELIANCE ON FICTIVE KINSHIP

To supplement the lack of extended kin ties and to personalize important relationships, Chinese have recourse to *ch'i* ("fictive kin") relationships with other people and with local deities. In his study of Yuen Long Market, John Young (1974:83) found that "fictive kinship ties are formed . . . between individuals of similiar origin and background." In Sai Kung, such ties are used to formalize patron-client ties not only within but *across* ethnic boundaries. The patron takes the position of "*ch'i*-father" or "*ch'i*-elder brother" and the client becomes the "*ch'i*-son" or "*ch'i*-younger brother" respectively. (Similiar relationships may be formed among females.) Traditionally the Hakka villager, shopkeeper, fishmonger, moneylender, or local deity fills the elder role and the boat man takes the junior role. This institutionalizes the boat person's dependency while it guarantees his family access to fresh water, grass from the hills to cook food, a safe haven from storms, a place to market fish, to buy supplies, and to obtain credit. The most obvious benefit to the patron is the supply of fish which constitutes a major source of protein for south coastal Chinese. The Hokkien boat people still try to find fictive kinsmen in the market town and in the spirit of Tin Hau. By contrast, the Cantonese boat people who are organized into cooperatives have rationalized most of these relationships out of existence. And for the poorer stratum of Cantonese boat people who are members of the Catholic church, the Chinese *ch'i* relationships are incorporated into Catholic godparent relationships.

Townspeople, especially immigrants, also form fictive kin ties among themselves and sometimes with locals. But all of these people express negative attitudes toward such relationships: "We don't form *ch'i* relationships anymore." "All that stuff is superstitious." "It's troublesome." These negative attitudes are based on the fact that fictive kinship binds people for life into a hierarchy of ritual exchange. Whereas this has great adaptive value where material want is constant, it has limited or maladaptive value in contexts of rapid economic expansion where one may not want to be bound by a network of unalterable economic obligations such as kinship imposes.

The Hokkien boat people are not directly involved in the commercial prosperity of Sai Kung market. They are in no position to take advantage of the changing opportunities. They therefore rely on ritual purity and fictive kinship as their best bet for survival. Only they are unabashed in their persistent regard for *ch'i* relationships and ritual obligations.

CHAOCHOW PROJECTIONS

At the opposite end of the socioeconomic spectrum from the Hokkien boat people are about two thousand Chaochow. About one-third of the Chaochow community are joined in a tight syndicate of immigrants from different counties of the native prefecture (see note 4) and from all relevant occupational classes. Eighteen percent are laborers and shop assistants; 37 percent are shopkeepers; and 45 percent are commercial farmers.

The organized Chaochow community projects itself as a highly civilized and virtuous people. In a public speech to commemorate the opening of the Chaochow Association in Sai Kung, the leader, Li Hung-Fuk, referred to the Chaochow as a *tsu* ("clan") with a long ancestry of virtuous men tracing back to Han Yu, the renowned scholar-statesman who was exiled to Chaochow during the Tang dynasty. In an interview, Mr. Li accounted for his personal success in terms of his Chaochow virtues:

> I never cheat anyone. I do charitable acts, and I try by all means to help other people. One must be polite, thankful, moderate, easy-going, and speak in a calm voice. Through humility and charity I ingratiate myself with the local Hakka people. To help others is to help yourself.

The Chaochow project themselves as urbane and mercantile. Mr. Li says that "Wherever there are cities, there are Chaochow people." Whether they are truck farmers or shopkeepers, most of the Chaochow in Sai Kung hail from Kowloon where they maintain most of their social and economic connections. In Sai Kung they pride themselves on their ability to work hard, to offer low prices for all customers, and to steer clear of the ideological struggles which at times rock the Sai Kung community. These abilities are the consequence of their ethnic organization which ipso facto accounts for their phenomenal success in the market. Their success is measured in their many "rags-to-riches" stories.

Ho Si-Yu is fairly typical. He peddled Li Hung-Fuk's cakes before he rented some land near Sha Kok Mei village and began raising vegetables and hogs. Today, he, his wife and young children wear the cheapest factory-made clothes and live in a one-room hovel adjoined to a large concrete pig sty. Well before dawn, Ho Si-Yu loads baskets of vegetables, cut the previous evening to take to the Kowloon market, onto a truck hired by the cooperative. When he returns from Kowloon, his wife is hoeing the vegetables. Mr. Ho eats a bowl of rice and then goes to hand water the fields. Later in the day they are joined by their children. Their day of toil in the fields and pig sty does not end until after sunset. Ho Si-Yu says he grosses about $100 per day. This places him in the second highest income bracket in the Hong Kong Census. In chapter 7 is additional case material on Ho Si-Yu and others which illustrates the pattern of Chaochow immigration.

VIEWS FROM THE OTHER SIDE

The local people are reluctant to acknowledge the Chaochow's self-image. A leader of a Cantonese village says that:

> The rich Chaochow help the poor Chaochow to set up small businesses by loaning money on easy terms. They really stick together. But they also like to fight (among themselves). Chaochow are very unreasonable people. They are barbaric: Why? Because Chaochow *feng shui* is like that.

"Chaochow *feng shui*" implies that Chaochow are immigrants and tenants and thus are in no position to effect a stable and proper relationship with the environment.

Chaochow character is, in fact, a product of a marginal adaptation and an ability to organize mutual aid independent from local Cantonese patronage. The increasing success and independence of the Chaochow has antagonized the Cantonese. Many Chaochow who were formerly tenants of the Cantonese villagers reoriented their patronage to a Hakka faction in the mid-1960s. Increasing Chaochow incomes enable some to take advantage of opportunities to purchase Cantonese village land. The Chaochow ability to acquire the Cantonese ancestral land further exacerbates the intergroup antagonism since it destroys the basic rationale of land ownership which underlies Cantonese identity as "Punti." It is relevant that the Cantonese villager who made the remark about "Chaochow barbarism" had just sold a large estate of his ancestral land to a Chaochow leader.

While the Chaochow project themselves as civil and virtuous, the local people generally think of them as "barbaric." In everyday language, the locals refer to the Chaochow as "Hoklo." For example, an old Hakka peasant woman remarked that "Hoklo grow vegetables, and they are extremely filthy because they scoop out the public cloacae to fertilize their vegetables." The old woman denied any distinction between "Chaochow" and "Hoklo," and used the terms interchangeably. A younger woman from Ho Chung, where the distinction has greater political utility and ritual visibility, retorted:

> The Chaochow and Hoklo are different. They have different celebrations during the Hungry Ghost Festival. The Chaochow stage a Chaochow opera, and the (Waichow) Hoklo stage a Hoklo opera. People say the Hoklo opera is no good, and the Chaochow opera, although bigger is still no good.

Another example of local rhetoric occurred during a wake being held by Hokkien boat people on the shore fronting a Hakka neighborhood. As the Hakka sat on benches watching the wake, an old Hakka woman exclaimed that "Those Hoklo eat *chuk* (H) all the time." (*Chuk* is thin rice gruel which Chinese eat for breakfast, or all the time, if they are too sick or too poor to eat steamed rice.) A young boy who attends the Catholic school and has a number of Chaochow classmates piped up: "No, that's what Chaochow eat!" The old lady shot back, "Chaochow, Hoklo, they are the same!"

In short, the economically successful Chaochow find it difficult to win public acceptance of their self-ascribed name and image. Compared to the Cantonese boat people they seem somewhat less successful in projecting their self-image to the local public. The difference is related in part to the position of each group vis-à-vis the locals. The Chaochow *compete* with the locals for customers, land, and political power. The Cantonese boat people *complement* the locals. The boat people have stimulated the market by expanding fish sales and by returning their profits in purchases from the local shopkeepers. Rather than vying with locals for political positions, the boat community enjoys a fixed quota of representation in the Rural Committee. Finally, where Cantonese boat people are moving ashore, it is onto unproductive Crown land provided by the government where there is no threat to displace land people.

The Emerging Waichow Hokkien

The two thousand Waichow Hokkien are among the least visible groups in Sai Kung. They are concentrated in Lok Mei, a new settlement on the hill behind Ho Chung. Most are truck farmers. A few have been able to open shops along the highway or in Sai Kung town. Presently they are trying to establish a native place association (see note 4). Although the Waichow and Chaochow share closer affinities in language, native place, and occupation than any other two groups in Sai Kung, their animosity for one another seems to be among the sharpest.

Chaochow, not to mention local people often refer to the Waichow Hokkien as simply "Hoklo." However, the Waichow leaders insist on being known as Waichow people rather than as simply "Hoklo." When asked to differentiate between themselves and Chaochow, a Waichow leader declared:

Chaochow are unreasonable, mean, and aggressive. They like to fight. We don't like to fight. We Waichow people just want our hand-to-mouth subsistence. We are diligent and live a hard life. I simply grow vegetables and sell them at the market to buy some rice and a little soy sauce for flavor. I can't even afford to eat vegetables and meat. When my crop is ruined by typhoon or is undersold by the China mainland producers, I can't eat my fill. More often I will sell my vegetables and buy pig feed. Only when the pig is sold can I afford to buy some meat and fresh fish.

Another Waichow leader who is a refugee (and was classified by the communists as a "rich peasant") states the difference in terms of money:

We are poor peasants and use the plow to turn the soil. We live from hand-to-mouth, compared to the Chaochow who have lots of money from their shops in the market. Just look at the Chaochow Hungry Ghost Celebration compared to ours! The goods they contribute are worth more than $10,000, and they get Kowloon people to contribute to their celebration.

Unlike the Chaochow, the Waichow maintain their patronage and therefore dependency on the local Ho Chung Cantonese establishment. We shall see that whereas the Chaochow receive substantial financial support from their ethnic cohort in Kowloon, the Waichow rely in part on the local Cantonese landlords for financial contributions to their Hungry Ghost Celebrations. From the Cantonese villager's point of view, the Waichow have kept their place and are perceived as friendlier and more trustworthy "Hoklo." A few of the more prosperous and hardworking Waichow men have married local girls. In contrast, the organized part of the Chaochow community tends to maintain its con-nubial connections within the wider Kowloon Chaochow circuit. In sub-sequent chapters I will examine the different adaptations which the Wai-chow and Chaochow have made to Sai Kung society. Suffice here that the Waichow are not as obtrusive in local society as are the Chaochow. The Waichow occupy a position between the Chaochow and the Hokkien boat people, and the names and images by which the Waichow are iden-tified reflect this intermediate position.

CONCLUSION

I have discussed the relationship between two dimensions of ethnic group relations. One dimension is the rhetoric of ethnicity. It consists of names and images which characterize and entitle social groups. The other dimension is the group's position in the political economy. The rhetoric identifies a group's position through the human ability to generalize and then to use these generalizations in the form of outgroup caricatures and ingroup mystiques. Chinese employ reptilian images (snakes, eggs, dragons) to caricature outgroups as "southern barbarians," while they employ the attributes of "civilization" to idealize their own group origins or to mystify the shortcomings thereof. Each of the groups in Sai Kung employs this rhetoric in claiming to be "more Chinese than" or "as Chinese as" the other. For example, the Hakka lump certain groups together as "superstitious," "extravagant," and "dirty" "Hoklo." The latter distinguish themselves in different socioeconomic strata as "religious," "benevolent," "ritually pure" "Chinese." In turn the Hakka are stereotyped by non-Hakka as "ill-mannered," "rootless," "rabble-rousers." But the Hakka mystique justifies their rudeness as "righteous," "independent," "progressive," and "nationalistic."

The degree to which a group is able to have its self-image acknowledged and honored by others in society is partly determined by the group's position in the society. It follows that as a humble group gains political and economic independence, its members are able to create and project a viable self-image. The groups which have done this with more or less success are the boat people and the Chaochow. The difference in the degree of success between these two groups seems to be contingent on the different roles each has assumed in the market vis-à-vis the politically dominant Hakka. Cantonese boat people have developed a position which complements that of the dominant Hakka, while the Chaochow have developed a more competitive role.

On a larger scale, the Hakka have been similarly successful in projecting their mysteries onto the political stage of modern China. Once a despised and vulgar term, the name "Hakka" attained more honorable connotations with the regional and international amalgamation of Hakka associations in the ferment of Chinese nationalism.

NOTES

1. Although she tends to reject what she labels as the productive labor hypothesis, elsewhere in the same volume Wolf (1975:134) postulates that Hakka women in Taiwan have a much lower suicide rate than Hokkien women due to Hakka fortitude and such institutions as "private room money" which allow Hakka women a certain amount of economic and psychological autonomy from the rigors of family life. In the most recent study of the Hakka in Taiwan, Myron Cohen (1976:190–191) rejects Wolf's interpretation of "private room money" as basically a Hakka institution. In fact it appears that this institution is embedded in the very structure of the Chinese family, especially in areas where the normative postpubertal form of marriage is practiced in which a large dowry accompanies a nubile woman in exchange for a handsome bride-price.

2. In Taiwan, Hakka are also known as "Kwangtung people" (that is, "Cantonese") vis-à-vis the local Hokkien-speaking Taiwanese.

3. American whites use the same slur against blacks: "Coloreds like loose shoes. . . ." Such slurs are considered so reprehensible that when uttered by a public official, even in private, it may cause an outpour of minority wrath and force the offending official from office (see "Ford Rebukes Butz for Slur on Blacks," *New York Times,* October 2, 1976:1).

4.   Ma Fat-Li is the oldest resident and the customary head of the Hokkien boat community. He maintains a list of his clients which he uses when dealing with other Rural Committeemen and government officials. He lists 64 male household heads and the number of members in each household. The total number of persons is 467. The list is arranged into surname groups. Within each group the household head listed first is the surname group's informal leader. He is responsible directly to Mr. Ma. (The surname groups are not based on genealogy.) There are eleven surname groups; and the Ma group, as might be expected, is the largest in number with 161 persons in 23 families. Not all of the people listed in Mr. Ma's group are resident in Sai Kung. A number live in Tai Po. Also, some of them are actually Cantonese boat people who are tied in various ways such as marriage, fictive kinship, and friendship to Mr. Ma and his followers.

         Mr. Li Hung-Fuk is the official head of the Chaochow Fellowship Association and the unofficial spokesman for the Chaochow community. Li gives the following, possibly inflated, round figures for the total numbers of Chaochow and Waichow Hokkien persons in Sai Kung:

Place	Chaochow	Waichow
Ho Chung (tenant villages)	1,200	1,500
Pak Kong (tenant villages)	30	100
Sha Kok Mei (tenant shacks)	200	10
Tai Mong Tsai New Village	30	10
Sai Kung town	500	300
Total	1,960	1,920

Note that these are not the numbers of members of the Chaochow or Waichow fellowship associations, and therefore, by their unincorporated nature, must be inexact. The Chaochow Association has 136 family head members (representing about seven hundred persons). Each family is identified in the membership book by its native county in Chaochow. The Chaochow, unlike the Hokkien boat people in Sai Kung, organize in terms of native places. If we count only the twenty executive committee members of the Chaochow Association we see that the Ch'aoyang county group with eight has the largest number among whom we find the chairman, Li Hung-Fuk. The Ch'aoyang group is followed by P'uning (7), Chiehyang (2), Tenglai (2), and Huilai (1).

         The Waichow Association is not (yet) registered with the government, and it is technically unincorporated. Its leaders were reluctant to divulge much information about its membership to me.

5.   If we view the boat community from within, we see a major dimension of socioeconomic grouping along lines of fishing techniques. Different techniques require different scales of capital investment, boat construction, and labor organization. The largest scale operations are the trawlers. Each has a crew of around twenty, and some of these have formed the nucleus of a fully rationalized deep sea fishing industry since 1960. Since 1955 there have been only a few trawlers operating from Sai Kung. Sai Kung is home for the more traditional family operated vessels. Within this group are some smaller shrimp trawlers, purse seiners, long liners, gill netters, hand liners, and trappers. Purse seining is the most lucrative inshore technique. A family can earn as much as $15,000 a year. Traditionally, it requires two boats working at night hauling nets. Often the two boats are manned by an extended joint or stem family. Long lining is

fairly profitable. It is conducted by one boat during the day, and often involves a two- or three-day trip along the coast. Except for the hand-to-mouth subsistence of hand-lining and trapping techniques, gill netting uses the least expensive tackle in shallow waters. A family engaged in gill netting may earn as much as $3,000 a year.

The techniques which are more dependent on inshore fishing grounds (that is, within several miles of shore) have decreased in productivity in recent years as the inshore waters around the colony have become polluted and overfished. This probably accounts for some of the decrease in purse seining and the increase in long lining. These and other changes in fishing techniques, which are reflected in the following statistics for Sai Kung, are also due to increased immigration and socioeconomic stratification. Between 1955 and 1965, shrimp trawlers increased from none to 20 vessels (160 persons) in Sai Kung harbor. Long liners increased from 27 to 71 vessels (212 to 575 persons). Purse seiners decreased from 124 to 100 vessels (992 to 900 persons). Hand liners increased from 20 to 50 vessels (120 to 250 persons). Gill netters increased from 30 Hokkien vessels (180 persons) to 220 Hokkien and Cantonese vessels (1,760 persons). Miscellaneous wrecks and houseboats increased from 60 to 170 vessels (360 to 850 persons). (Most of this data is from the Hong Kong government's Department of Agriculture and Fisheries Annual Reports, especially those of 1956b and 1966.) This apparent pattern of increasing stratification is partly explained by the capitalist mode of modernization by which the government has attempted to develop the fishing industry. (See Barbara Ward 1967 for an in-depth discussion of the stratification of the boat community.)

CHAPTER 5

Ethnic Group Culture

In Sai Kung, each group draws upon its ethnic heritage in an attempt to develop its position in society. In drawing upon its cultural traditions as a means of adapting to a new environment, each group borrows from a common pool of Chinese culture traits; or to use language differences in both a substantive and an analogical sense, each group uses a common grammar to articulate a different set of sounds and utterances.

Ethnic traits mark differences in both subtle and obvious ways. People may be conscious of their differences, but they may not be aware of, able, or willing to articulate the differences. The more subtle, inarticulate, largely domestic differences become relevant only in certain concrete interpersonal situations. At the opposite end of the cultural spectrum are the more obvious and consistently apprehended differences by which a group makes a living, or are stigmatized, or advertise themselves in the political-economic arena. In the previous chapters, I touched on some of the obvious instrumental differences by which groups earn a living. I now turn to some of the subtle domestic customs and the obtrusive politico-religious displays by which Sai Kung people identify ethnic group membership.

THE ORGANIZATION OF ANCESTOR RITES

The continuity of the male line is the mainstay of Chinese culture. I found that all group's share the basic Confucian values of patriarchal authority, patrilineality, equal inheritance among brothers, virilocal postmarital residence, and extended joint family. They honor forebearers. They have bona fide Chinese surnames and generational names.

Plate 10. Hakka ancestor hall. Single surname tablet in the center of the altar is characteristic.

They practice surname exogamy. And they practice terrestrial inhumation of the dead. But, there are some subtle differences in the organization of rites, particularly in the fetish that is set up to represent the souls of departed ancestors.

Land people who are in direct contact with a literate tradition have the names of their ancestors inscribed on sheets of red paper in their homes and on red wooden tablets in their ancestor halls. In Sai Kung, each "ancestor hall" *(chia tz'u t'ang)* incorporates about fifteen families descended from a single ancestor. Each group owns just enough land to finance the annual ancestor rites. Neither among Cantonese nor Hakka is there a "nesting" of halls indicative of the kind of economic stratification found elsewhere among Cantonese in the New Territories. However, within the halls, the Cantonese, as elsewhere, represent each of their significant forebearers with an individual soul tablet on the main altar. Hakka, as reported elsewhere, represent the ancestors of the entire group in a single surname tablet on the main altar.[1]

Nevertheless, in Hakka halls, one may see individually named ancestors represented on red papers pasted along the side walls, males on the right and females along the left wall facing the altar. These are the unfortunate ones who died before reaching sixty years of age. Those who live past sixty are incorporated into the main wooden tablet; they are much honored as "complete elders," who in rounding out their lives have become lineage leaders. Side altars are arranged in terms of the lineage's major genealogical segments. For example in Tai Mong Tsai, the Tseng lineage was founded by five brothers. There are five papers for the five segments, each containing the names of the unfortunate ancestors.

To what degree the different Hakka and Punti usages reflect culture-historical differences in social structure or the concept of the lineage is open to debate,[2] but the differences do constitute subtle points of ethnic demarkation in Sai Kung.

Cantonese boat people, who are not directly attached to the literate culture, and who live primarily in conjugal family abodes, set up small wooden icons. These are garish figurines between eight and fifteen centimeters high, each depicting a deceased family member. Grandfather may be a bearded warrior riding a tiger. Father may be represented as a standing official and mother as a woman of high rank. The smaller figures represent deceased unmarried children, who are not technically "ancestors."

Barbara Ward (1965:133) describes the boat people's icons as ethnic "badges," and furthermore, as "non-Han, or at least non-literati, items."[3] Land people regard the boat people's iconography as bizarre and rather crass, in somewhat the same manner that American middle-class Protestants disdain the vivid crucifixion pictures which adorn the walls of working-class Catholic homes. However, the boat people do not carve their own icons; they purchase them from the ritual shops in town, that is, from land people. And to these shops the boat people take their icons to be cleaned and repainted.

Traditionally, each ethnic group utilizes different iconic forms to represent its ancestors. However, at the level of epistemology, all the groups are culturally Chinese. For example, both land people and boat people know that the luminescent aspect of the deceased person's soul animates its respective tablet or figurine by the act of "dotting " the final ideograph on the tablet or the eyes of the figurine.

In recent times some of the superficial iconographic differences have eroded as the groups have shifted positions in the local social structure. There is a tendency for boat people, who are gradually becoming literate, to use the single surname tablet in their domestic altars. Many Chinese in urban highrise apartments also utilize the single surname tablet. This simplification of ritual seems to be associated with needs to conserve

Plate 11. Cantonese boat people's ancestral icons. These have been repainted and set out to dry on the counter of a local paper shop.

space and to facilitate transport and duplication. Structurally the single surname tablet embraces a larger number of relationships where exact genealogical relationships may be irrelevant in contexts of social discontinuity. This situation lies at the root of Hakka identity, and it characterizes floating, immigrant, and modern urban populations.

FIRECRACKER ASSOCIATIONS

Boat people and immigrants do not enjoy the benefits of extended kin groups organized around fixed agrarian estates and sanctioned by the ancestor cult. Boat people and immigrants utilize other identities to organize access to changing fortunes in the local economy. They organize mutual aid clubs on the basis of ethnicity, surname, occupation, neighborhood, age, or sex. These clubs are called firecracker associations (hua p'ao hui); and they are sanctioned by the local leaders in the name of the local deity. Firecracker associations are not normally incorporated by fixed estates, but operate on an annual renewable membership, and are therefore not regulated by the colonial government.

Table 1 lists the thirteen firecracker associations which participated in the Sai Kung Tin Hau Festival of 1972. We can see that the firecracker associations are popular among the boat people and immigrants and that ethnicity is an important criterion for their organization.

There are three other temples in the market area which sponsor firecracker associations. The Hung Shing feast on Kau Sai Island has

TABLE I. Sai Kung Tin Hau Temple Firecracker Associations of 1972

Association Name	Organizing Principle
Ch'ao Shing T'ang	Chaochow people
Hai Lien T'ang	Cantonese boat people (Sai Kung)
Ho I T'ang	Cantonese boat people (across Sai Kung harbor)
Hsieh Yü Lan	Cantonese boat people (across Sai Kung harbor)
Lung Chiang	Cantonese boat people (Yaumatei, Kowloon)
Lien Ho T'ang	Hokkien boat people (Sai Kung)
Hui Chou Ch'ing Nien	Waichow Hokkien youth (Sai Kung)
Hui Chou T'ang	Waichow Hokkien people
Hui Hai T'ang	Haifeng Hokkien people
Ho Shing T'ang	Sai Kung Road neighbors (mostly immigrant Hakka)
Lien Ta T'ang	Three generations of a Sai Kung family
Yü Shang Hui	Sai Kung fish buyers
Ho Hsi Ch'eng Shing Li T'ang	Patrons of Mrs. Ho, an immigrant Cantonese money lender and jewelry shop owner.

become the most outstanding in recent years. It is supported by twenty-six associations. The majority are boat people and others involved in the fishing industry from all around the colony. Several large firecracker associations composed of Sai Kung shopkeepers who have vested interests in the prosperity of the boat people regard the Kau Sai trip as one of the big events of the year. Second is the Tin Hau temple at Lung Shuen Wan. It is supported by thirty associations in a celebration held every three years. Associations of boat people from every major port in the colony, including many shopkeepers from Sai Kung, attend. Finally, the Kuan Yin Feast day at Pak Sha Wan is supported annually by twenty-two associations, primarily boat people and immigrant Cantonese and Hokkien truck farmers and shopkeepers from the immediate marketing area.

One of the main purposes of firecracker associations is to pool capital and to provide a credit fund for its members. Each association sells shares to its members. Association shares normally range between twenty and one hundred, each share costing an average of $50. The assets are used to finance the elaborate offerings of roast pork, buns, eggs, firecrackers, and a floral shrine on the annual feast day of the local deity. During the year the assets are used as a revolving credit fund. Such pools of capital are extremely important to immigrants and boat people who usually lack local sources for easy credit. However, these economic functions are completely encapsulated by the ritual fanfare which gives religious and local community sanction to each association.

During the year, each association keeps a small glass-encased icon of the temple deity in a member's home or in the association headquarters. The icons belong to the local temple and are numbered one through twenty (where there are twenty sponsoring associations). The members honor the icon and appeal to it when undertaking business ventures or in wishing for the birth of a son. In thanksgiving the members hang fish-shaped gold foil on the icon. Each foil is inscribed with a lucky phrase and the name of the contributor on the reverse side. Over the years particular icons may become known for their luck and wealth.

As the feast day of the deity approaches in late spring or early summer, the associations buy large paper-flower and figurine-decorated shrines which cost between $300 and $1000 to house the icons. The women of the association tie red eggs and ginger roots to the shrine to express the group's fertility and good fortune. On the god or goddess' feast day, the shrine is noisily paraded through the streets to the temple, preceded by its own or a hired martial arts team. There is competition among groups to position their ostentatious shrines in front of the temple deity. Afterward, martial arts teams execute public demonstrations of their fighting skills. In these, boat people's teams nearly always excel.

The temple Committee retrieves the numbered icons from each shrine to redistribute them for the coming year. They fire paper cartridges containing the numbers of the icons into the air, and the young men from the participating associations scramble fiercely to retrieve them, sometimes ending in melees. Each group wants to be sure to take one home. Smaller groups or shopkeepers hire martial arts teams to do their scrambling on the field. Groups that retrieve more than one number may keep them, or sell them, or give them to those who are less fortunate.

Local villagers, especially Hakka villagers, regard firecracker associations with their customary contempt for waste. However, Hakka Kaifong leaders, who are responsible for the Tin Hau feast day, sanction the firecracker associations. The leaders and the townspeople whose trade depends on boat people, often buy shares in the Kaifong Firecracker Association which patronizes the all important fishermen's Hung Shing temple at Kau Sai Island. However, the Kaifong Firecracker Association is managed by a Chaochow baker. The Hakka leaders seem to have as little to do with the firecracker association and the rituals surrounding the temple celebration as they can properly get away with.

The one exception to the rule that local villagers do not join these associations is a Cantonese lineage in Sha Kok Mei which organized a firecracker association in the 1920s. Their alleged motive was to increase the group's fertility. Having noticed the great fertility of the boat people, a lineage leader surmised that the boat people's secret lay in the power of their firecracker associations.

Plate 12. The floral shrines of various firecracker associations that are placed in front of the Sai Kung Tin Hau Temple

Of course many local people, including a few villagers, participate in the various feast days. The Hakka women's Elder and Young Sister Association attend the Tin Hau and Kuan Yin feast days with an offering of roast pig. A smaller group of women from Sha Kok Mei village, resplendent in Hakka costumes, presents a whole pig to Tin Hau on Lung Shuen Wan. But neither of these Hakka groups carries a floral shrine which is the sine qua non of the firecracker association.

DOMESTIC FESTIVALS

All groups in Sai Kung celebrate the standard cycle of family festivities: Lunar New Year, Ch'ing Ming, or alternatively the Double Nine. Double Five (Dragon Boat), Hungry Ghost, Harvest Moon and the Winter Solstice festivals. However, there are some differences which serve to mark group boundaries.

Cantonese Village Festival of Heavenly Things in Early Spring

The Festival of Heavenly Things is an unobtrusive family festival on the nineteenth day of the first moon. Cantonese village women light candles and burn incense and offer a chicken, pork, fruit and special "tea cakes" to the myriad heavenly spirits. The "tea cake" is made from sweet potato, sticky rice, five spice powder, green onion, and is fried like a pancake.

Locally the festival is known as *T'ien chi chieh* ("Heavenly Things Festival"), and everyone describes it simply as *pai t'ien* ("honoring Heaven") or *pai shen* ("honoring spirits"). However, the only people I found doing this were Cantonese village women. I did not observe boat people or Hakka celebrating this day, and when I inquired of the Hakka women if they ever did this, they were emphatic in their assurance that the "Heavenly Things Festival is Punti; we Hakka do not celebrate it." One woman used the rhetoric of the "Punti" as "hosts" and the Hakka as "guests" by jesting: "The Punti make tea cakes, and we Hakka eat them!"

The festival seems to be a fertility rite. In urban Hong Kong, a "Hundred Spirits Festival" is held on the same day by Cantonese women (Burkhardt 1955, II:160). Women who want to become pregnant beseech the magical intervention of various gods. In Sai Kung the rites on the nineteenth are situated at a critical point in the agricultural cycle, that is the interregnum between the end of winter's dry spell and the beginning of spring's wet spell. The onset of the spring rains is most critical to the spring sowing.

The Hakka Field Festival in Late Summer

The Hakka emphasize the fourteenth day of the seventh lunar month, or what they call *T'ien chieh* ("Field Festival"). (Other groups in Sai Kung begin a related celebration on the next day, the fifteenth, called "Hungry Ghost Festival.") The Hakka Field Festival is also a fertility rite geared to allay the peasant's anxiety over the ripening crop when late summer storms threaten to devastate it. Thus, the village women offer supplication to the village earth shrine in hopes of an abundant harvest.

The women bake a special tea cake for the occasion called *vo chhon pan* (H) ("rice cash-string dumplings"). *Vo chhon* refers to the grain-bearing rice stalk which will hopefully mature like copper cash on the string (old-style Chinese coins). Women make long rolls of sticky rice flour and press a chopstick lengthwise onto each roll to make a depression. The chopstick is also a phallic symbol, the word being a homophone for "quickly bear seed." Each cake is wrapped in a banana leaf and steamed.

These cakes, along with a roast chicken, joss sticks, and paper money are carried to the earth shrine and offered in hopes of gaining the earth god's influence for abundant crops. At the same time the women burn offerings of paper money to the wandering ghosts to appease all the malcontents in the area.

The Cantonese and Hakka fertility festivals complement each other. The Cantonese rites attempt to induce the spring rain, and the Hakka rites aim at retarding the late summer storms and increasing the autumn harvest.

COMMUNITY FESTIVALS

Rather than focusing on family or lineage ancestors or on the hamlet's earth deity, community festivals center on the temple housing the patron deity in the village or market. Community festivals may be one of two kinds, either the birthday of the particular deity or an elaboration of one of the basic Chinese family festivals. In the former category are Tin Hau's feast day at Sai Kung and Lung Shuen Wan, Hung Shing's on Kau Sai Island, and Kuan Yin's at Pak Sha Wan. In the latter category are two, the Double Five and Hungry Ghost festivals.

Double Five (or Dragon Boat Festival) was a traditional community celebration which the Kaifong sponsored prior to 1967. On the fifth day of the fifth moon, two canoes of Cantonese boat men and one canoe of Hokkien boat men raced through Sai Kung harbor cheered on by festive crowds along the shore. After 1967, the Dragon Boat celebration in early July gave way to the Hungry Ghost Festival in early August, and in some ways this reflected the loss of local power to the immigrant groups (see chapter 6, A Local Hakka Merchant Family).

The Hungry Ghost Festival (or the festival of deliverance) has become an important community event among immigrant groups. It is generally called the "Seventh Moon Fifteenth Day." On the fifteenth all the souls in hell are released for a month, and the world of the living is besieged by the myriad ghosts. During this period each family offers food and incense to its own ancestors as well as to the anomalous ghosts wandering about outside one's door. The sacrificial offerings are made with the hope of protecting the living from any malevolent ghost and to mercifully deliver the dead from the scourges of hell. This provides the opportunity for community observances among Chaochow and Waichow Hokkien and boat people. Each of these groups displays their benevolence toward the dead in a collective *ta chiao* or "rite of cosmic renewal" (see Saso 1972).

On the fifteenth day the boat people's representatives, both Cantonese and Hokkien, join together in sponsoring a small Taoist-led *ta chiao* for the ghosts in their harbor. The Chaochow and Waichow land people each stage separate grandiose celebrations along the road in Ho Chung. There is intense competition between the latter two, but they agree to hold their respective celebrations on different days of the thirty-day period.

The Chaochow erect two large matsheds (of bamboo and tin) that face each other across an open space. One shed houses their Chaochow opera which plays four days and five nights. The other shed is sectioned into three huge open-air rooms. On the left is the business office where contributions are accepted. There are long sheets of red paper publicizing the names and amounts of each contributor. The visitor is invited to sit in the breeze of the electric fan and to drink tea or beer provided by the association. In the center section of the shed is the offering table piled high with contributions from members: small appliances, lamps, figurines, trinkets, and baskets of fruit and buns, to be auctioned on the final night. This display of the group's wealth attracts much public scrutiny, commentary and comparison with other groups' displays. In front of the table is the main shrine, and around the area are shrines for other local deities including one shrine for the group's collective ancestors. The right section of the shed, draped in yellow and black, contains the *ta chiao* in which a troupe of hired Buddhist monks chants sutras and performs an assortment of rites to deliver the souls from hell. The sides of the walls are hung with pictures of the gruesome tortures of hell. This last most esoteric aspect of the whole event receives little or no attention from the crowds of visitors. Sociologically, the object of renewal is none other than the group's ethnic identity and its position in the local society. Here we witness one of the great ironies in all cultures in which people use the rhetoric of respect for the dead to finesse political influence among the living.

The Chaochow visitors, many from Kowloon, first go to the office to pay their respects and make their contributions. They make the rounds quickly, offering incense to each of the various shrines while taking little or no cognizance of the particular deity's identity. The visitors then survey the spread of goods on the main table, and finally they proceed to the matshed where the opera is being noisily staged. A major attraction is the opera, especially because it affords people the opportunity to socialize. Local people are drawn to the bright lights and the noise of the opera, although none can understand it because the opera is sung in Chaochow. But it is the auction on the final night which attracts the largest crowd. Liquor flows freely and members, as well as some locals (nonmembers), receive much limelight in bidding large, sometimes overly generous, amounts for an item.

The Waichow Hokkien *ta chiao* is similar in form to that of the

Plate 13. The Chaochow spirit place during the Sai Kung Tin Hau Festival

Chaochow. However, the Chaochow are able to erect their matsheds prominently along the highway where they own some land, whereas the Waichow hold theirs on a back road in Lok Mei hamlet above Ho Chung village. The Waichow also receive much greater financial support from their Cantonese patrons and landlords, while the Chaochow affair maintains more independence from the local community by substantial contributions from the Kowloon parent association.

The Chaochow erect another "spirit place" during the Tin Hau celebration in Sai Kung. The matshed is erected close to the Tin Hau temple, and it is sectioned similarly to the one in Ho Chung. The difference is that during the Tin Hau celebration the right-hand section of the shed houses the group's flower shrine (their offering to Tin Hau) rather than the *ta chiao* as during the Hungry Ghost Festival.

During the Tin Hau Festival, the Hakka-dominated Kaifong sponsors four days and five nights of Cantonese opera. This is extremely popular, and the enormous expense is partly offset by sales of seats to local shopkeepers. However, the Chaochow take advantage of the huge matshed which seats well over a thousand persons to sponsor an additional four days and five nights of Chaochow opera. The Chaochow Association bears the entire cost of their opera, and, thus, it is free to the public. To encourage local attendance, they flash "subtitles" onto a screen next to the stage for those who can read.

In 1967 the Chaochow spent $65,000 on their Hungry Ghost Celebration and $50,000 on the Tin Hau Festival. In 1972 they spent $80,000 and $65,000 respectively. In other words, the Chaochow spend at least $145,000 per year (not counting other substantial contributions) providing free opera and spiritual deliverance to the Sai Kung people. In such demonstrations of benevolence they are claiming to be Sai Kung's benefactors. They are in effect saying, "We are not mean, stingy, aggressive, violent-prone outsiders. We are a becalming influence." "We are peace-loving and generous Chaochow."

The Hakka do not concede this image. Some Hakka scoff at the veneer of religiosity and simply say the Chaochow are trying to *ch'u t'ou* ("thrust out their heads"). Another Hakka view is that this gaudy religious performance is "typical Hoklo superstition." One Hakka neighbor sarcastically said, "The Chaochow have plenty to feed the spirits but have nothing for the living." Another Hakka leader who is in fact allied with the Chaochow faction put it more diplomatically but hardly less condemnably: "Chaochow buy all those special offerings to present to the gods; they are very religious but toward living people they have no real sympathy!"

A more neutral view is that the Chaochow are very frugal. My Hakka friend pointed out that they wear threadbare clothes, live in hovels, eat poor food such as rice gruel. "They are not extravagant in any of the three necessities, clothes, shelter, and food. Yet at festivities each Chaochow contributes a large sum of money."

The Cantonese *Ta Chiao*

Sai Kung Cantonese villagers also mark their boundary by a festive *ta chiao* held late in the year once every decade. They say their observances originated with an imperial decree during the Ching dynasty. The district magistrate mobilized local leaders to pacify the ghosts and malevolent creatures which had gathered in their areas over the decade.

In Ho Chung, the *ta chiao* is customarily organized by the men of nine Cantonese lineages in, or originally from, Ho Chung proper. These lineages reside in hamlets scattered throughout the Ho Chung valley: Tai Lam Wu, Mok Tsa Che, Tai Po Tsai, the Lim lineage of Sheung Si Wan, Nam Pin Tsuen, Wan Wo, Tsuk Yuen, and the Chang lineage (C) of Wo Mei (H). Each Cantonese household is levied a charge of $10 per member. In 1970 the overall cost was $60,000, including $20,000 for opera, $10,000 for monks, and a large sum for the matshed. Hakka households in the surrounding hills and the Hokkien tenants in Lok Mei to the east, and the new factories in Ho Chung are all "encouraged" to help defray the immense cost of the *ta chiao,* but the show is a Cantonese one.

The *ta chiao* in Ho Chung is vigorously maintained, and the celebration centers on their temple deity, Che Kung. In past years, Che Kung was placed in a palanquin and noisily paraded through the neighboring Cantonese villages, Pak Kong and Sha Kok Mei, and the center of the Hakka dominion, Sai Kung town, so his beneficence could be felt and Cantonese influence could be known throughout the market area.

The other two large Cantonese villages are less vigilant in their maintenance of the *ta chiao.* Pak Kong has one every decade, but Sha Kok Mei is said to have given it up many years ago. (They may never have observed one.) The degrees of dedication to the *ta chiao* among the three villages is a measure of their respective claims on local Cantonese identity. In this and other ways, Ho Chung is the center of Cantonese identity in Sai Kung.

The Cantonese dedication to the *ta chiao* contrasts with the Hakka's complete lack of *ta chiao.* One Hakka leader in Sai Kung town said the Hakka Kaifong does not support a *ta chiao* during the celebration of Tin Hau's birthday because it is not a Hakka custom. This is certainly in keeping with the Hakka's more rational attitude and concern for frugal and simple religious displays as expressed in their criticism of the Chaochow people.

ASPECTS OF ETHNIC DRESS

In many societies around the world ethnic dress correlates with differences in sex, age, and class. In Burma, for instance, Edmund Leach (1965:20) notes that: "The dress of the highland males . . . is nearly everywhere a scruffy imitation of that of the local lowlander males, but women's dress is sharply contrasted as between highlanders and lowlanders and shows many regional variations among both groups." This observation applies equally well to China and to Sai Kung, in particular, where ethnic dress is largely the domain of young women presenting themselves to the public on feast days. One reason is that women's roles are primarily domestic, while men's roles require more cosmopolitan attributes—men must communicate outside the domestic sphere. Differences among men tend to be class differences, that is, differences in dress based on occupation and sphere of economic influence.

For example, the truck farmers dress in inexpensive factory-made clothes, undershirts, shorts, and rubber thongs. Boat men and small shopkeepers dress in "traditional" (Republican Period) tunics. While the wealthier shopkeepers, especially those aspiring to leadership positions, wear Western ("cosmopolitan") clothes: white shirt, tie, leather shoes. There are some counterculture alternatives such as the blue cadre coat which was popular among local activists in the late 1960s and early 1970s. There are also the young people who return from England sporting long hair, tight trousers, and elevator shoes. They call themselves "the new tide." A local Hakka leader calls them "the new filth."

Thus we could say that there are basically three "classes" of dress in Sai Kung. The highest class are the cosmopolitan leaders who wear Western suits and speak standard Cantonese and Hakka—a few of them speak English. Their political and economic horizons include interaction with the colonial government. The second class are mostly men who wear Republican-Period Chinese attire. Their socioeconomic horizon is the local market town. The lowest class are women who tend to wear particular ethnic attire; and their spheres of interaction are the ethnic communities of village or boat.

WOMEN'S ETHNIC ADORNMENTS

There are certain configurations of feminine adornment which distinguish local (Hakka) village women, Cantonese and Hokkien boat women. Their respective presentations are most apparent on festive occasions.

Since the end of the Japanese occupation, virtually all Hakka village women bob their hair, pulling back the bangs and securing them with a silver hair-band or comb. While working in the summer sun the Hakka woman shades her face with the calico-fringed bamboo hat tied around her chin with a black string. Her ears are pierced with modest jade earrings, and around her wrists dangle one or two thin silver bracelets along with the ubiquitous jade bracelet. Her tunic is black. Her dark blue or black apron, which in the old days she embroidered, is secured around the neck with silver buttons and chain. The apron is fastened around the back with a woven red (married) or green "patterned band."[4] (The patterns are mostly symbolic of fertility.) The Hakka woman wears black tunic and trousers and black canvas or cloth shoes. In the winter, she wears a dark shawl over her head which is tied around her chin with her woven waist band.

Local Cantonese village women do not have a distinctive attire. People say that in the old days the difference between Cantonese and Hakka was that Hakka tunics were much longer. In recent years the Hakka adopted a shorter urban style; and Hakka tunics no longer reach to the knees. While village Hakka have adopted more urban-style tunics, village Cantonese generally wear the same outfit as their Hakka neighbors. This results from the fact that many women in Cantonese villages are Hakka, that Hakka garb is adapted to field work, that Cantonese villagers patronize a Hakka market town where many of these accoutrements are manufactured and sold, and that the market town is plugged into an urban Cantonese circuit.

Chaochow and Cantonese immigrants do not have distinctive adornments. In accordance with their mercantile modes of adaptation and their adoption of the dominant urban lifestyles, Chaochow and other immigrant women's apparel are distinguished by occupation. Housewives and shopkeepers wear the urban styles, the short tailored tunics and tapered trousers and have short hair set in permanents, or for grandmothers, long and knotted at the back of the head.

Young Cantonese boat women have two rather distinctive hairstyles for festive occasions. One involves winding the hair into an oyster-shell-shaped coiffure. Pomade is used to hold it in place. In the other style the short permanent-waved hair is combed back from the face with a rippling effect and is secured with a hairnet. The boat woman is generally distinguished by her jade and gold earrings and her numerous jade and gold rings and bracelets. In Sai Kung she wears the bowl-shaped bamboo hat tied around the chin with a colorful plastic beaded string. Following the Chinese custom, older and middle-aged women tend to wear solid dark-colored tunic and pants. The younger boat women tend to display themselves in colorful pastel or flowered tunics and trousers. (This contrasts *somewhat* with the young village women's propensity for dark peasant colors.) The boat women wear plastic slippers or black flats.

The Hokkien boat woman is the most outstanding in the market when dressed in her festive clothes. Her long hair is wound in a large hemispherical bun propped with false hair. This is secured with a hairnet, gold and silver pins hung with silver chains and laced with red threads. She may also wear the high conical bamboo hat tied around her chin by a colorful plastic beaded string. Her ears are pierced with gold pendant earrings; around her wrists are gold and jade bracelets; and her fingers glitter with gold and silver rings. Most traditional and unique is her long hand-sewn dark blue or black lacquered tunic, fastened with silver buttons and bordered with leather strips along the neck and shoulder seams. She carries her baby in a colorful patchwork carrier. Often to this carrier is attached a colorful bonnet.

PHENOTYPES

Before continuing with the descriptions of body adornments, a word on phenotypes is in order. Western observers often insist that Hakka, Cantonese, Hokkien, and boat people "show differences in physical appearance . . . which suggests they are racially distinct. . . ." (HKG 1956a: 21). Wolfram Eberhard (1965) observed that serious historical Chinese texts never mentioned racial factors. In a survey of educated expatriot Chinese he found that their "regional stereotypes included very few images of a racial nature, and dark skin color was rarely mentioned. When it was mentioned, the image was of lighter color among the northern Chinese and among the upper classes" (1965:600). We know, of course, that the fair Chinese skin can absorb large doses of solar radiation and color is therefore a distinguishing feature among groups engaged in different occupations. In Sai Kung light and dark skin are sometimes elicited (rarely spontaneously) as distinctive features between "us Hakka and those Tanka" or between "us Cantonese (city folk) and those Hakka (villagers)."

While some people said it is possible to tell ethnicity by looking at the face and eyes, very few ventured to specify how it is possible. At most people mentioned the strong backs of Hakka women or the rolling gait of the boat women.[5]

HAIRDRESSING

Hair is a universal symbol of female fertility and male potency. The traditional Chinese girl lets her hair grow long, and by the age of seven years she braids it. When she becomes a bride, her elder brother's wife combs her hair in a rite of fertility and pins it up with a hairpin sent by the groom's side to symbolize impregnation (see Blake 1978 and 1979). A married woman unbinds her hair for washing only during the lucky days of the month.

Before 1950, married village women in Sai Kung generally kept their tresses knotted at the back of the head or on festive occasions, bound in coiffures much as the Hokkien boat women still do. However, after 1950 Sai Kung women began to bob their hair in accordance with progressive Chinese styles.[6] Nowadays young Hakka girls have their short hair permanent-waved in the popular urban style when they are married or leave the labor force for any length of time.

At present the most distinctive hairdo is worn by the Hokkien boat women. Commensurate with their ultraconservative domestic role, they spend a great deal of time washing, combing, and adorning their long hair for public display even for minor festivities.

JEWELRY

Chinese adorn themselves with jewelry for a number of reasons. Jewelry expresses a person's (and a group's) worth and prosperity. Jewelry also has magical medicinal properties which enhance one's fertility and longevity. For instance all Chinese consider jade to have soothing properties. With the exception of the male merchant class, members of the various ethnic groups cannot be distinguished in their use of the jade bracelet. However, there are a few subtle adornments which tend to distinguish groups.

In general boat people (men, women, and children) wear more jewelry (and more jade) than other groups of people. Parents decorate their children, notably little boys, with jewelry and medicinal charms. Boat children generally have a jade bracelet or silver anklet, with a bell attached, gold or silver earrings and finger rings. Infant boys often have a magical charm sewn in a small cloth packet and pinned onto their clothes. Although similar charms were worn previously by village children, such charms are much less prevalent today.

Most women in Sai Kung have ears pierced for earrings. The boat people seem most distinctive in their choice of earrings.[7] Cantonese boat women, and sometimes their infant sons, wear a flat jade button on their earlobes. Hokkien boat women wear earrings shaped either in a modest gold ring, small pendant, or jade droplet. The Hokkien boat women are most outstanding in their jewelry when we include their decorative coiffures.

While boat people tend to wear more traditional jewelry and magical charms, many of them wear the symbol of modernity and industrial discipline—the wristwatch. In fact the wristwatch does not distinguish ethnicity. Many boat women and Hakka women, not to mention men, wear watches. These people need to keep time in places where the economic base has begun to turn with the clock. These include the educational institutions, the construction companies, and the fish and vegetable markets. These three sites are coordinated with the urban social organization where everything is disciplined by the clock.

Sai Kung people spend a great deal of time shopping for jewelry. It is considered a good investment during periods of economic flux, and it is one category of property which a woman can personally own. It has the aforementioned magical medicinal properties relating to prosperity, fertility, and longevity; and these are categories which the Chinese traditionally feel to be interrelated.

The identity of boat people with jewelry and their image as "big spenders" is dramatized in the following incident, which I recorded in my diary, May 26, 1972:

Today in the temple square a Cantonese woman from Kowloon was selling jade jewelry displayed in a small suitcase. Many boat women were gathered around. Occasionally a village woman or man would pause for a look, but the boat crowd remained. One young boat man was eager to buy his young wife a jade bracelet. The wife tried to fit a few he had selected; each was too small. Her husband was excited about buying one, and the one he turned in his hand had been bargained to fifty dollars. Finally the vendor took hold of the wife's arm and soaped her hand and wrist with a bar of soap in a bowl of water. The vendor tried to force the bracelet over the wife's hand. The crowd began to take interest. The husband stood watching, shifting his weight, frustrated at the slow progress. The wife's hand turned red, and her knuckles became raw. The vendor gave up.

A few of the other boat women grabbed the wife's arm, soaped the red hand and raw knuckles. They each grabbed a part of the arm, hand or bracelet, yet with much pushing, huffing and puffing, failed to get the bracelet over the hand. Just then a burly village woman, who had just come for a look, folded her umbrella, set down her load of groceries, and pushed her way through the gathering crowd. She was going to have a go at it. She picked up the bracelet, but the wife at this point was recuperating from the great pain and wearily waved the village woman away. So the latter soon left.

The determined husband hunkered down, soaped his wife's hand once more and started to push the bracelet on. The wife's hand turned red, then purple, as the husband strained and pulled with every bit of his might. He was not succeeding. Again, four boat women joined the struggle, each trying to tuck small folds of the skin on the wife's hand under the path of the bracelet. The crowd was large now and people were tightly packed as each jostled to get a glimpse of the show. The audience even began to cheer each advance of the bracelet over the woman's purple hand. Some old Hakka women stopped at the edge of the crowd with their baskets of groceries curious about the commotion. They could see the wife's face in painful contortions. They made some barely audible disparaging remarks to each other as they looked on.

Then catharsis! The arduous struggle ended as the bracelet slid onto the wrist. There was audible relief from the crowd. The husband and his helpers smiled broadly while rubbing the wife's hand vigorously to stimulate circulation. Fresh water was poured over the bruised flesh. The wife's face was a study in pain and pride as if she had just given birth. Her husband stood up, swaggered in his place, threw back his head and waved a hundred dollar bill in the vendor's face. He was proud. After receiving his change, he opened the umbrella to shade his wife and himself from the morning sun; he handed his wife the heavy basket laden with the day's food, and they marched off side by side. Even after they had made their grand exit, a crowd of boat women continued to chatter about the event, each excitedly offering her advice on how to put on a small bracelet.

HATS

In the popular culture of Hong Kong, the hats worn by rural folk are the most distinctive ethnic markers perhaps because of their quaint styles, visibility, and the fact that they do, in some quantitative sense, mark ethnic boundaries. There are many coverings for the head, but here I consider only summer bamboo hats popularized in Hong Kong folklore (see, for example, Burkhardt 1955, II:83; Osgood 1975, III:998).

All people emphasize the need to protect the head from the heat of the sun. The important men of Sai Kung never wear hats; instead they carry umbrellas. The laboring men, especially the immigrant vegetable farmers, wear cheap wide-brimmed straw hats or bamboo hats with hemispherical crowns. The Cantonese fishermen wear the bowl-shaped bamboo hat.

One of the most unique bamboo hats is the so-called Hakka hat. This hat consists of a flat bamboo woven disc about forty centimeters in diameter. A hole in the center fits over the head. Over the head hole a towel is folded and tied down with a tie string which goes over the brim and under the chin. The top of the bamboo disc is used to carry small items (comb, paper, knife, and so on) which are slipped under the tie string. Around the edge of the disc is sewn a pleated calico curtain about ten centimeters wide. This calico fringe is the all important *female* part of the hat; it has both practical and expressive value. It shades the face from the sun and preserves the facial skin. It is also a veil and enhances the wearer's feminine modesty. This hat is the only one worn exclusively by women.

According to a Chaochow gazetteer (Han 1971:2), this calico-fringed hat is worn by the women of Waichow Prefecture. As a regional characteristic it is even further refined in different parts of the prefecture. In Sai Kung, a Hakka seamstress imports the bamboo discs from markets in Paoan county. Then she sews on a heavy, black, deep-pleated cotton fringe. She sells her Sai Kung hat for seven dollars, which makes it the most expensive hat in the market. However, the calico-fringed hat is assembled in other markets such as Tai Po. This results in hats with different styled pleats, cloth weight, and color. Thus, Hakka women from the northern slope of Sai Kung who patronize Tai Po market wear different styled hats from those who patronize Sai Kung market. These distinctions are not simply fortuitous. The Sai Kung and Tai Po village women on either side of the Sai Kung peninsula are each aware of the other's style. At times I have heard Sai Kung Hakka say that the Tai Po hats are "Punti style" and that they are "cheaper." (See note 4 for symbolic differences.)

Although the calico-fringed hat is usually associated with the Hakka speech group, it is primarily a regional manifestation expressing intraregional variations and exclusive of other Hakka areas in South China.

In fact women in other groups may wear the Waichow "Hakka hat" on such occasions as when Cantonese women work in the fields or when boat women pole their small boats or work in the streets. When I asked non-Hakka women why they wore "Hakka hats," the usual response was that "it is convenient to work in" or that "it is all the same."

The "Hakka hat" is obviously useful in shading the face and preserving a fair complexion. This utility, when coupled with the dominant position which Hakka occupy in a region, motivates non-Hakka to adopt the "Hakka hat." At the same time, however, the non-Hakka may alter the hat to express their own ethnicity. For example, the Hokkien boat women "jazz up" the hat by replacing the black cotton tie string with their gaudy plastic strings.

The cheapest ($2) hat in Sai Kung is the conical shaped bamboo hat which is distinguished by its high point sharply curving out to a broad brim. Unlike the "Hakka hat," which is exclusively female, the conical hat and all other hats may be worn by either men or women. According to Burkhardt (1958, II:85), the conical hat is originally Cantonese. However in Sai Kung, this hat is most popular with the Hokkien boat people, and for that reason, it is sometimes referred to as the "Hoklo hat." Nonetheless, all peasant households have one or more of these hats; and Hakka women call it their "rain hat." One sunny day at a construction site I asked a Hakka woman why she wore a "Hoklo hat." All other women wore a "Hakka hat." She explained that when she left home early in the morning she thought it would rain. Many, in fact, wear these hats on rainy days.

The third bamboo hat is a bowl-shaped hat. It is a cheap but substantial hat which sits like an inverted bowl on the head. It does not succumb to gusts of wind as readily as the broad-brimmed bamboos, and therefore is favored among boat people. Land people refer to it as the "Tanka hat," while boat people call it the "bamboo hat." I observed very few land people wearing it.[8] The only other group which preferred it were Hokkien fishermen, although not their womenfolk. Among Cantonese boat men, women and young people, this bowl-shaped hat is ubiquitous. The young people especially like to decorate the brims with plastic beaded bands.

The various bamboo hats are popularly identified with various ethnic groups. However, each type of hat also has certain utilitarian values. Their use in different working situations or festive contexts expresses different degrees of utilitarian or ethnic value or a complex mixture of the two.

SPEECH

Language and dialect is a primary ethnic criterion for interaction in Sai Kung. As with other aspects of the culture of ethnicity, there is much similarity in the underlying grammars of the different languages, while the unbridgeable gaps are largely phonological and to some extent lexical. From an objective point of view, the phonetic and lexical distinctions are superficial. In the subjective organization of ethnic boundaries, even the slightest phonetic difference may be blown out of proportion.

Before 1960, Hakka was the dominant language spoken in the market town and in the surrounding Hakka villages. To be successful, one had to speak Hakka in public. This is one reason Hakka women were desired as wives on the local level. Even for a Hakka woman to marry into a Cantonese village was not too traumatic, for she could expect to continue speaking Hakka with other Hakka women in the village and at market. On the other hand, when on occasion a Cantonese maiden married a Hakka villager, the situation could be more traumatic. In one case, a Cantonese woman married a Hakka village leader. They lived in the village for the first fifteen years of their married life before moving to the market. She tended to remain somewhat aloof from her neighbors and never quite mastered Hakka speech. In the village her local Cantonese accent was a stigma; and she was acutely aware of her linguistic handicap. "I can't speak Hakka, but I can't speak much Punti either! I speak half *Sa* and half Hakka! I speak a half-salted Hakka!"

However, standard Cantonese has great utility for men conducting business in the market town and beyond. Sai Kung market town is an interface between the local society and the larger Cantonese-controlled Hong Kong. Success in the larger social and economic spheres requires fluency in standard Cantonese, and the sanctions against males speaking impure Cantonese are becoming severe. The mastery of Cantonese is a source of pride for Sai Kung Hakka. One young Hakka man said that he is so fluent that his Cantonese schoolmates in Kowloon could not believe he was Hakka when he told them. Older Hakka who grew up speaking only Hakka are unable to master Cantonese, and for aspiring leaders this became a real handicap after 1960.

For instance, one important leader in the town is originally from a remote Hakka village and speaks Cantonese with a heavy Hakka accent. The local people feel that his speech gives outsiders the idea that Sai Kung is a jerkwater town. During the Tin Hau festivities, he publically addressed an audience of townsfolk, Hong Kong government officials and urbanites, and I heard embarrassed local Hakka schoolchildren snicker at the man's heavily accented speech.

While the Cantonese language was subordinate to Hakka before 1960, Cantonese subsequently became the lingua franca of the market town. As one now walks through the streets one is apt to hear more Cantonese than Hakka being spoken. The majority of shopkeepers and itinerants, not to mention the many boat people, speak Cantonese. Moreover, all schools, whether controlled by the department of education, the Christian missions, or the patriotic (procommunist) establishment, are conducted in standard Cantonese. All young people are extremely sensitive about the quality of their Cantonese speech.

As with other forms of ethnic expression in the town, bilingual Cantonese and Hakka speakers tend to mix the languages. Among the young Hakka who concentrate on perfecting their Cantonese there is a tendency to use Cantonese words and sounds when speaking their native Hakka. In fact the heavy infiltration of Cantonese into Hakka language among the young receives only slight disapproval from older Hakka townsfolk these days.

The only ones who, out of necessity, preserve the pure Hakka speech rich in diphthongs and fricatives are the older Hakka village women. In the village context the loss of their native speech is sometimes a point of contention between young and old. For instance, the young daughter of a Hakka villager was reared in the market town and speaks only standard Cantonese. On the eve of her cousin's wedding she returned to her village to be with the bride. That evening her aunt ostracized her as "Useless . . . a Hakka who cannot speak Hakka!" Other village women chided and laughed at her. The young daughter was humiliated and went to sit by herself.

While it is imperative that a successful man speak Cantonese in the presence of outsiders, this does not detract from the fact that, in Sai Kung, the ability to speak Hakka is a matter of pride, and for those with local political aspirations it is a necessity. The only Cantonese who ever headed the Sai Kung Rural Committee, Chan Yat-Kuan, is often identified as a Hakka because of his fluency in Hakka. Every member of his faction, which included a number of immigrant Cantonese, also spoke Hakka. Still, the sanctions against "impure" Hakka speech in the local context have diminished while those against "impure" Cantonese have increased. In other words, standards for Hakka speech are more relaxed than ever before while standards for Cantonese are more rigid.

The sanctions against nonstandard Cantonese begin to be felt early in a child's schooling. In the market town, children who speak Cantonese with an "ethnic" or "rustic" accent are mercilessly ridiculed by their classmates. Such situations are usually avoided since the Cantonese and Hakka village children and boat children have their own village schools. But until a few years ago, boat children did not have their own school. During the 1950s and 1960s they were allowed to attend the Kaifong school in the market. Their intermittent attendance was due to the constraints of living aboard fishing vessels. When they did attend school they were always in the minority and frequently humiliated by their mispronunciation of standard Cantonese. A friend who attended the Kaifong school in 1960 recalls, for example, a boat child who stood to recite a lesson and mispronounced the word for "foot" saying instead "horn." (In standard Cantonese the word for "foot" is /koek/, and in boat dialect it is /kɔk/, which means "horn" in standard Cantonese.) The whole class erupted with laughter, and after school the Kaifong boys chased after the boat boys yelling "Horn! Horn!"

Many boat men do speak standard Cantonese, although, according to Eugene Anderson (1970:2), they tend to overcorrect for their dialectical handicap by inserting the /oe/ sound into standard Cantonese words where it does not belong. This is comparable to upwardly mobile white Americans who overcorrect their lower-class English when saying "Between you and I."

Most boat men still speak their own dialect aboard their boats where the dialect is preserved by women just as Hakka and the local Cantonese ("sa") dialect is preserved among village women.

Hokkien dialects have no status in Sai Kung public domain. They are spoken within the home or ethnic organization. Yet even in these private recesses, especially among the young, Cantonese is frequently used since the effort to master the lingua franca is so critical to their success outside. In fact one of the stated purposes of the Chaochow Association is to shield those Chaochow who are unable to speak Cantonese.

The local people treat Hokkien sounds as exotic and somewhat humorous. Based on my impression, Hokkien speech is richer in bilabial sounds than Cantonese or Hakka. In fact Hakka refer to it as "Hoklo pipa." Chaochow are careful how they flout Chaochow signs. For example, at the Chaochow auction attended by many locals the auctioneer speaks in Cantonese, although he sometimes injects a Chaochow word to add some flavor, to remind the audience of their benefactor, and to provide laughs and a relaxed atmosphere which loosen the strings on the pocketbook. Another manifestation of their reticence to use their language in public is among Chaochow children who dread that they will make sounds which are foolish to local ears. Chaochow children take great care to speak standard Cantonese or not to speak at all when they are the minority. On the other hand, when they are the majority, they may slander and curse the locals in their native tongue. The locals' inability to understand makes them into "great fools!"

The various Hokkien dialect groups in Sai Kung also draw sharp distinctions in manner of speech. Among themselves slight alterations of sound give rise to feelings of ethnic estrangement and occasion for ridicule, that is, of course in contexts of ethnic competition. However, in contexts where Waichow and Chaochow Hokkien are facing hostile locals, they will gloss over their already minimal linguistic differences emphasizing a common Hokkien speech group.

The linguistic boundary between Cantonese and Chaochow is clearly marked, while that between Hakka and Cantonese in Sai Kung is muddled, at least in practice. The "clarity" of these linguistic boundaries is, of course, a reflection of social behavior and organization more than objective linguistic differences.

CONCLUSION

In this chapter I have touched on some of the particular traits by which people in Sai Kung distinguish their membership in social groups. I call this the culture of ethnicity insofar as it is a conscious, though not in every context apprehended, means of local level adaptation, interaction, and expression.

These traits are expressions of an underlying Chinese universe of discourse—a grammar in point of fact or by analogy (see Lehman, 1967:106). The "grammar generates" traits which express differences between conservative and progressive, outside and inside, immigrant and local, rural and urban, provincial and cosmopolitan, poor and prosperous. In antagonistic situations these dichotomies are expressed in the rhetoric of the "civilized" versus the "barbarian." In such situations, these traits seem to become insurmountable barriers to intergroup communication. In situations or periods of alliance or commonality, the ethnic markers are played down by claims that "we are the same underneath."

Another aspect of these ethnic traits is symbolic. They symbolize a group's prosperity, fertility, and potency, which translate into expressions of the group's economic vitality and political power. These ethnic displays may be arranged along a continuum between small-scale customary domestic rites at one end and large-scale corporate community extravaganzas at the other end. The domestic level includes the family-oriented festivals and interpersonal usages of dress and dialect, which are preserved by women. The community level includes the organized religious festivities which have more direct political consequences and which are conducted by men.

Also there is a correlation between these levels of symbolic action and the positions of groups in society. Among Hokkien speakers, for example, the Chaochow tend to be acculturated to urban Cantonese styles of dress and speech. They preserve their ethnic group solidarity and social position in large-scale politico-religious displays twice a year. In sharp contrast are the Hokkien boat people whose women are most conservative in their dress and speech. During the Tin Hau Festival the Hokkien fishermen form a firecracker association and set up a small "spirit place" after the fashion of the Chaochow. But here all similarity ends. The boat people's "spirit place" is located in a back alley next to their leader's house. It consists of one small table under an awning, set with a few contributed trinkets for auction to the members at a private feast of the firecracker association.

The Chaochow "spirit place" is a huge matshed located along the highway into the market town. The whole center section of the shed is piled with hundreds of goods for public auction on the last night of the Chaochow opera. The Chaochow do this twice a year. The Waichow display is slightly smaller than the Chaochow, and it is held along a back road and only once a year during the Hungry Ghost Festival.

In conclusion, there is a tendency for the different sexes and the different ethnic groups to express their ethnicity differently. The female and the poor tend to be more personally attached to their displays, while the male and well-to-do tend to be more corporate and cosmopolitan in their community fanfares.

NOTES

1. Others have noted the distinctive character of Hakka ancestor tablets (Freedman 1970:169; Aijmer 1967:47; Pasternak 1972:71). Reverend Piton (1870:219) noted that Hakka who are in want of a proper ancestral hall "write the name of their ancestor on a paper, burn it with some ceremonies, and put the ashes in a little

bag, which they hang up in the hall or in some other part of the house, and there burn incense; and this they call *hsiang-huo* ("fragrant fire"). Obviously, the iconic representation of the ancestor is extremely flexible, and there are millions of Chinese who maintain no fetish and who are nonetheless Chinese in their regard for family and ancestors.

2. Scholars such as Freedman (1966:93–95) and Pasternak (1972:131–134) are skeptical of any suggestion of substantive differences between Hakka and Cantonese or Hokkien social structures. Others such as Göran Aijmer (1967:57) and Manabu Nakagawa (1975:221) argue for a particular kind of social structure which is identifiable as "Hakka." Aijmer suggests, partly on the evidence of the single surname tablet, that Hakka maintain a more unified concept of the "major lineage," while Nakagawa boldly states "the principle of unification in social structure among the Hakka settlements. . . ." My position, which is developed in the concept of "ethnic group culture," is between that of Freedman's and Nakagawa's.

3. There is, in fact, a basis in the literary tradition for such iconography as boat people practice. In the *Classic of Filial Piety* (Koehn 1944:11) is a story about the origin of the ancestor fetish. During the Han dynasty, Ting Lan remembered his dead parents but could not see them, so he carved their images in a pair of wooden statues.

4. According to an interesting study by Elizabeth Johnson (1976), these "patterned bands" serve as an assertion of Hakka identity, although the custom of weaving and wearing them may have been adopted from non-Chinese aborigines in East Kwangtung. Johnson describes differences in style and usage among Hakka who patronize different markets in the New Territories such as between Sai Kung and Tai Po. For example, Tai Po-oriented Hakka on the northern slope of the Sai Kung peninsula leave large white tassels on each end of the band, and they use the band as a chin strap for the bamboo hat. Sai Kung-oriented village women leave small multicolored tassels on their woven bands, and they use their bands for apron or winter scarf ties. I found comparable distinctions in the manufacture of the so-called Hakka hat, which I describe in the text. It is significant that *within* the Sai Kung market area, these traits do not readily distinguish Hakka and Cantonese village women for reasons cited in the text.

5. Barbara Ward (1965:119) says that the few physical traits that distinguish boat people (darker complexion, rolling gait, small leg muscles, heavy shoulder development) are best explained as phenotypic adaptations to living aboard boats. Another claim that I heard Taiwan Hakka make is: "You can tell a true Hakka by the cleft in his/her little toenail." However, I also heard this claim for Hokkien and Manchu identities in the Philippines and in Honolulu respectively. The cleft toenail is, in fact, a trait found among many East Asians, and it has some interesting symbolism associated with it. However, no person in Sai Kung ever elicited this as a distinguishing mark. Scientific attempts to discern ethnic phenotypes (for example: head shapes, body statures, hair whorls, ear wax, and blood types) for Cantonese, Hakka, and Hokkien are generally inconclusive. (See Zaborowski 1879; Whyte 1911; Vaillant 1920; Shirokogoroff 1925; Liu 1937; Yamashita 1939; Alley 1943; Woo 1947; Simmons 1950; Ts'ai and Yen 1950; Grimmo 1961 and 1964.) However, recent research has revealed significantly different rates of nasopharyngeal cancer among different Chinese groups in Malaysia, Hong Kong, and Hawaii. The Cantonese have the highest incidence; the Hokkien have the lowest; and Hakka have moderate rates. These

studies are suggesting that the different rates may be due to different genetic predispositions coupled with socioeconomic (environmental) factors. (See Ho 1967; Shanmugartnam and Tye 1970; Shanmugartnam 1971 and 1973; Armstrong, Kutty, and Dharmalingan 1974; Armstrong 1977; Shem and Armstrong 1977; and Armstrong, Kutty, and Armstrong 1978.)

6. The progressive custom of bobbed hair is a symbolic violation of the traditional distinction between male and female. During the early decades of this century the bobbing of hair was a revolutionary act. As a sign of radicalism it was sometimes punished by death (see Chou 1941:63–64; Isaacs 1968:290). One rite of passage by which a woman was accepted into the East River Guerilla Brigade was to bob her hair (Chin 1947).

7. Charles Piton (1870:219) used evidence of similar trumpet-shaped earrings to trace an historical connection between the "Hia-K'ah" of Chekiang province and the Hakka of Paoan county, Kwangtung. He says that the Cantonese women wear two interlaced rings on each earlobe. Neither of these earrings are worn today in Sai Kung; and what is more, the differences that do exist are so subtle that as far as they constitute conscious ethnic demarcations, they are hardly apprehended.

8. In Sai Kung these bowl-shaped hats distinguish ethnic groups. However, in other local systems they may distinguish other social identities. For example I observed in several films from a commune in southern Paoan that the laboring women wore "Hakka hats" while the laboring men wore the bowl-shaped hat.

CHAPTER 6

Formation of the Local Hakka Establishment

Around the turn of the century Sai Kung developed from a Hakka village into a small marketing center. Most of its trade was seaborne between Hakka areas of Paoan and Hong Kong. Analysis of the 1915 Tin Hau temple reconstruction contributions indicates that 80 percent of the town's shopkeepers were Hakka. About half of these were local born villagers; the other half were immigrant traders from markets in eastern Paoan and southwestern Waichow. The other 20 percent were evenly divided between native Cantonese villagers and Cantonese traders from the Pearl River estuary.

Until about 1960, Hakka was the lingua franca, and immigrants who wanted to do business in Sai Kung market had to accommodate local Hakka interests and language. In this chapter I have selected several prominent leaders in Sai Kung to illustrate how each established himself and his family in the market. Although each has diverse ethnic roots, all are generally considered to be among the old Hakka families of Sai Kung town.

AN IMMIGRANT HAKKA FAMILY

One of the many Hakka who immigrated to Sai Kung shortly after the turn of the century was a sojourner named Kong from Hengkang, a large market in the Hakka area of southwestern Waichow. Young Kong was a carpenter. He rented land on the shore to build and repair boats. Some years later he bought land around the edge of the market town, and, together with his first son, ventured into other small enterprises such as a tea shop. He was never able to buy the land upon which his boatyard stood. To this day, his sons pay the same rent to the descendants of an earlier Cantonese immigrant family named Chan (described below).

Kong married a Sai Kung town woman whose own father had immigrated from Puchao market in north central Paoan county. However, most of his sons married women from Hakka villages surrounding Sai Kung market. In the 1930s Kong's eldest son became one of Sai Kung's leaders. Just before the Japanese occupation, he emigrated to Malaya, took a Malay wife, and is presently a smalltime neighborhood leader and businessman there.

The second and fourth sons spent most of their lives sojourning, occasionally returning to Sai Kung where the second son's Hakka wife and daughter manage a small sundries shop. The third son, who never sojourned, manages the deceased father's boatyard, which now provides only drydock facilities. He is a Kaifong representative, and as a member of the Rural Committee ruling faction, he is also the chairman of the Kaifong committee.

When their father died in the 1930s, the eldest son returned to his father's native place in Hengkang and retrieved the bones of his father's father, father's mother, and father's elder brother, which together with the father, they buried in the hills around Sai Kung town. The Hakka custom of carrying the ancestor's bones to a new place, rather than the usual Chinese instinct to inter the sojourner's bones in his "native" soil is distinctive. The brothers' mortuary rite, as much as the purchase of land, was a gesture by which this little band of agnates established their identity as "local Hakka." Every Ch'ing Ming the Kong brothers, dressed in business suits, visit their ancestors' graves.

AN IMMIGRANT CANTONESE BOAT FAMILY

A number of early immigrant merchants were Cantonese. They did not always come directly from their native places to Sai Kung but followed a series of kinship and ethnic networks.

One case is that of a young immigrant surnamed Chung. He was born in Nant'ou, the county seat. During the latter part of the nineteenth century, Chung sailed to Lan Tau Island just west of Hong Kong. Lan Tau has a number of fishing and Hakka farming settlements much like Sai Kung. Chung married a woman from his native place, and in the early years of the twentieth century settled in Sai Kung. They were Cantonese who spoke "a peculiar dialect" according to an old man who knew Chung. (From this and other evidence it is likely that Chung and his wife were Cantonese boat people.)

In Sai Kung, Chung first earned a living by hawking ritual paraphernalia. In later years he opened a small paper goods shop. He and his wife reared two sons and four daughters.

His first son married a Hakka woman from a small village near the market. Both of them died in the 1950s leaving their children to be reared by the second son. Between the eldest and second son were four daughters. The first and fourth daughters both married Cantonese men from Hong Kong. The second daughter was given to a local boat family (around 1910) when she was quite young. She later married a boat man and bore four sons. Her sons and grandsons all prospered either working overseas or aboard the large fishing trawlers. The third daughter married a Hakka from Sai Kung market.

The second son, Chung Hoi-Sun, married a boat woman whose family was a long-term resident in Sai Kung harbor. Hoi-Sun claims that she was actually a Hakka who was given to a boat family to rear. The ambiguity over her identity is useful to Hoi-Sun who solicits the business of both boat people and land people.

While keeping one foot planted in the life of the local boat community through kinship and commerce, Chung Hoi-Sun identified as a local Hakka through his speech and associations in town. During the Japanese occupation, rather than returning to his father's native place in Nant'ou, he and his family followed a Hakka friend to Waichow where he earned a living hawking cloth on the streets. He was able to open a small dry goods store and to sell Chinese medicines on the side. But during a Japanese attack his store was burned, and he lost his investment. After the occupation he returned to Sai Kung.

Hoi-Sun gave up his father's trade in ritual paraphernalia and concentrated on the trade in dry goods. Today he employs his old friend, a Hakka tailor from Waichow, who lives with the Chung family above the store. Hoi-Sun still plies one part of his father's original trade. On request, he sews cloth accoutrements for boat people's weddings and funerals. In addition, Hoi-Sun is known to be one of the biggest moneylenders in town. Most of his money is lent on easy terms to fellow townsmen.

Over the years Chung Hoi-Sun earned the respect of boat people, townspeople, and villagers alike. He became a Kaifong representative, and in 1964 he became an executive of the Rural Committee, a position which he continues to occupy. In 1965 he contributed a large sum of money to the Tin Hau temple reconstruction which placed him among the top ten on the town's social registry. As a testimony to his local renown, the funeral of his wife in 1972 was the largest and most elaborate funeral ceremony that I witnessed during my two years in Sai Kung. Many people believe that Chung Hoi-Sun could easily become the chairman of the Rural Committee since he commands the respect of the different ethnic and ideological interest groups in Sai Kung. In fact, it was to Hoi-Sun that the district officer turned in a desperate appeal during the turmoil of 1967 to form a group which could compromise the radical elements and defuse the situation. But Hoi-Sun did not feel up to such a task. According to his testimony, he has never been willing to spend the large sums of money required to participate in the potlatch politics of Sai Kung. If he decided to compete, he, the son of a Cantonese boat man, would be Sai Kung's "Hakka" leader.

AN IMMIGRANT CANTONESE MERCHANT FAMILY

That it is possible for a non-Hakka to become the market area leader is exemplified in the case of Chan Yat-Kuan. He attained leadership of Sai Kung district at an early age by acting as a local Hakka, although his ancestral origins are Hsinhui (Szeyap) Cantonese.

Chan Yat-Kuan's great grandfather, Kun-Hau, came from a village in Hsinhui county to Kowloon City during the closing years of the last century. In Kowloon City, Kun-Hau opened a general store which catered to customers from Sai Kung. When the British acquired the New Territories in 1898, Kun-Hau moved to Sai Kung market, and set up his store called "Warehouse of Expanding Abundance" (see Figure 5). With his profits, Kun-Hau expanded his business and invested in commercial land around the town. By 1915 he was prosperous enough to be one of the main sponsors of the Tin Hau temple reconstruction.

As a successful immigrant, Kun-Hau brought a wife from his native village. They had three sons, who were reared and educated in Sai Kung. Upon reaching marriageable age, each of the three sons returned to seek wives from their father's native place. The native lineage was a prosperous one, judging by the present generation's descriptions of their ancestor hall. Their wives were brought from Hsinhui, and in the great house in Sai Kung, they maintained Hsinhui (Cantonese) manners, such as bound feet, unadulterated by the dominant Hakka customs outside.

However, the three sons spoke Hakka and took Hakka secondary wives from the market area. The first brother took a Hakka woman from Sai Kung market whose father was a Meihsien immigrant and a practitioner of Chinese medicine. The second brother took a Hakka woman from a village in the Hang Hau area. If these secondary wives were situated as secondary wives are today, each occupied a commercial and residential niche in the lineage organization. The Hsinhui wives maintained the central domicile, while the Hakka wives were crucial in the commercial organization.

Each of the three sons in the second generation also began to build his own estate in commercial property while they maintained the original business together with Kun-Hau's estate for a full decade after his death.

The third generation, Kun-Hau's grandchildren, who are today grandparents themselves, numbered at least ten males and three females. (The oral genealogy lacks information on the female offspring. Hsinhui wives living in Sai Kung returned to Hsinhui on such occasions as childbirth. Many daughters were married to Hsinhui men outside Sai Kung, while the male offspring of the three sons were brought to Sai Kung and reared in the family store.) During the 1920s and 1930s the third-generation boys went to the Kaifong school, the Catholic school just outside town, and the Cantonese village school in Sha Kok Mei. Some of them also attended Chinese secondary schools in Kowloon, Hsinhui, Chiangmen, and Canton.

In selecting brides, the older members of the third generation followed the lineage tradition of marrying Hsinhui women from outside Sai Kung. Two of the younger agnates married local Sai Kung village women after the Japanese occupation. However, it is interesting that with one exception (described below), none took secondary wives. I surmise that by the third generation, the Chan lineage was sufficiently affiliated with the local Hakka so as to obviate secondary alliances with local Hakka.

As long as the old patriarch, Kun-Hau, lived, Hsinhui was home, and this is where his bones were interred in 1940. However, this pattern was not followed by later generations who considered themselves Sai Kung residents. Their residential orientation was due in part to the closing of the Hong Kong-Chinese border after 1950. By this time, the lineage founder was dead, the second generation was in its dotage, and the older members of the fourth generation were young adults. At this point Kun-Hau's original estate was divided among and within the three major branches.

The original warehouse was partitioned by a great wall down the center. The first and third segments each took a half and renamed their stores incorporating a part of the original name, "Abundance." The new names reflect divergent business and local political orientations. The southern half was named "Southern Abundance" and came under the management of the second brother of the third generation of the first branch. His marketing connections were oriented toward the Hakka villages to the east and southeast of the market. The other half, owned by the third branch, increasingly came under the management of the young second brother, whose patrons were mostly from old Hakka and Cantonese villages to the east and north of town. This third branch manager married a "Punti" woman from the Fourteen Villages, a remote mixed Cantonese and Hakka valley to the northeast. Around 1965 he obtained a franchise to sell products from mainland China. He named his store "China's Abundance," thus combining his patriotic sentiments with his commercial interests.

This left the second segment with no part of the original warehouse;

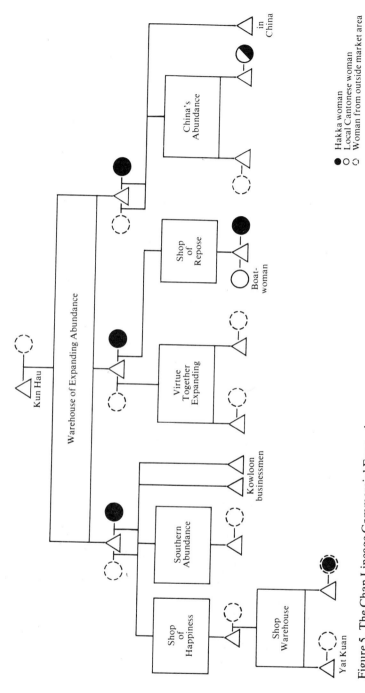

Figure 5. The Chan Lineage Commercial Expansion

instead they took their share in the lineage properties and set up smaller shops oriented toward the greatly expanding trade in fishing supplies. The two much older brothers of the Hsinhui mother had already taken Hsinhui wives before the Japanese occupation and set up small businesses.

The third brother, a younger man and the son of the Hakka mother, simply continued to manage a shop in his father's establishment. He married a Hakka woman from the western end of the district. Some years ago he obtained a second woman from the boat community at Leung Shuen Wan. It is relevant that he simultaneously reoriented his entire business toward these boat people. Today he lives with his secondary wife and their infant daughter in an apartment at the edge of town, while his legal wife lives with their older children in a room behind the shop. Everyday the third brother, his children, and his boat wife work together in the little shop on Main Street. There, surrounded by stocks of fishing supplies and barrels of rice, the older children do homework or hold and humor the infant daughter while the boat wife casts molten lead alloy weights onto premanufactured fishhooks, and the third brother, the proprietor, sits at the counter working on his books or waiting on a customer from the boats. The boat wife makes no attempt to appear as a land person. She cannot speak Hakka. On the contrary, she displays all the personal accoutrements of a boat woman while the Hakka first wife, suffering from a chronic illness, remains in a room behind the store.

Thus the three main segments of the Chan lineage continue to expand into different economic niches and literally into different directions in the market area. As the genealogy shows, in each succeeding generation, members left for opportunities outside the market area. Some returned to China in a professional capacity. Others returned to Kowloon in a commercial capacity. Many of those in the fourth generation sojourned to England and France for work and school.

In the fourth generation, descendants number at least seventeen males and thirteen females, ranging in age from the forty-five-year-old son of a Hsinhui mother who had bound feet to a six-month-old daughter of the boat woman. The children of the boat woman will probably never speak Hakka or the Hsinhui dialect, while the forty-five-year-old Chan Yat-Kuan is fluent in both.

Chan Yat-Kuan came of age during the Japanese occupation of Hong Kong (1941–1945). During the occupation, rice stores dwindled along with the motivation and means for cultivating rice on land being contested between Japanese soldiers and Chinese guerrillas. Some people in Sai Kung starved to death. The Japanese forced all nonnative residents to return to their homes in China. The Japanese also suspected nonnatives of being guerrillas and killed a number of such persons in Sai Kung. The entire Chan lineage therefore returned to their "home" in Hsinhui. This move cost them their claims on native Sai Kung status. This fact makes the postoccupation accomplishments of Chan Yat-Kuan the more remarkable. However, before describing these accomplishments, we need to describe what Sai Kung looked like when the Chans returned.

In 1945 the East River communist guerrillas relinquished control of Sai Kung to the British army. The guerrillas had organized the remote Hakka villagers in a resistance network during the occupation. Although they voluntarily withdrew to their bases in Waichow to continue the fight against the Kuomintang, the guerrillas left behind a large number of sympathizers. In 1947 the East River Brigade was annihilated by Kuomintang onslaughts, and Hong Kong became a refuge for communist guerrillas and United Front intellectuals. In Hong Kong they organized a propaganda mill, which was partly directed toward arousing Hong Kong youth. According to a recent study (Catron 1971), the propaganda failed to recruit Hong Kong youth as guerrilla fighters in China. However, according to my friends in Sai Kung, about a hundred Sai Kung villagers, most with resistance experience in Sai Kung, did go to China to fight on the side of the communists. Other young people in Sai Kung were also affected by the United Front appeal for national unification and an end to the civil war.

At exactly what point in his life Chan Yat-Kuan tied his fortunes to the communist cause in China is unknown to me. I suspect it was during his stay in Hsinhui where there was communist-led anti-Japanese resistance similar to that in the Hakka areas of the East River. In any case, upon his return to Sai Kung, Chan Yat-Kuan set out to organize local sentiment for the Chinese revolution. He found support from Hakka villagers who had been part of the resistance to Japan or who had relatives in the civil war. Another source of support included refugees from the civil war.

Chan was never an idealogue. Organizing sentiment for the communist cause was tied to trade and commerce in Hong Kong. Chan bought real estate around the town, which he rented to refugees. He finessed business contacts with urban Cantonese commercial interests and communist credit facilities on behalf of his local cohort. The communist-managed commerce in Hong Kong became substantial after 1950, and this strengthened Chan's position in Sai Kung.

The Rural Committee was established in 1947. In 1952, Chan Yat-Kuan was elected vice-chairman. In 1960, the chairman, a Hakka villager who owned a shop in the market, was forced to resign the chairmanship. Chan Yat-Kuan was elected to be the new chairman. In this role, Chan was identified as a "local Hakka." However, his native ability to speak

Cantonese and to operate in important Cantonese circles outside Sai Kung made him an extraordinarily effective advocate of Sai Kung native interests.

One example of Chan's effectiveness as a local leader was his maintenance of the Tin Hau temple. In the early 1960s, the government-sponsored temple preservation committee attempted to assume trusteeship of Sai Kung's Tin Hau temple. Their stated purpose was to insure the temple's historical preservation by the collection of entrance fees. Chan protested that entrance fees would deny Sai Kung's religious supplicants unhindered access to their own religious properties. He also articulated the feeling that the temple was not an artifact at which tourists could gawk. It was an integral part of local cultural integrity and vitality. Chan's resistance was successful, and the Tin Hau temple, for better or for worse, remained in the trust of local leaders. Actually, the temple faired better than it might have otherwise. In 1965 Chan sponsored the first reconstruction of the temple since 1915.

Ironically and tragically, the Cultural Revolution in China brought an end to this balanced and competent leadership in Sai Kung. Suffice to say that Chan Yat-Kuan and his faction, under the direct pressure or indirect influence of the radicals in Canton, organized resistance to British colonial authority. While a number of his cohort were detained in prison, Chan and others fled to the mountain villages where they hid from the police until 1968 when Mao Tse-Tung reasserted his leadership in Peking, thus enabling the British to reestablish their authority in Sai Kung.

A LOCAL HAKKA MERCHANT FAMILY

Chin Fuk-Loi succeeded Chan as head of the market area. His background and leadership contrast with Chan's at almost every point. Chin was a local Hakka villager; his fortune was self-made; he won and ultimately lost power in Sai Kung by organizing support for British authority.

Chin was born in a remote Hakka village on the peninsula, but he spent much of his boyhood during the 1930s in the market town. There, two of his uncles (agnates from a different major segment of the village lineage) were establishing their own businesses in the town. Both Hakka uncles had taken Cantonese women as secondary wives, a strategy which Chin Fuk-Loi would follow in later years. One of the uncles also became the first chairman of the Sai Kung Rural Committee. However, Chin Fuk-Loi's own career was never linked to his uncle's. We need to consider this point for a moment.

In Sai Kung there is little utility in organizing agnatic (or lineage) interests with the aim of controlling the market. The previous case of the

Chan lineage is a clear example, for it constituted one of the most formidable agnatic groups in the market town. Yet it was never large enough to control the town. There was little utility in maintaining its corporate solidarity. The lineage splintered over the division of estates with the result that different lineage members joined different factions in the town. Chan Yat-Kuan never enjoyed the support of any Chan other than his younger brother and father. His uncle in the third segment was the only other agnate who shared patriotic sentiments with Yat-Kuan. Yet in the 1960 Rural Committee's executive session vote for a new chairman, this uncle was the only executive who did not vote for Yat-Kuan.

In fact agnatic bonds seem to be less effective than affinal bonds in mobilizing factional support. The domain of affinal relations tends to be coterminus with various levels of ethnic group consciousness. Sai Kung people rely as much on their affinal kinsmen and their ethnic cohort as they do on their agnates in seeking political and economic support.

Thus, Chin Fuk-Loi could not expect help from his uncles purely on the basis of shared ancestry. Chin's first job was not in his uncle's shop, but in the New Unity Tea House owned by another Hakka named Chin who was not a relative.

The Japanese occupation created conditions which provided wily young men like Chin Fuk-Loi an opportunity to gamble with their lives in the hope of large rewards. During those years of extreme deprivation Chin sailed a boat carrying contraband between Hong Kong and the guerrilla controlled bases in eastern Paoan. By his own and other people's testimony, Chin was not a guerrilla. But many of his relatives and neighbors were guerrillas, and they did not interfere with his trade because he inadvertently undermined the Japanese position while he also paid duties on guerrilla levies. In those days he was very daring according to his own story; had the Japanese known of his exploits he would have been shot on the spot, yet he was never afraid to fraternize with the local garrison on his forays into town.

In 1945 Chin Fuk-Loi returned to Sai Kung town "with the purpose of setting up one shop after another," as he put it. He maintained his old trading connections with eastern Paoan where imports of batteries, kerosene, dry goods, truck tires, and medicines, and exports of refugee cargoes continued to pay ever more handsome profits. This unregulated trade with China is reported for other parts of the New Territories as well. James Watson (1975:71–72) describes how the profits from this trade enabled members of the Man lineage of San Tin village to invest in the burgeoning Chinese restaurant business in London.

During the early 1950s Chin bought two shops, one to sell Chinese medicines and the other to sell general household supplies to remote villages accessible only by boat. Today, these two stores are each managed by one of his first two wives, a Hakka child-bride and a later Cantonese mistress. His drugstore employs several herbalists and a pulse doctor. All are Hakka refugees from Waichow. The pulse doctor is also head of the Sai Kung Sun Yat-Sen Memorial Association whose members supported Chin's bid for power in 1967.

In keeping with his far-flung connections in the movement of refugees and sojourners, Chin opened a travel agency in 1963. His agency organized the movement of local villagers to newly opened restaurant jobs in Western Europe. Today the travel service has branches in seven other marketing centers and Kowloon. Every spring, Chin gives a mammoth feast to celebrate the anniversary of the opening of his travel agency in Sai Kung. All the Hakka men who use his travel service and vote for him are invited. Such feasts are the typical offerings to curry favor with clients which any man seeking prominence in local politics must provide.

There is one other smaller travel agency in Sai Kung town which is owned by a Cantonese village leader. The Hakka and Cantonese travel agencies are in bitter competition, and they represent two of the several factions which animate market town politics, in part, along speech group lines. Chin's travel agency is another example of a market level organization formed along ethnic rather than agnatic lines. This contrasts with the lineage organized travel industry in the San Tin area of the New Territories (see Watson 1975).

While Chin enjoyed enormous economic success, he lacked political influence and prestige. Even before his uncle was forced to resign from the Rural Committee in 1960, Chin Fuk-Loi was organizing disgruntled Hakka. However, when his uncle suddenly resigned in 1960 and Chan Yat-Kuan assumed leadership of the Rural Committee, the symbolic edges of the conflict were sharpened between Chin the Hakka villager and Chan the Cantonese merchant.

Chin's first move against Chan's entrenched Kaifong was to mobilize the Native Fellowship Association. Chin's Hakka-led village faction doubled the membership and forced the Cantonese founder from his position of executive secretary. After Chin was elected to this post he launched one struggle after another against Chan's leadership of the Kaifong, Chamber of Commerce, and Rural Committee. Chin rallied support around the rhetoric that Chan headed a faction of "propertyless immigrants," and they were excluding local merchants from positions of power and prestige in their own market.

My analysis of Chan's Rural Committee executive officeholders shows that 19 percent were born outside the market area (three Hakka and one Cantonese). About half of the executive officers were elected from the

Kaifong which was Chan's base of power. The Kaifong consisted of nine Hakka, seven Cantonese, and one Chaochow. Half of them were born outside the market area. However, it is significant that all of Chan's close faction members, even non-Hakka immigrants, spoke Hakka.

The irony of Chin's protest that Chan was aligned with outsiders was that he, Chin Fuk-Loi, began to garner support for his local Hakka-led faction from the financial backing of immigrants. My analysis of Chin's 1963 faction (based on forty-seven members of the Chamber of Commerce who signed a letter to the district officer supporting Chin's accusations against Chan) shows that 38 percent of the faction was born outside the market area (nine Hakka, five Chaochow, two Cantonese, and one Waichow). Over the course of the four years, Chin's rhetoric against Chan's non-Hakka, nonlocal base of support seemed to increase in direct proportion to the increased support that his own faction received from other immigrant and outside groups. What is more significant, the immigrants that began supporting Chin Fuk-Loi made no attempts to speak Hakka.

Each of Chin's electoral challenges of Chan's leadership was defeated until the summer of 1967. That summer Chan transformed the Rural Committee into the Sai Kung All Circles Struggle Committee. The colonial government lost political control and barely managed to keep police control of Sai Kung during the summer and autumn of that year. The radicals' bombing campaign and the government's detention of radicals without due process completely polarized the situation in Sai Kung and other parts of the colony. The government issued urgent requests for "responsible men" to organize support for the government and to reconstitute the Rural Committee.

To facilitate the process, the government authorized creation of semivigilante groups called Public Security Advancement Associations. Members were to patrol the local area, report suspicious activities, gather intelligence on the social backgrounds and whereabouts of radicals, and to disseminate government rewards and information. This proved to be Chin's opportunity to replace Chan. Using the Sai Kung Native Fellowship Association as his leadership base, Chin organized a public security association. Through the latter association, he recruited large numbers of Cantonese-, Hakka-, and Hokkien-speaking immigrants. In this way, Chin formed regional links with the urban economic and political muscle of secret societies, the Kuomintang, and the Royal Hong Kong Police. Through this process many immigrants and some persons living outside Sai Kung altogether were awarded honorary memberships in Sai Kung's Public Security Association. Later these memberships were extended to the Native Fellowship Association itself!

In the spring of 1968 the district officer in Kowloon held a meeting for all Sai Kung village and Kaifong leaders who supported the government. Chin Fuk-Loi's faction were elected to fill the executive seats in a new Rural Committee. Almost all of these men were Hakka with roots in the local villages.

Now, however, the contradictions within his larger base of support began to create problems. I will mention only two more relevant ones. Having received enthusiastic Chaochow support in the organization of the Public Security Association, Chairman Chin now felt obliged to reciprocate. He therefore supported the election of Chaochow members to leadership positions in the Chamber of Commerce. Chin also accorded a number of Chaochow leaders honorary memberships in the Sai Kung Native Fellowship Association. I will treat this blow to local hegemony more fully in the next chapter.

A second severe contradiction was Chin's dependency on the colonial government. The government had suspended open Kaifong elections in the wake of the riots. A simple nomination system was substituted for elections. The nomination system gave Chin and the district officer much tighter control over access to political office in Sai Kung.

A couple of events dramatically illustrate Chin's dependency on the government. In 1972 the government was filling in the harbor in front of the Tin Hau temple. The government attempted to persuade the boat people, who are the backbone of local commerce, to move away from the market. On top of the fill, the government planned to construct resettlement housing for villagers whose lands were condemned for the purpose of building a reservoir. Chairman Chin complied with the government's request that the matshed housing the opera for Tin Hau's feast be moved from its traditional place in front of the temple in order not to interrupt the landfill. Recalling the kind of opposition that Chan Yat-Kuan could muster against a government meddling in local religious affairs, some people concluded that Chin was a "puppet" of the government.

Some local people also recall that while Chan Yat-Kuan was in control, Sai Kung was the site for a traditional dragon boat race at the Double Five Festival. They complained that since Chin had taken over, his faction was "too cheap" to sponsor the races. Members of Chin's faction argued that the festival was too expensive and the people were not willing to foot the bill for such extravaganza. It was, therefore, difficult for Chin and his supporters to rationalize their compliance with a government request to hold a Hong Kong Festival Celebration in the market. The Hong Kong Festival was instituted by the colonial government in the years following the 1967 disturbances to celebrate Hong

Kong's prosperity and to reassert the colony's credibility and reputation with foreign investors and resident workers alike. In Sai Kung, Chin and his faction supporters worked with the Catholic mission setting up displays and preparing programs. They collected contributions from the public to sponsor an operatic performance. Several members of Chin's faction expressed great displeasure at having to collect money for what seemed to most people to be a meaningless, if not altogether pernicious, celebration. Thus, while Chin had cut back on traditional ceremonial expenses, he was obliged to organize a "foreign" festival at the government's behest.

In 1973 some of Chin's Hakka supporters broke with him in a contest which almost ended in violence, had it not been for the intervention of the district officer; the new faction blocked Chin's reelection to head the Native Fellowship Association. The following year, with the reinstitution of more open Kaifong elections, the new faction successfully contested Chin's leadership of the Rural Committee. In the short history of the Sai Kung Rural Committee, the first two chairmen had been forcefully removed by the government, but Chairman Chin was the first to be forced out by the people.

Chan Yat-Kuan and Chin Fuk-Loi exemplify the problematic relationship between local Hakka society and the larger arena of Cantonese society. A leader must be competent in both the local and the external spheres of political influence. The failure of Chan and of Chin, in each case, was due to an overcompensation in that sphere of influence where each lacked native credentials.

Chin, from a rural Hakka village, espoused local Hakka hegemony while organizing support for the colonial government by mobilizing immigrant groups and outside muscle. This crucial component of Chin's support had little interest in local customs, much less speaking the Hakka language. Instead, they used Chin's position to organize their own ethnic and partisan interests.

Chan, the Cantonese outsider, emphasized Hakka language—all members of his Kaifong faction which included a number of non-Hakka immigrants, spoke Hakka. Chan stressed the integrity of local customs and worked for local automony partly on the strength of Hakka identity and patriotic sentiments.

Chin and Chan each had a different strategy for sharing power with immigrant groups in attempts to maintain a modicum of local Hakka hegemony in Sai Kung. The different strategies were products of different ethnic identities and cultural competencies attempting to cope with radical changes in Sai Kung society caused by outside events such as The

Great Leap Forward and the Great Proletarian Cultural Revolution. In the next chapter I examine this process from the point of view of the most successful immigrant groups, especially the Chaochow.

CONCLUSION

Sai Kung always had an immigrant population as a result of growing commercial traffic between Hong Kong and China. Before 1960 persons with different ethnic roots interacted in ways that maintained the dominant "local Hakka" identity of Sai Kung market. Immigrant families, including Cantonese merchants and boat people, are now identified as old Hakka families insofar as they affiliate with local Hakka in matters of speech, wives, and support for local religious affairs. Such immigrant Cantonese prove to be effective and popular local leaders because they are able to maintain important connections with the Cantonese establishment surrounding Sai Kung. These connections are facilitated by their maintenance of Cantonese speech and wives inside their homes. These case studies illustrate the proposition that successful ethnic group leaders are not necessarily native to the groups they lead!

Local Hakka, on the other hand, have to cultivate outside Cantonese connections to be successful Sai Kung town leaders. Often, a local Hakka marries a Cantonese woman, who not only connects him to Cantonese patronage but from whom his children are exposed to Cantonese customs and speech. Having a Cantonese wife helps a man become a successful Hakka leader at the local level.

Immigrants to Sai Kung tended to become part of the local establishment before 1960. After that date, the volume of immigration became too great to accommodate in traditional fashion, and among the new waves of immigrants were a large number of Hokkien speakers for whom there were no traditional hosts in Sai Kung. Discrimination and exclusion on the part of local Hakka and Cantonese forced the Hokkien immigrants to organize around their own native identities.

In the next chapter, we see how Li Hung-Fuk early adapted to local Hakka society by organizing fellow immigrants on the basis of their Chaochow identity. This process amounted to a reorganization and restructuring of Sai Kung society, which took place during a period of rapid change and political upheaval throughout the region.

CHAPTER 7

The Chaochow Renegotiate
Sai Kung Social Organization

For a century the Hakka maintained dominion over Sai Kung market. Beginning in 1950, and in particular after 1960, refugees from the economic rigors of China's socialist transition along with other immigrants seeking opportunities outside the concrete jungle of Kowloon filled economic gaps left by Sai Kung natives sojourning to Europe.

Among the most formidable groups to organize themselves in Sai Kung were the Chaochow. The Chaochow were a new group, and they competed with others, natives and immigrants, for land and market. The local villagers organized a Sai Kung Native Fellowship Association in order to retain unified control over local resources. However, the very act of providing access to outsiders caused factional infighting which such immigrant groups as the Chaochow manipulated to their own advantage.

Today the Chaochow, qua "Chaochow," occupy leading positions in the market order. Most engage in business, and many manage commercial vegetable and pig farms in the Cantonese valleys. A significant number, who began as commercial farmers, itinerant traders, or shop assistants now manage small rural industries, hardware, plastic wares, crockery shops, bakeries, and rice stores in the Sai Kung market. They have achieved leadership positions in the Kaifong and the Chamber of Commerce. Their attempts to gain political influence are described in such local speech as "the Chaochow are thrusting out their heads," while "the Hakka have lost their gall."

HOKKIEN-SPEAKING IMMIGRANTS

In the late 1930s a Chaochow rice merchant opened a store in Sai Kung. He was introduced to the town by a local Cantonese villager who worked in the main Chaochow store in urban Kowloon. The Sai Kung branch, of the Together Achieving Company, became a funnel through which other Chaochow were introduced to Sai Kung.

One of the early shop assistants was a man named Yeong Wai-Sin. When he arrived in Hong Kong from Chiehyang county, he was barely eighteen, illiterate, unskilled, and unemployed. A fellow Chaochow who worked in the Sai Kung store introduced him to work there as an assistant. During the next twenty years Yeong worked his way up to the counter where he calculated prices and received payments. In the process he learned to manage a business, to read, and to speak Cantonese.

Yeong married a Chaochow woman from Kowloon. In 1965 he built a hut on some lowland between Sha Kok Mei village and Sai Kung town. Although the location was subject to floods, Yeong and his wife began raising chickens and pigs there. Following the post-1970 influx of picnickers from Kowloon he began selling soda and beer. Today he has a total monthly income of over $5,000; and he is trying to obtain the best schooling for his five young children. They attend the semiprivate Catholic school in Sai Kung.

Another early Chaochow was Li Hung-Fuk. Most local people identify Li as "the first Chaochow in Sai Kung" because of his role in founding the Chaochow Association.

Li Hung-Fuk is from a Ch'aoyang county farm family. His father sojourned in Vietnam. As a very young man in 1940, Li Hung-Fuk settled on Cheung Chau Island, southwest of Hong Kong, which is inhabited by many Chaochow and boat people. During the Japanese occupation he went back to his native place, but returned to Hong Kong at the end of the occupation. He took a job hawking seeds and baby animals—this is a Chaochow monopoly in the New Territories. To the villagers he brought access to other goods and services, easy credit, investment opportunities in lucrative ventures, and not least of all, a charming and gregarious personality.

Li chose Sai Kung because the "environment of Sai Kung was most suitable for hawking these products." He concentrated his trade on the Cantonese and Hakka villages north and east of the market. Although he was merely a "Hoklo" in the eyes of the Hakka villagers, he learned to speak Hakka and established a fictive brother relationship with one of the Hakka villagers in that area.

Another focus of his trade was the immigrant miners at Ma On Peak.

There he opened a small soda, cracker, and cake shop that was supplied from the Sai Kung market.

Within a decade, Li Hung-Fuk was well known in the market town and throughout the northeastern hinterland. By 1962 he was able to open a bakery on Common Street. A few years later he moved his bakery near to the wharf on Big Street, and he introduced another Chaochow merchant into his old premises on Common Street. In 1964 Li purchased land in a Hakka village at the end of the newly constructed road a mile east of town. There he established a pig farm and employed village women to tend his pigs. This purchase was just the beginning. Around 1970, he bought a large tract of land from a Cantonese leader in Ho Chung. Today Li is a prominent landlord in Sai Kung.

In the bakery Li's Chaochow wife and children tend the counter. The bakers are mostly Chaochow, a few Waichow Hokkien, and one boat youth. Several of the Chaochow whom he employed earlier, including a "younger brother," and another man, Pang Wan-Hei, have established their own bakeries.

A third case is a man named Ho Si-Yu (see chapter 4, Chaochow Projections). His natal family owned a small cosmetic and crude-oil shop in Chaochow. He went to school for four years before he was recruited into the army at fourteen to fight the Japanese. He married in Chaochow at the age of twenty-two. Encouraged by an uncle, he sailed to Hong Kong in a boat with thirty young Chaochow men. Most of them returned to Chaochow, but Ho stayed in Hong Kong as an unskilled laborer. First he worked in the iron mine at Ma On Peak. There he met Li Hung-Fuk who owned the small soda and snack store. Ho subsequently worked in the mines at Tsuen Wan and Lan Tao Island before returning to Sai Kung.

Li Hung-Fuk recruited his old friend Ho to hawk the noodles and cakes which Li's little bakery produced daily. Ho bought noodles and cakes from Li at the wholesale price of sixteen cakes for a dollar. He sold them to farmers around Ma On Peak at a slight profit of fourteen cakes for a dollar. He earned three to four dollars a day, when rice was 50¢ per catty. With the money he saved, Ho invested in four piglets and embarked on an occupation that was altogether new to him. Today his farm on the outskirts of Sai Kung town grosses $100 per day.

Some of the early Chaochow immigrants learned to speak Hakka and Cantonese. However, they did not attempt to affiliate with the local people in part because of local prejudice against "Hoklo." Most did not marry local women. Rather they married Chaochow women and maintained their Chaochow affiliations in Kowloon. Their strategy for integrating into the Sai Kung economy developed around the incorporation of their ethnic identity and their concomitant use of pecuniary power.

Chaochow Business Strategies

The Chaochow are extremely competitive businessmen, and they are tightly organized. However, these characteristics derive less from behavior which can be identified as exclusively Chaochow and more from the organization of the Sai Kung market in which the Chaochow participate as Chinese immigrants.

Chinese and students of Chinese often assume that people prefer to patronize their ethnic cohort because native brothers are less likely to cheat each other, and each may expect to receive special consideration. However, there are equally compelling reasons for commerce to flow *across* ethnic boundaries, and in Sai Kung this does happen. The main motive for conducting one's business outside the ethnic cohort is the freedom to turn a profit. If one feels constrained to give a good deal to the ethnic cohort, then one's profit margin is reduced. In his study of the Mississippi Chinese, James Loewen (1971:48) points out that Chinese grocers orient their trade toward the outgroup blacks which obviates mixing friendly, that is particularistic and diffuse, relationships with hard-nosed business practices. The vendor does not feel compelled to give a good deal or to comply with a customer's credit request where the two are members of different ethnic groups.

In Sai Kung there are other reasons which compel interethnic commerce. Immigrants tend to patronize local merchants and local villagers often buy from immigrant shopkeepers. Looking at it from the point of view of the immigrant Chaochow marketing strategy we can see that it is largely a product of their immigrant status. First, Chaochow have to attract customers from other groups if they want to do any sizable business. Second, they have to pay rent. To compete with the local establishment they have to sell in volume and cut profits to the bone. Their slogans are: "The cheapest price for every patron" and "Everyone is treated the same!" To compete successfully, they must labor harder and consume less than the local shopkeepers. It is ironic that the Chaochow who are organized into the tightest ethnic syndicate develop a marketing strategy which requires minimal ethnic prejudice and discrimination.

The local Hakka marketing strategy, on the contrary, thrives despite a smaller turnover of inventory. They may charge higher prices depending on the customer, and they receive higher profits on each sale. The local shopkeepers calculate their assets in the provision of credit, the ownership of land, political influence in the Rural Committee, and in social and economic connections in the Native Fellowship Association, all of which attract clients and customers despite the sometimes higher prices.

Immigrants patronize local merchants and pay the few cents more to establish local connections, whereas local customers take advantage of the Chaochow and other immigrants who need to sell their goods at more competitive prices.

These differences are illustrated by the case of a Hakka village representative on the Rural Committee. In 1960 he was able to rent a shop in the market to sell groceries, but at this time of heightened immigrant competition, he found himself having to work and live like an immigrant. However, as a local Hakka with political connections, he managed to be elected a Kaifong leader. After several years, he closed the shop and utilized his local influence to buy and sell real estate. He reaped handsome profits from land that was rapidly escalating in commercial value.

By 1970 real estate had become more lucrative than shopkeeping, and it was easily monopolized by local leaders (that is, landowners). It became the political foundation for the Native Fellowship Association and the factionalism which animated local politics during my stay in Sai Kung.

The different strategies of local Hakka and immigrant Chaochow provide some of the behavioral bases for the stereotype that the Hakka men are "lacking in gall" or "lazy," and that the Chaochow are "threadbare," "hardworking," "aggressive," and "clannish."

The last two labels, "aggressive" and "clannish," have to do with the corporate tenacity of the Chaochow Native Place Association. Although local identity is incorporated in the Sai Kung Native Fellowship Association, it does not appear to be so "clannish" because it is essentially "defensive" and an integral part of the overall Sai Kung leadership which is diffused in a number of organizations. However, the Chaochow success in Sai Kung is a function of Chaochow organization. The Native Place Association facilitates their successful competition in that it provides an independent basis for securing loans and insuring their repayment. It keeps a lid on the intense competition among themselves, at the same time enhancing their competitiveness with locals and other outsiders by lowering prices and cornering the market in legitimate trades such as bakery goods.

I have argued that Chaochow business strategy is mainly a product of Sai Kung social organization. However, the "clannishness" is often perceived to be characteristic of their native culture. H. B. Morse noted that,

> people of the country and coast around (Swatow) are . . . industrious workers and hardy fishermen, and the merchants are adventurous traders,

whose influence is felt in every port along the coast. The people are exceedingly clannish, and to injure a Swatow man is to plunge the hand into a nest of hornets. The trade of the port is absolutely, in its minutest detail, under the control of the *Wai-nien-feng,* and the Swatow men in other ports are as completely organized in provincial clubs, working in conjunction with the home guild and under its guidance (1932:61).

In exactly this way, the tight Chaochow organization in Sai Kung is an extension of the powerful parent association in Kowloon. It is important to realize, however, that other groups, notably Hakka and Cantonese in Thailand, where among the Chinese the Chaochow constitute the "locals," have been stereotyped similarly as "aggressive" and "clannish." If Chaochow strategies have cultural roots, they are simply Chinese. For the overriding factor in determining their strategies is their position in Sai Kung society.

Why have other immigrant groups not organized in these ways? The Waichow Haifeng and Lufeng people have begun to. They seem to lack the kind of organizational support from long-established parent associations in Kowloon. Perhaps more importantly, they made different choices during the crucial local faction fight of 1967. I shall discuss this in more detail later.

Immigrant Hakka and Cantonese, on the other hand, tend to maintain organizational connections in Kowloon, and in Sai Kung they cultivate informal networks with local Hakka and Cantonese, respectively, on the basis of common speech. The early Hokkien immigrants who could speak Hakka and Cantonese followed a similiar pattern of local patronage. But with the influx of Hokkien speakers, they found increasing advantage in organizing their monolingual Chaochow brethren. Undoubtedly, much of the emphasis for the Chaochow organization came from decisions made by Kowloon parent organizations. Part of the evidence is the large amount of money they contribute to the fledgling Sai Kung Chaochow Association.

ORGANIZING THE CHAOCHOW FELLOWSHIP ASSOCIATION

Several factors account for organization of a Chaochow association in the heart of Sai Kung's Hakka and Cantonese enclave. One is the lack of an established Hokkien-speaking host through whom the immigrants might establish themselves. Second is the particular Chaochow ability to organize certain niches in the local economy and to manipulate local factions in the process. Third is the revolutionary disorder in China which spilled over into Sai Kung and provided the Chaochow an opportunity to help reorganize the local community along new lines.

The early and successful Chaochow spoke Hakka and Cantonese

which helped to ingratiate them with the local people. But most Chaochow never bothered to affiliate with the Hakka. The Chaochow were acutely aware of their "Hoklo" and, more particularly, their Chaochow identity which in the context of greater Hong Kong had practical and affective value. Their first organization in Sai Kung was the Chaochow Achievement Society, a firecracker association, which included a revolving credit fund. In 1965, the association erected its first "spirit place" and sponsored the first Chaochow opera in honor of Tin Hau's feast day. This cost them $50,000.

In the process of organizing on the basis of their native place identity, the Chaochow differentiated themselves from the other "Hoklo" with whom they had been identified hitherto. According to Ho Si-Yu, during the early attempts at organization, the Chaochow invited the Haifeng and Lufeng people to join them.[1] However, most of the Hai-Lufeng Hokkien declined to join with the Chaochow, and instead they attempted to organize a Waichow group.

Ho Si-Yu did not offer any reasons for the Waichow refusal. It is possible the Waichow feared domination by the Chaochow. I suspect the more important factor was that the Waichow were aligned with a local Sai Kung faction which differed from the factional links which the Chaochow were forging.

The Waichow group allied themselves with the Ho Chung village Cantonese. The Waichow cluster in a new village, Lok Mei, on the hill behind Ho Chung. Many of the Waichow are refugees and together with their Ho Chung Cantonese landlords affiliate through Kuomintang networks and institutions. The Cantonese village leaders are also connected to the central political agencies of Sai Kung and Hong Kong and are therefore in a position to distribute the considerable refugee aid which flows from the United States and its client government on Taiwan. Thus, the Waichow success in Sai Kung was closely tied to their status as reliable tenants and clients of the village Cantonese.

Here it is necessary to digress slightly to examine the relationship between the Ho Chung Cantonese villagers and the Kaifong establishment in Sai Kung market. Holding important executive positions in the Rural Committee, the Cantonese village leaders were in close association with Chairman Chan Yat-Kuan and his Kaifong faction. In fact, the Ho Chung Cantonese had a vested interest in Chan's leadership for every reason except ideology. The Ho Chung leaders were Kuomintang loyalists, and the Kaifong leaders were communist partisans. However, both leaderships were Cantonese. Moreover—and this is crucial—each occupied a niche which complemented the other in the local economy. The Ho Chung villagers were landlords and sojourners, while the Kaifong members were shopkeepers. Neither group coveted the other's resources. The Ho Chung leaders could never muster enough votes to control the chairmanship of the Rural Committee. There developed a keen sense of balance between the two Cantonese factions.

When the village Hakka under Chin Fuk-Loi contested Chan's leadership in the town in 1960, the Ho Chung Cantonese spent no small effort in supporting Chan Yat-Kuan.[2] The Waichow Hokkien, who were clients of the Ho Chung leaders, remained loyal to the Chan establishment.

In contrast, the Chaochow, who were seeking to advance themselves into the market town as an organized group, threw their considerable financial weight behind Chin's faction. Indeed, Chin Fuk-Loi's faction was made up of Hakka villagers who were trying to gain political influence in the market where they owned shops. They felt that their market had been taken over by immigrant Cantonese. Ironically, these "immigrant Cantonese" were allied with local Hakka communist partisans, and they all spoke Hakka and promoted local customs. On the other hand, Chin, the bona fide Hakka allied himself with powerful outside financial interests and political muscle which had little appreciation for local customs much less for the speaking of Hakka. When the Chan faction revolted against the colonial government in the riots of 1967, Chin's decade-long bid for local leadership finally found support from government officials. The Chaochow, as close allies of Chin, were then in a position to carve out a piece of the market pie for themselves.

During the summer and fall of 1967, the colonial government was desperate for public support. The pro-Hong Kong press printed lists of organizations which publically supported the government, while the patriotic press printed its count of insurgent organizations. The Sai Kung district officer was literally beleaguered; 13 percent of the Sai Kung Rural Committee openly joined the revolt, including most of the executive leadership. The average defection in other townships of the New Territories was only 4 percent (Catron 1971). The district officer kept a list of local leaders who professed loyalty to the government along with the number of loyal followers vouched for by each leader.

In the midst of this turmoil Li Hung-Fuk seized the opportunity to organize support for the government and at the same time organized the Chaochow in Sai Kung. In his petition to the district officer, Li pointed out that Chaochow residents in the Sai Kung district had increased very much in recent years. He asserted that Chaochow are law-abiding. However, to prevent them from being exploited by agitators, Li argued, a Sai Kung Chaochow Association should be formed. Such an association would provide Chaochow both with a place to meet and with a base of support for the government's move to maintain law and order.

This appeal to organize support for the government by a group with the reputation of being "outsiders" and "truculent" carried great weight during the months of turmoil. The district officer gave strong support when the Chaochow preparatory committee forwarded a draft of its constitution to the Registrar of Societies in October 1967. The Chaochow Association received official recognition in May 1968.

The new Chaochow Association backed the Hakka leadership which was trying to bring about order through its Public Security Association. At the inauguration of the Chaochow Association, Li Hung-Fuk praised Chairman Chin Fuk-Loi as "a farsighted local leader who is not only kind and honest but is also zealous in extending help to others." Li further pledged the Chaochow Association to create greater prosperity and to build a new Sai Kung under Chin Fuk-Loi's leadership.[3]

THE CHAOCHOW RECONSTITUTE THE CHAMBER OF COMMERCE

Before 1967 Chin Fuk-Loi's village faction controlled the Sai Kung Native Fellowship Association, but it had not been able to wrest control of the Chamber of Commerce. The Chamber was headed by the faction which also controlled the Kaifong and the Rural Committee, namely by Chan Yat-Kuan. Only after Chin consolidated his power in the Kaifong and the reconstituted Rural Committee was he in a position to deal out leadership posts in the Chamber. In January 1968 elections were finally held for offices in the Chamber of Commerce. Chin Fuk-Loi persuaded his followers to elect the Chaochow Li Hung-Fuk to chair the Chamber of Commerce. Many local people, including some within Chin's own faction felt betrayed. Not only was the Chamber chairmanship placed in the hands of a Chaochow, but seven of the seventeen management positions were allotted to the Chaochow. This included five of the twelve executive positions. However, Chin's supporters argued that all the powerful positions under the chairmanship, that is two vice-chairmanships and two treasury posts were still in the hands of local Hakka.

In 1969 Li Hung-Fuk began to exercise his executive power by submitting a list of requests to the district office. His requests generally called upon the government to promote the urbanization and industrialization of the market area. One specific item requested government to provide Crown land on which to build a new Chamber of Commerce. By 1972, most people agreed that the Chamber had accomplished at least one thing—the erection of its new building. It was not altogether surprising that half of the building was financed and occupied by the Chaochow Fellowship Association.

Local shopkeepers generally say, "Yes, of course I'm a member of the Chamber of Commerce!" Queried further, they respond, "The Chamber is useless." "Its only functions are the annual spring dinner, and membership in the New Territories General Chamber of Commerce." Some shopkeepers point out that since it is run by the Chaochow, it does not have the confidence of a large number of its local members. Commercial disputes and financial problems are rarely taken to the Chaochow chairman. That action is now negotiated through the Kaifong committee or the Sai Kung Native Fellowship Association.

MEMBERSHIP IN THE CHAOCHOW ASSOCIATION AND THE NATURE OF CORPORATE ETHNICITY

The ethnic association is altogether distinct from the ethnic community. As a group becomes organized and uses ethnic identity to incorporate its boundaries, the criteria for membership become more objective and exclusive. It seems that the criteria become more subject to political-economic considerations and less a matter of cultural competence. In any corporate group the criteria for membership must specify precisely who has access to the organization's properties. The Chaochow organization's properties are considerable, and about one-third of the Chaochow community hold membership in the Chaochow Association.

In Sai Kung the Chaochow assets include connections to Li Hung-Fuk, whose own self-made fortune guarantees the group's credit. The association provides a crucial source of credit to the striving commercial farmer or shopkeeper. It also provides lucrative investment opportunities, farmland and shop space. The association has the wherewithal to support its members in disputes with locals as well as for solving disputes among themselves.

For example, one Chaochow monopoly is bakery goods. Many who are in the bakery trade started in Li Hung-Fuk's bakeshop. As each established his own bakery, he tended to specialize in different kinds of pastries and noodles. However, a major seasonal item which most bakeries sell is moon cakes to fill the heavy demand during the Mid-Autumn Festival. Most bakeries offer their customers an installment plan for buying moon cakes. A family can pay a little each month and collect their cakes at the time of the festival, thus saving their larger cash expenditures for fresh fruits and meat. Pang Wan-Hei found that he was not selling his usual volume of moon cakes. He felt that Li was taking his customers. Pang loaded his cakes on a dolly and hawked them in front of Li's bakery which is in the center of town. The squabble was settled behind the closed doors of the association. Shortly thereafter, Pang gave up his line in moon cakes and began selling factory-baked biscuits tinned in Kowloon.

The three requirements for membership in the Chaochow Association are: (1) A Chaochow resident in Sai Kung more than eighteen years old; (2) be a person of good character; and (3) be recommended by at least one other member and have the approval of the Executive Committee. When I asked Li what criteria constituted Chaochow identity, he merely stated that to be Chaochow means that a person is from one of the nine counties around the port of Swatow. He indicated that speaking a Chaochow dialect is usually taken as proof that the person is from Chaochow or is of Chaochow ancestry. However, the rules do not specify any test for cultural competence.

Li expressed great sensitivity when I asked how certain individual members, such as Pang Wan-Hei and Chow On, whom other townsfolk said were not really Chaochow, could be included as Chaochow. Li snapped that "Pang is from Tenghai, and Chow is from P'uning!" (Both counties are part of Chaochow Prefecture.) The two cases of Pang and Chow illustrate the nature of corporate Chaochow identity in Sai Kung, as well as the role of political-economic criteria in corporate ethnicity.

Pang Wan-Hei is an ectomorph, a tense, nervous little man. He is an immaculate dresser, always in a starched shirt and tie and leather shoes. He labors diligently, pushing his dolly of tinned crackers through the market town while his wife and daughter watch the store. As a distributor of canned crackers he is imminently successful in Sai Kung market. In 1972 he was the head of the Kaifong Firecracker Association, a Chamber of Commerce executive, and a leading member of the Chaochow Fellowship Executive Committee. During the Tin Hau Festival he was listed as the third ritual head, responsible for inviting the gods to take their positions in the spirit place.

Some local politicians scoff that Pang is merely a (Haifeng) "Hoklo." Yet the head of the Chaochow Association testifies that Pang is a bona fide Chaochow. Pang's Haifeng dialect is probably accepted within the Chaochow orbit by "the social fact" that his native place in Chaochow is Tenghai. Tenghai is just south of the Fukien-Kwangtung border, and it includes the heterogeneous port of Swatow. Even if Pang is a native of Haifeng, he might trace his ancestry to Tenghai for purposes of being Chaochow in Sai Kung.

Another somewhat different case is that of Chow On. He is also a member of the Sai Kung Chaochow Association, although he holds no formal office in that or any other association in the market area. When I first began buying vegetables from his shop on Common Street, he referred to himself as "Hoklo."

Chow and two of his wives worked very diligently buying and selling vegetables all of their waking hours. Although he does not waste his time sitting at mahjong tables, he still manages to squander much of the profits gambling. When a collector from the local syndicate comes around, Chow interrupts his work to hand the man a week's profit to bet on the horse races in Hong Kong. Chow's older children are always out in the streets, and they are infrequently available to help their old father and his wives. Periodically they come into the shop to reach into the change bucket for a handful of coins before their father can do anything more than give a scowl and utter a cry of exasperation.

Chow sleeps on a cot amid the litter of baskets and crates emptied of their second-grade vegetables from the Kowloon wholesalers. Some of the children bed in the loft at the rear of the store. Others sleep with his third wife, a Hakka, in a small farm outside of town, while the second wife, a Chaochow, lives with her nephew who helps her hawk vegetables on Wharf Street. Chow and his Hakka wife work together in the vegetable shop. She quietly tolerates his gambling while the older Chaochow wife berates him for gambling.

Next to his phone amidst piles of papers and bills, the shrill sounds of "Hoklo opera" often bellow forth from his record player.

When the man from "the Chairman Mao group" next door comes to sell $20 tickets for the October First celebration, Chow buys five tickets, discards four, and sends his eldest son to be warmly wined and dined at the restaurant. Chow feels constrained to purchase only one or two tickets for the Kuomintang's Double Ten (October Tenth) celebration. Five to two is about the ratio of influence which the Chinese Communist Party enjoys over the Kuomintang in Sai Kung. As most Chaochow, Chow On is strictly bipartisan. The top of Chow's refrigerator is cluttered with trinkets—plastic lanterns and flowers, a Buddhist figurine, a communist-worker statue, small animal molds, and other tokens of his generous contributions to the Chaochow Association during their biannual auctions.

Chow was born in 1915 in P'uning county, Chaochow. He quit school after one year because he could not stand the constant beatings. Nevertheless, he could, as he demonstrated, recite passages from the *Four Books*. At the age of seventeen (1932) he journeyed to Hong Kong and performed various kinds of work with his elder brother in Kowloon. In the late 1930s, he traveled "all over China" as a soldier in the predominantly Hakka Nineteenth Route Army. After the Japanese defeat, he married a woman in his native place by whom he had a son. He soon left to find work in Hong Kong, again, where he took a Chaochow mistress with whom he had three more sons and a daughter. During the 1950s, Chow lived in Tai Po market where he worked for a sand and cement consortium. There, he joined the Waichow Hakka Fellowship Association. Why?

> . . . for the welfare benefits, especially the burial insurance, and because we are all the same kind of people after all! I joined to establish relations, to develop *kan ch'ing* (good sentiments) among people who are the same as I.

In 1960, the consortium supplied sand and cement for the road being built into Sai Kung. Chow On moved to Sai Kung to work. He decided to rent a few fields near Sha Kok Mei to grow vegetables and to raise pigs. Competition with mainland China producers forced him out of business, so he began hawking vegetables in Sai Kung market in 1965. He then took another mistress, a Waichow Hakka, who worked for him and later bore him two daughters. However, as an immigrant to Sai Kung, he associated with people who were the same as himself—this time they are Chaochow.

When speaking with me—we both used Hakka—Chow says he is of the sixteenth generation as recorded in his lineage genealogy. Both his father and grandfather were born in P'uning county, Chaochow. However, his previous ancestors were born in Wuhua county, upriver from Meihsien and before that, in Fukien, a typical Hakka genealogy.

"Are you then Hakka?" I asked.

"Indeed," he replied: "I am the true Hakka" *(Ngai he chin shi Hakka)* (H)!

In Sai Kung society, as Li Hung-Fuk so adamantly stated, Chow On is Chaochow. Membership in the association gives his ethnic identity corporate significance and obligates him to participate consistently as a "Chaochow." Still, it is theoretically significant that Chow On, who is not an official of the association, was willing to discuss his non-Chaochow background with me, while Pang, an important Chaochow leader, skirted all conversation which began to impinge on his background. As Maurice Freedman (1957:94) pointed out for Chinese associations in Singapore: "There is a world of difference between those who actively participate in association affairs and those who remain passively on the rolls. The difference is essentially that between the status-seekers and the ordinary members: each category pursues different ends." Hence Pang's reluctance was due, at least, in part, to the corporate need to preserve consistency in his ethnic affiliation, a need which was highlighted by the fact that the Waichow and Chaochow compete with one another and that he is an officer in the latter association. The cases of Pang and Chow indicate that criteria for membership in corporate ethnic groups are political and economic and not simply cultural.

CONCLUSION

The corporate Chaochow identity emerged out of two decades of generalized Hokkien immigration and gradually increased socioeconomic differentiation of the slightly earlier and less partisan Chaochow sojourners from the Waichow Hai-Lufeng refugees. The Chaochow incorporation was accomplished by the daring and determined leadership of such multilingual virtuosos as Li Hung-Fuk through alliances with local factions in the midst of local disorders. Essentially, the Chaochow won their place in Sai Kung society by providing financial support for a particular Hakka faction which, after it won power, was in turn obliged to support Chaochow demands for positions of power and prestige in the local order of voluntary associations. These positions are maintained by the large expense account of the Chaochow in public festivals, in support of local factions, and by their collective ability to sell their merchandise at cut rates. Their positions in Sai Kung include honorary memberships in the Sai Kung Public Security Association and in the Sai Kung Native Fellowship Association, executive offices in the Chamber of Commerce and on the Kaifong Committee.

The creation of a formal ethnic association among outsiders is tantamount to a fundamental shift in the (ethnic) organization of Sai Kung society. It is important to note that the purpose of Chaochow corporate ethnicity is not so much aimed at cultural conservation much less segregation but rather to facilitate their integration into the local political economy. This requires their acculturation of the increasingly dominant Cantonese. In this case, and perhaps in general, the ultimate aim of ethnic organization in complex social systems may be acculturation, assimilation, and integration. At least, let us say that in many places, one approach to ethnic (or racial) integration may be through ethnic organization. The dialectic of sociocultural integration through ethnic incorporation is a process which requires further inquiry.

NOTES

1. The two counties of Haifeng and Lufeng are geographically and historically related to Hakka-dominated Waichow. However, they have been peopled by Hokkien speakers. Since the end of the Ching dynasty the two counties have been administratively attached to Chaochow rather than, as previously, to Waichow.

2. Although the Chin Fuk-Loi faction was never pro-Kuomintang, they did not hesitate to seek the backing of Kuomintang elements. It is possible that the Chin Hakka faction cut into the Ho Chung village's Kuomintang support. Hence, the Ho Chung faction, although anticommunist, found it more to their benefit to support the procommunist Chan faction than the nonpartisan Chin faction. It is also noteworthy that the procommunist faction led by Chan Yat-Kuan was "embarrassed" to distribute the refugee relief which was funneled through the Rural Committee. This relief found its way into the hands of the Ho Chung faction which based some of its political patronage on the distribution of relief. In a sense then, the procommunist and the pro-Kuomintang factions were allied before 1967 against the nonpartisan factions led by Chin Fuk-Loi. Only in the summer of 1967, when Chan's Rural Committee was dissolved and the ideological confrontation was violently polarized, did the Ho Chung leaders abandon Chan Yat-Kuan. They still found it impossible to ally with the Chin Hakka faction until Chin finally consummated his power in the new Rural Committee.

3. While Chin Fuk-Loi and Li Hung-Fuk formed a close working alliance and praised each other in public speeches, their respective ethnic cohort maintained less praiseworthy opinions of the outgroup's leadership. According to one member of the Chaochow Association, "Li Hung-Fuk is the richest man in Sai Kung; he can read and write. But Chin Fuk-Loi is illiterate, unprincipled, and a mere puppet of the Government. . . . Yes, all the Hakka leaders are like that; they don't protect the common people's interests."

CHAPTER 8

Conclusion: Ethnicity as
a Sociocultural Process

Many social scientists have viewed ethnic groups in a structural-functional framework and therefore as a conservative and static phenomenon. The current "root metaphor" of these studies is the "maintenance of ethnic boundaries." As I have shown, such a metaphor does not describe adequately my data on ethnic groups in Sai Kung. In fact, the assumption of boundary maintenance is an important question for empirical verification. We might begin to ask: What is the purpose of social or ethnic boundaries? How then do they form? Under what conditions are they maintained? relaxed? dissolved? And how do these processes take place? The overarching question has to do with how we study social grouping in general and ethnic grouping in particular. Ethnic groups are not static either culturally or socially. They are in a dynamic state of formulation and dissolution. As such, the ethnic group is not a simple product of culture, nor is it a simple product of interest group articulation. It is a product of both. Perhaps more than any other kind of social grouping, ethnic groups are variegated amalgams of both the symbolic motivational dimension and the social organizational dimension of human existence.

THE ROLE OF CULTURE

The cultural approach to the study of ethnic groups is inadequate to understand what it means to be a member of such an ethnic group as the Hakka. The late Maurice Freedman correctly warned that: "There is great danger in the study of southeastern China that people will assume for all Hakka or Hokkien or Cantonese or Teochiu (Chaochow) that what some of them do in one place is characteristic of the behavior of all of them" (1966:95). Burton Pasternak (1972:131–134) went on to conclude that the ethnic background of Hakka and Hokkien in southern Taiwan explains very little of the divergent adaptations and social organizations between a Hakka and a Hokkien village. In the larger realm of general theory, Fredrik Barth (1969:15) dismisses the "cultural stuff" as a factor in ethnic grouping. At first glance Barth's point is immediately applicable to the study of Chinese ethnic groups among which there are few significant differences in basic values, technological sophistication (including boat people and land people), social structures, and grammars. The ethnic cultures along the southern coast of China constitute a broad range of superficial variations on an underlying Chinese pattern.

This situation is not peculiar to China. We observe the same lack of technical and cultural cleavage among ethnic groups which even today engage in mutual carnage for control of little bits of real estate. In "Israeli Palestine" and "British Ireland" the protracted blood feuds are between groups rooted in the same traditions. In the former case, the feud flares between brothers in the bosom of Abraham, and in the latter case the war wears on between brothers in the love of Jesus. Neither of these modern conflicts equals the ferocity of the Hakka and Cantonese feuds during the last century, then, between brothers in the humanity of Confucius.

Having pointed out the weakness of a cultural analysis, the danger lies in dismissing the cultural aspect of ethnicity altogether. We need to bring the cultural dimension back into focus, since it is clearly a crucial component in the process of ethnic grouping. An ethnic group cannot exist without a cultural identity which includes sets of instrumental and expressive practices, reference to a historical experience or collective condition expressed in rhetorics of names and reputations.

The point I am developing here is that particular cultural traits are relevant to particular adaptations and interaction systems. Many of the culture traits that identify a particular group in Sai Kung are derived from a common Chinese heritage, and secondly they are the product of a particular adaptation. For example, in Sai Kung the difference between "Hakka" and "Chaochow" business strategies is, by and large, a product of local and immigrant organizational adaptations in which each draws on relevant traits in Chinese culture. This becomes clearer when we collapse the different speech groups into the larger ethnic categories of "local" (Hakka and Cantonese) and "immigrant" (Hakka, Cantonese, Hokkien), or when we compare the situation in Sai Kung with Bangkok where the Hakka and Chaochow are reversed in their older versus newer immigrant roles.

The cultural dimension of a group's life may not be reduced in every case to a dependent variable. Certain aspects of an ethnic group's culture have deep historical and widespread geographical roots. These may transcend localized interaction systems and exert more "independent" influence on the group's adaptation. For example, the role of Hakka women has deep roots in the Hakka rejection of foot-binding; and it has broad geographical representation in South China as a crucial subsistence strategy. I stop short of suggesting that the role of Hakka women involves a substantive difference in social structure from other Chinese groups. It is rather the "democratic" pole of the Chinese social structure in which domestic activities are extended to include subsistence labor. This cultural trait facilitates survival in niches which non-Hakka are reluctant to fill. In this case ethnic tradition plays a "compelling" if not altogether "determining" role in the process of ethnic grouping.

Many culture traits facilitate certain kinds of adaptation, even such apparently fortuitous traits as festivals and body decor. I have already mentioned the former tradition of foot-binding. Today, in Sai Kung, the Cantonese and Hakka villagers are distinguished by different annual fertility festivals. Closer scrutiny along lines which Marvin Harris suggests (1975) may demonstrate that these fertility festivals are geared to differences in local Cantonese and Hakka agricultural cycles—the Cantonese occupy double-crop land, and Hakka occupy single-crop land. This needs much further study. I have shown that the calico-curtained hat worn by Sai Kung village women is useful for working under the summer sun. However, in Sai Kung this hat does not distinguish Hakka from Cantonese village women. In fact, the stylistic aspects of the hat and the decorated straps which village women weave for their hat and waistbands do distinguish women who live on opposite sides of the Sai Kung peninsula and who use Tai Po and Sai Kung markets.

While I can easily agree with Freedman that what one Hakka does in Sai Kung may not be generalizable to what Hakka do everywhere, the more pertinent question for ethnic studies is: What constitutes the cultural identity of the Chinese groups such as the Hakka? Given my insistence on relating culture and behavior, it follows that for a widespread ethnic group such as the Hakka, different symbols and traditions are manifest at different levels of the social system. From my study of the Hakka in Sai Kung and elsewhere, it seems there are Hakka traits which tend to identify group membership in all parts of the "global village." Perhaps we should call these "global Hakka traits." They include obviously the language, and a legacy of poverty, political partisanship, and the subsistence role of women. Focusing on regional and village levels, we observe different configurations of Hakka traits. Use of the calico-curtained hat is relevant to Hakka women in the Waichow orbit which in border areas extends to their neighboring Cantonese sisters-in-law oriented toward Kwangchow. The subtle ways in which the hat is constructed and strapped on differ between lower-level interaction systems, such as between the Sai Kung and Tai Po markets in the New Territories. Within Sai Kung the hat does not distinguish Hakka from Cantonese, whereas different annual festivities do distinguish membership in the two communities.

Differences in ethnic cultures are not only manifest at different regional levels of integration but more specifically between different sexes and social strata within the same local system. Lower class groups and females tend to carry the group's culture through the personal mode of speech, dress, and domestic customs. Higher class groups and males tend to be more competent in the dominant or outgroup culture and tend to display their ethnic identity through the political mode.

The most dramatic example of ethnic stratification in Sai Kung is between two communities in the same speech group. The Hokkien-speaking boat people and the Hokkien-speaking Chaochow land people are sharply stratified in Sai Kung society. The Hokkien boat people lack political clout and opportunities for economic mobility, assimilation, and acculturation. They maintain a modicum of cultural integrity by elaborating traditional styles of ritual purity, dress, and dialect, which are well within their means of control. The boat people focus on these personal and domestic forms to enhance their self-esteem in a system which discriminates against them. Local land people look down on "Hoklo" boat people's displays as quaint and exotic.

On the opposite side are the Hokkien-speaking Chaochow. Many of them, especially their leaders, are highly acculturated in all forms of personal expression. The Chaochow are nonetheless "ethnic." Their ethnic displays involve large-scale activities organized by the men during the feast of Tin Hau and the deliverance of the Hungry Ghosts which advertise Chaochow prosperity and charity. By comparison with the more personal, exotic displays of the boat people, the Chaochow seem more psychologically superficial and politically expedient. Hence, the political organizations and cultural expressions of ethnic groups in the same general language group and in the same local system may have very different modes of expression. Each group's display is divisive and integrative; each display articulates the group's interests in and play for position in a particular social system.

An ethnic group is not identified everywhere by the same cultural configuration or mode of symbolic expression. It is defined rather by its role in a particular social system. It is a product of political economic adaptation coupled with the need to express its reason for being through a selected set of symbols. In the Chinese case, the selected symbols may be part of the larger pool of Chinese traits.

THE ROLE OF SOCIAL ORGANIZATION

Related to the different modes of cultural expression are the different *degrees* of ethnic group organization. In view of my data I do not agree with Freedman's contention (1966:94) that there has been no "consistent pattern in which being Hakka or Punti has been a basis for social organization" in the New Territories. When one simply looks beyond the lineage-village one is struck by the incongruity of Freedman's statement. In fact, Freedman had some second thoughts on the kind of order which lay beyond the lineage-village as expressed in his next phrase: ". . . although one might argue that ethnic solidarity, by being one of several bases of extra-village organization . . . contributed to that very complexity of social ties which made it possible for some sort of order to be maintained in a part of China that one might have superficially supposed was well on the road to anarchy" (1966:94). The difference between Freedman's conclusion and my own is focal—Freedman focused on localized institutional continuity and I focus on the regional process of social grouping. I view the study of social organization as the study of how people use their social identities to create and to cope with changing conditions. The use of ethnic identities among Sai Kung folk is a matter of degree, subject to situation and change. We see that ethnicity constitutes one means by which the Chinese organize with great flexibility —rather than perfect consistency—their group interests in both the rural and the urbanizing contexts of Sai Kung society.

Ethnic groups are like other social groups. They range from named categories lacking organizational boundaries and functional utility to communities with more intensive interpersonal affiliations, to corporations which have highly specified long-term memberships actively committed to political and economic goals. From one end of the organizational spectrum to the other, ethnic identity ranges from a purely personal matter to matters of jural authority. The continuum of ethnic group consistency may be analyzed in terms of the following variables: (1) categorization, (2) interpersonal affiliation, (3) occupation, (4) incorporation, and (5) government regulation.

The process of categorizing and naming ethnic groups is primary. The actual process of categorization itself may involve different epistemologies when the groups are as different as Chinese and Westerners. According to Joseph Needham (1956, II:243) Chinese categories are relational; Western categories are substantive. However, I have restricted my study to the Chinese community in which there are no differences in epistemology, world views, or basic values. Among the Chinese, surname (and genealogical connection), language (and dialect), native place, and occupation constitute traditional criteria for categorizing humans and for structuring interaction.

These categories are used to structure interpersonal relations for affective and practical purposes. At the hamlet and village levels, agnatic relationships proved useful to the original Cantonese and Hakka settlers. Whereas at the market-town level, people tend to affiliate on the basis of speech, native place, and occupational niche. The more these criteria overlap—for example, where speech and occupational boundaries coextend—the stronger is the visible organizational basis for ingroup affiliation and outgroup discrimination. Where there is some such unspecifiable degree of overlap we may consider such groupings ethnic communities. The boundary of an ethnic community is fluid and ambiguous, though not situational *in extremis;* leadership is informal; and the community's culture (technology, dress, dialect, ceremony, rhetoric, and so on) is more or less apprehended in the public domain. In the preceeding chapters I have described a number of ethnic communities, the boundaries of which intersect or combine to form higher-order communities.

Under conditions which vary with each case, a portion of an ethnic community may incorporate and form what is called a "voluntary association" or syndicate. Such corporate groups provide their members access to particular political and economic resources managed by formally selected leaders. Membership is exclusive; and compared to membership in the ethnic community, there is much less ambiguity of boundaries and very little room for the situational manipulation of a member's identity in other local settings. This distinction may also hold for different classes of membership within the syndicate as suggested in chapter 7. Corporate officers have little or no room for play in their ethnic identities while nonofficeholders may enjoy somewhat greater scope in their repertoire of ethnic identities.

The ethnic association does not, and by definition cannot, include every member of the surrounding ethnic community, although the association often presumes to speak for the larger community. It is altogether possible, and perhaps inevitable, that the boundaries around larger ethnic communities may be dissolved through acculturation and assimilation while the ethnic associations maintain their corporate lives. In fact, ethnic associations may be created in the midst of a community dissolving through acculturation and assimilation. The ostensible goal of an immigrant association, such as the Chaochow Association in Sai Kung, is to cushion newcomers against the strange and often hostile host society. The paradox is that as the immigrants attempt to fit into the host society they tend to operate within their own ethnic enclaves. This paradox is described by Oscar Handlin (1952:185) for the immigrant associations of nineteenth-century America. However, there is a more profound paradox, which I prefer to think of in terms of a dialectical process. As members of an ethnic group become more incorporated, the criteria of ethnic competence become more utilitarian in the political and economic sense and less expressive in the personal, psychological, or cultural sense. Increasing corporate ethnicity may spur cultural cosmopolitanism.

Further demonstration of this phenomenon comes from Maurice Freedman's (1958:137) study of Chinese lineages. Where the agnatic lineage increased its corporate character in its stand against the state, agnatic principles of recruitment had to be pushed aside, and the agnatic character of the lineage diminished. Perhaps there is a general principle of social organization at work here: Roughly stated, as a kinship or ethnic grouping becomes more corporate and more successful, its cultural charter is attenuated.

The idea that corporate ethnicity is associated with cultural cosmopolitanism is poignantly true for the ethnic group's leadership. On the one hand, ethnic leaders must be able to inspire collective identification and action through the use of native symbols while, on the other hand, they must be able to communicate the group's interests to the larger society. In stratified societies, therefore, successful ethnic group leaders are often acculturated, cosmopolitan, and well-to-do persons. They are able to operate in their own ethnic camp as well as in other, especially dominant, camps. In fact, ethnic group leaders often promote their own integration into the mainstream political economy by organizing their ethnic cohort. Some may find it to their personal advantage to keep their ethnic cohort unacculturated and unassimilated.

In Sai Kung a crucial measure of ethnic competence is language ability. The most successful ethnic group leaders are multilingual men. Chan Yat-Kuan, the leader of Sai Kung between 1960 and 1967, is among the most illustrative. While strongly affiliating with local Hakka in speech and custom, he was, in fact, Cantonese. His Cantonese facilitated his successful management of Hakka interests in the larger Hong Kong arena. The case of Chan's successor illustrates the proposition that the native leader is not necessarily more competent to represent his ethnic group than the nonnative. Chin Fuk-Loi was a local Hakka villager who lacked the urbane Cantonese styles of his predecessor. Chin seemed to compensate this lack by overidentifying with outside government and immigrant interests. Chin failed to uphold important local customs. Also, he coped with the flood of immigrants in new ways which accommodated their ethnic group interests. He was the first, and to this day the only, chairman of the Rural Committee to be voted out of office by the local people.

Other studies have demonstrated the link between ethnic group leadership and bilingual competence. In his study of Chinese leadership in Thailand, G. William Skinner (1958:93) found that the one characteristic common to the most influential Chinese leaders was their "Thailand orientation." According to Skinner, the most influential leaders speak good or adequate Thai, while many of the least influential leaders speak little or no Thai: "This relationship is all the more striking when it is realized that the community within which the leaders are leaders is defined by its Chineseness" (1958:93). Skinner goes on to suggest that the top leaders function as the community representatives vis-à-vis the Thai government so that speaking adequate Thai is almost a prerequisite of high influence. Skinner's findings lend further support to my contention that, in complex societies, the acculturation of the native elite facilitates their efforts to organize ethnic groups. Or more abstractly, cosmopolitanism at one level facilitates "retribalization" at another level. And "retribalization" represents an attempt to participate and integrate into the mainstream of a changing society. This point is extremely relevant to our understanding of the ancient historical development of South China and Vietnam as well as to the recent history of the relationship of blacks and whites in the United States.

The process of incorporation involves ultimate political sanctions, which, in stratified societies, reside in the central political agencies (Smith, 1966). In Hong Kong the central political agency is a colonial government. The relationship between the colonial government and Sai Kung society is crucial in understanding the existence and form of local social organization and ethnic grouping. In a study of the Chinese in Cambodia, W. E. Willmott (1970) concluded that differences in colonial regime determined differences in the structure of Chinese communities. The Chinese communities in French Indochina were ruled indirectly, and, consequently they did not segment to the extent they did under British colonial rule. The British follow a laissez faire approach which does not interfere with native customs and which allows a rather free expression of native social organization so long as it serves to maintain the colonial status quo. The Hong Kong government exercises the authority to legalize and regulate associations through a system of registration.

The government does not attempt to control associations which own miniscule amounts of property and which have periodical corporate lives. For example, firecracker associations have an annual renewable membership, and they are regulated and constrained by local Kaifong leaders and public opinion. The Hokkien boat people represent this level of corporate ethnicity. More permanent groups, which own larger assets, are regulated by the system of government registration. This system requires government and police surveillance of association leaders, constitutional charters, and group activities, none of which may in any way threaten the security or authority of the colonial regime. This level of incorporation includes the Chamber of Commerce, the Fresh Fishdealers, the Chaochow Association, the Kuomintang's Sun Yat-Sen Association, and the network of procommunist associations.

Finally, an association may acquire legal standing under Hong Kong law as a company with limited liability. Disputes over control of its assets are adjudicable in a court of law. The Sai Kung Federation of Fishermen's Cooperatives and the Sai Kung Native Fellowship Association are legally incorporated. I suspect this is because their assets are immense, and at least in the latter case, the organizational membership is heterogeneous and the infighting is correspondingly intense. Since the late 1960s the Fellowship Association's assets include access to commercial land and public office; and its membership includes upwardly mobile Hakka, Cantonese, boat people, and others.

While the Hong Kong government's approach to native social organization can be characterized as comparatively laissez faire, I have shown how its exercise of authority directly influences the organization of ethnicity in Sai Kung.

With the end of the Japanese occupation and the rise of the People's Republic of China, the colonial government felt a need for tightened security. The need to control international boundaries and to stimulate production of fresh food led to the organization of the boat people and the local land communities. The same need, which became critical in the 1967 riots, prompted the government's support for the Sai Kung Native Fellowship Association which it had earlier spurned. The beleaguered government accepted support from wherever it could get it. The government drew locals and immigrants into a Public Security Association. This association was controlled at the local level by the leaders of the Sai Kung Native Association. The Native Association became the basis for reconstituting the Rural Committee which had been dissolved by the radicals. In this way local Hakka maintained their political dominion of Sai Kung in keeping with the colonial policy of native hegemony. However, the Chaochow, by demonstrating their support for the loyal Hakka, were able to help reconstitute the Chamber of Commerce. This also gave formal recognition to the fact that the Chaochow, as a group, constitute a dominant power in the market economy.

Thus, while the central government exercises the authority to determine the basic shape of local communities as Willmott suggests, the forces within local communities may be active also in manipulating and influencing government actions, even where, as in Hong Kong, government is not democratically constituted.

Throughout my study of ethnic groups in general and Chinese ethnic groups in particular, I have been most impressed with the manifold forms which they take not only in different social systems but within the same system. I have been equally impressed with the labile nature of ethnic grouping, that is, with that aspect of people's identity which was once assumed to be fixed and rooted in a racial or cultural mode of existence. However, some of the newest sociological views which tend to dismiss the cultural dimension as epiphenomena are still inadequate for understanding the experience of ethnic identification much less for explaining the *process* of ethnic grouping. Ethnic groups are social groups which are created by people to forge relationships or to cope with problems of political and economic concern. The act of creation involves the use of symbols to motivate and express interpersonal and group affiliation. The Chinese, as do other European and Middle Eastern ethnic groups, orient toward distinct (symbolic) origins as a means of enhancing group solidarity, while each draws its tools and symbolic motifs from its respective pool. The objective cultural cleavages among groups have little or nothing to do with the subjective organization of ethnic prejudice, discrimination, and conflict. Often an ethnic group organizes itself to promote the success, or to protect the position, of its members in the mainstream society. In some cases, the more successful the ethnic group becomes, the more acculturated its members become. Similarly, ethnic group leaders are often successful group leaders to the degree they are themselves acculturated to the larger society or to dominant outgroups.

Glossary of Chinese Words

Ch'aoyang 潮陽
ch'i 契
chia tz'u t'ang 家祠堂
Chiehshih 碣石
Chiehyang 揭陽
Ch'in ch'i 親戚
ch'u t'ou 出頭
chuk(H) 粥
feng shui 風水
fuk(H)(C) 福
gaai-seuhng-yahn(C) 街上人
Hakka-lao(H) 客家佬
Hakka-ma(H) 客家媽/嬤
Haifeng 海豐
Hengkang 橫崗
Hoklo-ma(C) 學佬媽/嬤
hsiang 鄉
hsiang hsia 鄉下
hsiang huo 香火
Hsinan 新安
Hsinan hsien chih 新安縣志
hsü ch'ang 墟塲
hua p'ao hui 花炮會
-ka(H)(C) 家
kan ch'ing 感情
ka-siu-lao(H) 家滫佬

K'unkang 坤崗
-lao(H) 佬
Liu yüeh 六約
-lo(C) 佬
Lufeng 陸豐
Min 閩
Minchia 民家
Nant'ou 南頭
Ngai he chin shi Hakka(H) 吾係眞是
    客家
pai shen 拜神
Paishih 白石
pai t'ien 拜天
Paiyüeh 百越
Paoan (old name for Hsinan) 寶安
pao chia 保甲
P'inghai 平海
Puchao 布隔
P'uning 普寧
Punti 本地
sa(H) 蛇
sa-lao(H) 蛇佬
sa-ma(H) 蛇媽/嬤
sa-va(H) 蛇話
seui-seuhng-yahn(C) 水上人
Shunte 順德

ta chiao 打醮
Tan 蛋
Tanka-ma(H) 蛋家媽/嬤
Tanka-tsai(H) 蛋家仔
Tenghai 澄海
T'ien chi chieh 天機節
T'ien chieh 田節
ti fang 地方
tou chung 斗種
-tsai(H) 仔
tso sheng li 作生利

tsu 族
tsuen 村
Tungkuan 東莞
vo-chhon-pan(H) 禾串粄
wai-lai-jen 外來人
Wuhua 五華
Yao 猺
Yent'ien 鹽田
Yüeh (kingdom) 越
yüeh (alliance) 約

References Cited

Aijmer, Göran
  1967   Expansion and extension in Hakka society. *Journal of the Hong Kong Branch of the Royal Asiatic Society* 7:42–79.
Anderson, Eugene N., Jr.
  1967   Prejudice and ethnic stereotypes in rural Hong Kong. *Kroeber Anthropological Society Papers* 37:90–107. Berkeley, California.
  1970   *The Floating World of Castle Peak Bay.* Anthropological studies number 4. Washington, D.C.: American Anthropological Association.
  1972   *Essays on South China's Boat People.* Asian folklore and social life monographs Volume 29. Taipei: Orient Cultural Service.
Alley, Otis E.
  1943   The M, N, types of Chinese from Canton. *American Journal of Physical Anthropology* 1:301–304.
Armstrong, R. Warwick
  1977   Nasopharyngeal Carcinoma: Opportunities for International Collaborative Research in Malaysia and Hawaii. *National Cancer Institute Monograph No. 47:*135–141.
Armstrong, R. W., M. Kutty, and S. K. Dharmalingam
  1974   Incidence of nasopharyngeal carcinoma in Malaysia, with special reference to the state of Selangor. *British Journal of Cancer* 30 (86):86–94.
Armstrong, R. W., M. K. Kutty, and M. J. Armstrong
  1978   Self-specific environments associated with nasopharyngeal carcinoma in Selangor, Malaysia. *Social Science and Medicine* 12D:149–156.

Baker, Hugh
1968   *A Chinese Lineage Village: Sheung Shui.* Stanford: Stanford University Press.

Balfour, S. F.
1970   Hong Kong before the British. *Journal of the Hong Kong Branch of the Royal Asiatic Society* 10:134–179.

Barnett, K. M. A.
1957   The Peoples of the New Territories. *The Hong Kong Business Symposium* J. M. Braga (ed.). Hong Kong, *South China Morning Post,* pp. 261–265.

Barth, Fredrik
1969   Introduction. *Ethnic Groups and Boundaries* F. Barth (ed.) Boston: Little, Brown, pp. 9–38.

Bayard, Donn
1975   North China, South China, South East Asia, or Simply "Far East?" *Journal of the Hong Kong Archeological Society* 6:71–79.

Berreman, Gerald D.
1972   Social categories and social interaction in urban India. *American Anthropologist* 74 (3):567–586.

Blake, C. Fred
1978   Death and abuse in marriage laments: the curse of Chinese brides. *Asian Folklore Studies* 37 (1):13–33.
1979   The feelings of Chinese daughters toward their mothers as revealed in marriage laments. *Folklore* 90 (1):91–97.
n.d.   Racial slurs and ethnic humor: the rhetoric of race relations in Hawaii (manuscript).

Bracey, Dorothy Heid
1967   The effects of emigration on a Hakka village. Ph.D. dissertation, Department of Anthropology, Harvard University.

Burkhardt, V. R.
1955   *Chinese Creeds and Customs* Volume 2. Hong Kong: *The South China Morning Post.*

Campbell, George
1912   Origin and migration of the Hakkas. *The Chinese Recorder* 43:473–480.

Catron, Gary Wayne
1971   China and Hong Kong, 1845–1967. Ph.D. dissertation, Department of Government and Political Science, Harvard University.

Chin, Fan
1947   Nü chung tui, Li Yu-Chen. *Yeh Huo Chi* (Wild fire annals) Hong Kong: Yin shua kung yeh he tso she, pp. 41–47.

Chou, Shu-Jen (Lu Hsun)
1941   The story of hair. *Ah Q and Others, Selected Stories of Lusin.*

Wang Chi-Chen (trans.). New York: Columbia University Press, pp. 59-64.

Chu, T'ung-Tsu
1965   *Law and Society in Traditional China.* The Hague: Mouton and Company (originally, 1961).

Ch'ung Cheng Editorial Staff
1971   Hsiang Kang Ch'ung Cheng Tsung Hui hui shih (History of Hong Kong Hakka Association). *Hsiang Kang Ch'ung Cheng Tsung Hui chin hsi ta ch'ing chi nien t'e k'an,* Hong Kong: Chin ch'iang yin wu kung so, pp. (1-21).

Cohen, Abner
1974   Introduction: the lesson of ethnicity. *Urban Ethnicity.* A. Cohen (ed.). A.S.A. monograph number 12. London: Tavistock, pp. 1-36.
1976   *Two-Dimensional Man: An Essay on the Anthropology of Power and Symbolism in Complex Society.* Berkeley and Los Angeles: University of California Press.

Cohen, Myron L.
1968   The Hakka or "guest people": dialect as a sociocultural variable in southeastern China. *Ethnohistory* 15 (3):237-292.
1976   *House United, House Divided: The Chinese Family in Taiwan.* New York: Columbia University Press.

Creel, Herrlee Glessner
1970   *The Origins of Statecraft in China, Volume 1: The Western Chou Empire.* Chicago: University of Chicago Press.

Crissman, Lawrence
1967   The segmentary structure of urban overseas Chinese communities. *Man* 2 (2):185-204.

Davis, S. G. (ed.)
1964   *Land Use Problems in Hong Kong.* Hong Kong: University of Hong Kong Press.

D'Estrey, Comte Meyners
1890   Les Hakkas et les Hoklo, l'autonomie des villages en Chine. *Revue de Geographie* 27:29-35, 95-103.

Eberhard, Wolfram
1965   Chinese regional stereotypes. *Asian Survey* 5 (12):596-608.
1968   *The Local Cultures of South and East China.* Leiden: E. J. Brill.

Egerod, Sorod
1967   Dialectology. *Current Trends in Linguistics, Volume II: Linguistics in East Asia and South East Asia* T. A. Soebeok (ed.), The Hague: Mouton 91-129.

Fei, Hsiao-Tung
1947   *Peasant Life in China: A Field Study of Country Life in the Yantze Valley.* London: Kegan Paul, Trench, Trubner.

Fitzgerald, C. P.
 1941   *The Tower of Five Glories: A Study of the Min Chia of Ta Li
           Yunnam*. London: The Cresset Press.
Forrest, Robert Andrew Dermod
 1965   *The Chinese Language*. London: Faber and Faber (originally,
           1948).
Freedman, Maurice
 1957   *Chinese Family and Marriage in Singapore*. London: Her
           Majesty's Stationary Office.
 1958   *Lineage Organization in Southeastern China*. London School of
           Economics Monographs on Social Anthropology, number 18.
           New York: Humanities Press.
 1966   *Chinese Lineage and Society: Fukien and Kwangtung*. New
           York: Humanities Press.
 1970   Ritual aspects of Chinese kinship and marriage. *Family and
           Kinship in Chinese Society* M. Freedman (ed.). Stanford: Stan-
           ford University Press, pp. 163–187.
Greenberg, Joseph
 1953   Historical linguistics and unwritten languages. *Anthropology
           Today* A. L. Kroeber (ed.). Chicago: University of Chicago
           Press, pp. 265–286.
Grimmo, A.
 1961   A survey of blood groups in Hong Kong Chinese of Cantonese
           origin. *Oceania* 31:222–226.
Grimmo, A. and Lee Shun-Keung
 1964   Further blood groups of Hong Kong Chinese of Cantonese
           origin. *Oceania* 34:234–236.
Han, Ch'ao
 1971   *Ch'ao chou feng wu* (Chaochow customs) Hong Kong: Shanghai
           shu chu.
Han, Su-Yin
 1972   *The Crippled Tree*. New York: Bantam Books (originally, 1965).
Handlin, Oscar
 1952   *The Uprooted*. Boston: Little, Brown and Company.
Harris, Marvin
 1975   *Cows, Pigs, Wars and Witches: The Riddles of Culture*. Vintage
           Books: New York (originally, 1974).
Hashimoto, Mantaro J.
 1973   *The Hakka Dialect: A Linguistic Study of its Phonology, Syntax
           and Lexicon*. London: Cambridge University Press.
Hashimoto, Oi-Kan
 1972   *Studies in Yue Dialects 1: Phonology of Cantonese*. London:
           Cambridge University Press.
Hayes, James
 1967   Chinese temple in the local setting. *Some Traditional Chinese*

Ideas and Conceptions in Hong Kong Social Life Today. M. Topley (ed.). Hong Kong: The Hong Kong Branch of the Royal Asiatic Society, pp. 86–98.

1977   *The Hong Kong Region 1850–1911: Institutions and Leadership in Town and Countryside.* Hamden, Connecticut: Archon Books.

Ho, H. C.
1967   Nasopharyngeal carcinoma in Hong Kong. *Union Internationale Contre le Cancer Monograph Series I.* Copenhagen: Munksgaard: 58–63.

Hong Kong Government (HKG)
1956a   *Hong Kong Annual Report 1955.* Hong Kong: Government Printer.

1956b   *Department of Agriculture, Fisheries and Forestry Annual Departmental Report.* Hong Kong: Government Printer.

1962   *Report on the 1961 Census by K. M. A. Barnett.* Department of Census and Statistics. Hong Kong: Government Printer.

1966   *Department of Agriculture, Fisheries and Forestry Annual Departmental Report.* Hong Kong: Government Printer.

1969   *A Gazetteer of Place Names in Hong Kong, Kowloon and the New Territories.* Hong Kong: Government Printer.

1972   *Hong Kong Population and Housing Census, 1971* Department of Census and Statistics. Hong Kong: Government Printer.

Hsieh, T'ing-Yu
1929   Origins and migrations of the Hakkas. *The Chinese Social and Political Science Review* 13 (220):208–228.

Hsinan Hsien Chih (Paoan county gazetteer)
1819   Introductory chuan. Original copy at the University of Hong Kong (21).

Hsu, Francis L. K.
1967   *Under the Ancestor's Shadow.* Garden City, New York: Doubleday and Company (originally, 1948).

Huang, Parker Po-Fei
1970   *Cantonese Dictionary.* New Haven: Yale University Press.

Huang, Wei
1957   Shui shang chü min. *Chu chiang feng wu* (Pearl River customs). Hong Kong: Shang hai shu chü, pp. 37–40.

Hurlbut, Floy
1939   *The Fukienese: A Study in Human Geography.* Muncie, Indiana: published by the author.

Isaacs, Harold R.
1968   *The Tragedy of the Chinese Revolution.* New York: Antheneum (originally, 1938).

Johnson, Elizabeth L.
1975   Women and childbearing in Kwan Mun Hau village: a study of

social change. *Women in Chinese Society* M. Wolf and R. Witke (eds.). Stanford: Stanford University Press, pp. 215–242.

1976   "Patterned Bands" in the New Territories of Hong Kong. *Journal of the Hong Kong Branch of the Royal Asiatic Society* 16:81–91.

Johnson, Graham Edwin
1971   Natives, migrants and voluntary associations in a colonial Chinese setting. Ph.D. dissertation, Cornell University.

Koehn, Alfred
1944   *Classic of Filial Piety*. Peking: Fu Jen University Press.

Kulp, Daniel Harrison II
1966   *Country Life in South China: The Sociology of Familism*. Taipei: Ch'eng-wen Publishing Company (originally, 1925, Columbia University Press).

Lamley, Harry J.
1977   *Hsieh-Tou:* The pathology of violence in southeastern China. *Ch'ing-shih wen-t'i* 3 (7):1–39.

Lattimore, Owen
1962   *Inner Asian Frontiers of China*. Boston: Beacon Press (originally, 1940).

Leach, Edmund R.
1965   *Political Systems of Highland Burma*. Boston: Beacon Press (originally, 1954).

Lebar, Frank M., Gerald C. Hickey, and John K. Musgrave
1964   *Ethnic Groups of Mainland Southeast Asia*. New Haven, Connecticut: Human Relations Area Files Press.

Lee, Rose Hum
1960   *The Chinese in the United States of America*. Hong Kong: Hong Kong University Press.

Lehman, F. K.
1967   Ethnic categories in Burma and the theory of social systems. *Southeast Asian Tribes, Minorities, Nations*. Volume II Peter Kunstadter (ed.). Princeton: Princeton University Press, pp. 93–124.

Li Chin-Fa
1970   *Ling tung luan ko* (Love songs of East Kwangtung). Taipei: Orient Culture Service (originally, 1926 Peking: Peking University and Chinese Association for Folklore).

Liu, Chungshee H.
1937   A tentative classification of races of China. *Zeitschrift fur Rassenkunde* 6 (2):129–150. Stuttgart.

Lo, Hsiang-Lin
1933   *K'e chia yen chiu tao lun* (Introduction to the study of the Hakkas). Hsingning, Kwangtung, China: Shi Shan Library.

1955   *Pai yüeh yuan liu yu wen hua* (Yüeh origins and culture). Hong Kong: Chung Hua Ts'ung hsu.

1965   *K'e chia shih liao hui p'ien* (Historical sources for the study of the Hakkas). Hong Kong: Institute of Chinese Culture, Ling Nam Printing Company.

Lo, Wan

1965   Communal strife in mid-nineteenth century Kwangtung. *Papers on China* Harvard University East Asian Research Center. 19: 85–119.

Loewen, James

1971   *The Mississippi Chinese: Between Black and White.* Cambridge: Harvard University Press.

MacIver, D.

1926   *A Chinese-English Dictionary Hakka-Dialect* (republished by Ku-T'ing Book Store, Taipei, Taiwan, 1970).

Mendel, Douglas Heusted

1970   *The Politics of Formosan Nationalism.* Berkeley and Los Angeles: University of California Press.

Morgan, W. P.

1960   *Triad Societies in Hong Kong.* Hong Kong Government Press.

Morse, H. B.

1932   *The Guilds of China.* New York: Russel and Russel.

Myrdal, Jan

1966   *Report from a Chinese Village.* New York: Signet.

Nakagawa, Manabu

1975   Studies on the Hakkas: reconsidered. *The Developing Economies* 13 (2):208–223 [Tokyo].

Needham, Joseph

1956   *Science and Civilization in China* Volume II. London: Cambridge University Press.

Ng, P. Y. L.

1961   The 1819 edition of the *Hsin-an Hsien-chih,* a critical examination with translation and notes. M.A. thesis, University of Hong Kong.

Oehler, Wilhelm

1922   Christian work among the Hakka. *The Christian Occupation of China* Milton T. Stauffer (ed.). Shanghai: China Continuation Committee.

Osgood, Cornelius

1975   *The Chinese: A Study of a Hong Kong Community.* Tucson: The University of Arizona Press.

Pasternak, Burton

1972   *Kinship and Community in Two Chinese Villages.* Stanford: Stanford University Press.

Piton, Charles
1870   The Hia-K'ah in the Chekiang Province and the Hakka in the Canton Province. *The Chinese Recorder* 2:218–220.
1873   On the origin and history of the Hakkas. *The China Review* 2:160–164, 222–318.
Potter, Jack M.
1968   *Capitalism and the Chinese peasant: social and economic change in a Hong Kong village.* Berkeley and Los Angeles: University of California Press.
Pratt, Jean A.
1960   Emigration and unilineal descent groups: a study of marriage in a Hakka village in the New Territories, Hong Kong. *The Eastern Anthropologist* 13 (4):147–158.
Rock, Joseph F.
1947   *The Ancient Na-Khi Kingdom of Southwest China.* Cambridge: Harvard University Press.
Ryan, Thomas F.
1959   *The Story of a Hundred Years: The Pontifical Institute of Foreign Missions in Hong Kong, 1858-1958.* Hong Kong: Catholic Truth Society.
Saso, Michael R.
1972   *Taoism and the Rite of Cosmic Renewal.* Washington State University Press.
Schafer, Edward H.
1967   *The Vermillion Bird: T'ang Images of the South.* Berkeley and Los Angeles: University of California Press.
Schurman, Franz
1973   *Ideology and Organization in Communist China,* 2nd Edition. Berkeley and Los Angeles: University of California Press (originally, 1968).
Shanmugartnam, K.
1971   Studies on the etiology of nasopharyngeal cancer. *International Review of Experimental Pathology* 10:362–414. New York: Academic Press.
1973   Cancer in Singapore—ethnic and dialect group variations in cancer incidence. *Singapore Medical Journal* 14 (2):69–81.
Shanmugartnam, K., and C. Y. Tye
1970   A study of nasopharyngeal cancer among Singapore Chinese, with special reference to migrant status and specific community (dialect group). *Journal of Chronic Diseases* 23 (5–6):433–441.
Shem, Pak, and R. W. Armstrong
1977   Survivorship among patients with nasopharyngeal carcinoma in Hawaii. *Hawaii Medical Journal* 36 (11):348–350.
Shirokogoroff, S. M.
1925   *Anthropology of Eastern China and Kwangtung Province.* The

North China Branch of the Royal Asiatic Society, Shanghai: The Commercial Press.

Simmons, R. T., J. J. Graydson, and N. M. Semple
1950   The A$_1$-A$_2$ B-O, M-N and Rh blood groups in southern Chinese: Hak-kas, Cantonese and Hokkiens. *Medical Journal of Australia* 2 (26):917-921.

Skinner, G. William
1958   *Leadership and Power in the Chinese Community of Thailand.* Ithaca, New York: Cornell University Press.
1964   Marketing and social structure in rural China, part one. *Journal of Asian Studies* 24 (1):3-43.
1965   Marketing and social structure in rural China, part two. *Journal of Asian Studies* 24 (2):195-228.

Smith, M. G.
1966   A structural approach to comparative politics. *Varieties of Political Theory* David Easton (ed.). New Jersey, Englewood Cliffs: Prentice-Hall, pp. 113-128.

Sessional Papers (SP)
Papers laid before the Legislative Council of Hong Kong in the years of 1905, 1910, 1912, 1914, 1915, 1917, 1920. Hong Kong: The Government Printer. (Held at the Library of the Colonial Secretariat, Hong Kong.)

Sparks, Douglas W.
1976   Interethnic interaction—a matter of definition in a housing estate in Hong Kong. *Journal of the Hong Kong Branch of the Royal Asiatic Society* 16:55-80.

Srinivas, M. N.
1971   *Social Change in Modern India.* Berkeley and Los Angeles: University of California Press.

Tobias Stephen F.
1977   Buddhism, belonging, and detachment—some paradoxes of Chinese ethnicity in Thailand. *Journal of Asian Studies* 36 (2):303-326.

Topley, Marjorie
1964   Capital, saving and credit among indigenous rice farmers and immigrant vegetable farmers in Hong Kong's New Territories. *Capital, Saving and Credit in Peasant Societies,* Raymond Firth and B. S. Yamey (eds.). Chicago: Aldine, pp. 157-186.

Ts'ai, H. S., and C. H. Yen
1950   *Kantoshō Kakkazoku no tēhatsu mōka ni tsuite.* (German title: *Ueber den Kopfaar wirbel bei den Chinesen vom Hakka-stamm in der Kwangtung Provinz.*) *Bulletin of Anatomy* 10:33-38, National Taiwan University Library, Taipei (in Japanese, filed under German title).

Vaillant, L.
1920   Contribution a letude anthropologique des Chinois Hak-ka de la
          province de Moncay (Tonking). *L'Anthropologie* 30:83–105.
Vogel, Ezra F.
1969   *Canton Under Communism: Programs and Politics in a
          Provincial Capital 1949–1968.* Cambridge: Harvard University
          Press.
Volonteri, M. G. R.
1866   Map of the San On District. (Reproduced from the copy held in
          The Braga Collection of the National Library of Australia,
          Canberra. Milton G. Simons, Director.)
Ward, Barbara E.
1955   A Hong Kong fishing village. *Journal of Oriental Studies* 1:195–
          214.
1959   Floating villages: Chinese fishermen in Hong Kong. *Man*
          59:44–45.
1963   Structure and environment: the fishermen of South China.
          Typescript prepared for the seminar on Problems of Micro-
          organization in Chinese Society. Castle Harbor Hotel, Bermuda
          (January 19–20, 1963).
1965   Varieties of the conscious model: the fishermen of South China.
          The Relevance of Models for Social Anthropology A.S.A.
          monograph number 1, Michael Banton (ed.). New York:
          Frederick A. Praeger, pp. 113–138.
1967   Chinese fishermen in Hong Kong: their post-peasant economy.
          Social Organization: Essays Presented to Raymond Firth,
          Maurice Freedman (ed.). Chicago: Aldine, pp. 271–288.
Watson, James L.
1975   *Emigration and the Chinese Lineage: The Mans in Hong Kong
          and London.* Berkeley and Los Angeles: University of California
          Press.
Weber, Max
1958   *The Protestant Ethic and The Spirit of Capitalism.* Talcott
          Parsons (trans.). New York: Scribner's (original English edition,
          1930).
1968   *The Religion of China.* Hans Gerth (trans.). New York: The Free
          Press (original English edition, 1951).
Wiens, Herold J.
1967   *Han Chinese Expansion in South China.* Yale University: The
          Shoe String Press.
Willmott, W. E.
1970   *The Political Structure of the Chinese Community in Cambodia.*
          London School of Economics monographs on social an-
          thropology number 42. University of London: The Athlone
          Press.

Wolf, Margery
1975   Women and suicide in Taiwan. *Women in Chinese Society.* Wolf and Witke (eds.). Stanford: Stanford University Press, pp. 111–141.

Wolf, Margery and Roxane Witke
1975   Introduction. *Women in Chinese Society.* Wolf and Witke (eds.). Stanford: Stanford University Press, pp. 1–11.

Woo, Ju-Kang
1947   Blood grouping of four aboriginal tribes in Kweichou Province, China. *American Journal of Physical Anthropology* 5:429–433.

Whyte, G. Duncan
1911   Notes on the height and weight of the Hoklo people of the Kwangtung Province, South China. *Journal of the Royal Anthropological Institute of Great Britain and Ireland* 41:278–300.

Yamashita, Seiichi
1939   *Kantokei Taiwanjin ni okeru ekishu to nanteidei to ni tsuite.* (German title: *Ueber den achselgeruch und das Klebrige ohrenschmalz bei den Hakka in Formosa.*) *The Journal of the Anthropological Society of Nippon* 54 (10):18–20. University of Tokyo (in Japanese, with German title and abstract).

Yang, C. K.
1965   *Chinese Communist Society: The Family and the Village.* 2 volumes. Cambridge, Massachusetts: The M.I.T. Press (originally, 1959).

Yang, Paul S. J.
1967   Elements of Hakka Dialectology. *Monumenta Serica* 26:305–351.

Young, John Aubrey
1974   *Business and Sentiment in a Chinese Market Town.* Asian folklore and social life monographs Volume 60. Taipei: The Orient Cultural Service.

Zaborowski, M.
1879   Sur cinq cranes d'Hakkas et les origines Chinoises. *Bulletin de la Societe d'Anthropologie de Paris* 3 (2):557–578.

Index

Acculturation: of Cantonese villagers, 66; of Chaochow people, 73, 146; and ethnic boundaries, 3, 153; of ethnic group leaders, 155; of immigrants, 12

Affinal relations: between ethnic communities, 62–63, 69; in politicial factions, 127; within ethnic communities, 25, 26, 87. *See also* Marriage

Agnatic relations: as basis for village organization, 25, 153, 154; in political factions, 126–127; versus affinal relations, 127; versus ethnic relations, 128

Aijmer, Göran, 22, 25, 58, 115n1, 116n2

Ancestor halls: Cantonese, 23; Hakka, 25, 45n4, 115n1; in Sai Kung, comparison, 92–93

Ancestor rites: of Cantonese boat people, 93, 116n3; of Hokkien boat people, 82; of land people, 92–93

Ancestor tablets, 82, 92–94, 116n2

Anderson, Eugene, 2, 3, 26, 113

Associations, development and alignment of, 33. *See also* Better Living Cooperative; Chamber of Commerce; Chaochow Achievement Society; Chaochow Fellowship Association; Firecracker associations; Fish Marketing Organization; Fishermen's Credit Cooperative Society; Fresh Fish Merchant's Association; Kaifong Association; Native Fellowship Association; Public Security Advancement Association; Rural (Affairs) Committee; Self-Administration Association; Struggle Committee; Sun Yat-Sen Memorial Association; Tsung Tsin Association

Barbarian, 1, 4, 6n1, 12, 50, 62, 85, 87–88, 114. *See also* Chinese

Barth, Fredrik, 3, 149

Basel Mission, 61, 71

Berreman, Gerald, 4

Better Living (Credit) Cooperative, 36, 79

Boat people: ancestor rites of, 93; and Chinese Imperial government, 13, 17n6; and credit cooperatives, 36, 38; economic influence of, 13–14, 26, 70–71; economic stratification of, 38, 89n5, 75; educational level of, 46n5; ethnic differences among, 73–76; *feng shui* as irrelevant, 13, 17n5; and firecracker associations, 26, 94–95; income levels, 70; intermarriage with land people, 63, 68; origins of, 2, 67; and People's Republic of China, 38, 48n11; relations with Catholic Church, 79, 83; relations with land people, 2, 14, 25–26, 69, 83; in Rural Committee, 32, 71; self-image of, 2, 61, 68–71, 88; settlement in Sai Kung, 14, 23, 25–26, 35, 68–69; stereotypes of, 14, 67, 68–71; *ta chiao* of, 99; use of fictive kinship, 83; and wage labor, 14, 43, 55; women, 55. *See also* Cantonese boat people; Hokkien boat people; "Hoklo"; "Tanka"

Bracey, Dorothy, 56, 66

British Colonial Administration. *See*
Government of Hong Kong
Burkhardt, V. R., 2, 69, 98, 109, 110

Cantonese boat people: adornment of,
105, 107, 108–109; associations of,
36–38, 79, 83, 94–95; boats of, 74;
changing image of, 68–71; dialect versus
standard Cantonese, 113; movement
onto land, 14, 23, 36, 79, 86; religious
iconography of, 93, 116n3; in Sai Kung
market, 68, 71; stereotype of, 66–67;
women, 55, 105, 107. *See also* Boat
people; "Tanka"
Cantonese immigrants: families, case
studies, 119–124; in Sai Kung market,
38, 132, 140; settlement of, 71, 138;
women's dress, 105
Cantonese language: to conceal Hakka
identity, 51, 112; dialects of, 8, 17n3,
60; as lingua franca, 61, 71, 76, 104,
111; in Sai Kung schools, 66, 112, 113;
standards maintained, 111–112, 113,
114
Cantonese people, 1–2, 8; ancestor rites
of, 92; and Chaochow people, 85;
defined, 60, 88n2; derogatory names
for, used by Hakka, 62–63; and Hakka,
61, 62–63, 149; Heavenly Things Festival, 98; Ho Chung, *ta chiao* of, 103;
intermarriage of, 54, 63–66, 132; political faction in Ho Chung, 139–140; in
Sai Kung market, 39, 47n8, 118; in Sai
Kung Native Fellowship Association,
34; self-image of, 2, 88; settlement in
Sai Kung, 21, 22–24; similarities with
Hakka, 53–54, 60; villages of, compared to Hakka, 45n4; and Waichow
people, 87; women, 51, 98, 105
Caste mechanisms, 67
Catholic mission, 23, 79, 83, 131
Chamber of Commerce (of Sai Kung):
establishment of, 34, 78; government
regulation of, 156; immigrant interests
represented in, 34; and political factions, 130, 133, 141–142, 146
Chan Yat-Kuan (pseudonym), 121–124;
and Chin Fuk-Loi, 131–132, 154; and
Communists, 125; as leader, 34, 113,
121, 125–127, 128–129, 131, 139–140,
147n2, 154; resistance to colonial
government, 125, 126, 129
Chaochow Achievement Society, 139
Chaochow Association. *See* Chaochow
Fellowship Association

Chaochow Fellowship Association: as
benefactors, 102; and Chamber of
Commerce, 141–142; community festivals, sponsors of, 99–103, 114, 115;
establishment of, 134, 138–141; functions of, 113, 137, 142, 146, 153–154;
government control of, 156; politics,
participation in, 130, 140–141, 146,
147n3
Chaochow Native Place Association. *See*
Chaochow Fellowship Association
Chaochow people: affiliations in Kowloon, 87, 135, 138; business strategies
of, 136–138, 149; dialects of, 11, 114;
and Hokkien boat people, 76–77, 115,
151; local attitudes toward, 85–86,
86–87, 135, 143; number of, 89n4; in
Sai Kung market, 39, 40, 133, 142, 146,
156; self-image of, 72–73, 84–86, 88,
102, 139, 143; settlement in Sai Kung,
133–135; stereotypes of, 85–86, 102,
137–138; and Waichow people, 139,
145–146, 146n1; women, 105
Che Kung Temple, 46n8, 103. *See* Ho
Chung village
Chin Fuk-Loi (pseudonym), 126–128; and
Chan Yat-Kuan, 128–129, 131–132;
dependence on colonial government,
130–131; as leader of Hakka, 71,
130–131, 140–141, 147n2, 147n3,
154–155
China, People's Republic of: and boat
people, 13, 38; and changes in Sai Kung
society, 44, 48n11, 54, 131–132, 133,
138. *See also* Cultural Revolution
Chinese, criteria for identity, 2–3, 4, 5,
6n1, 7, 12–13, 91, 93, 116n1. *See also*
Barbarian
Ching Ming festival, 24, 97, 119
Chuk (rice gruel), as ethnic marker, 86
Ch'ung Cheng Association. *See* Tsung
Tsin Association
Chung Wo Tong, 31. *See also* Secret
society
Clothing. *See* Ethnic groups, dress of
Coastal settlement ban, 23, 45n3, 47n9
Cohen, Abner, 4
Cohen, Myron, 10, 50, 88n1
Communist elements: boat people's sup-
port of, 38, 79; bookstore, 41, 42; rela-
tive strength of, 144. *See also* Chan
Yat-Kuan; China; Cultural Revolution;
East-River Anti-Japanese Brigade; Pro-
communist organizations; Riots
Construction labor. *See* Wage labor, con-
struction

Cooperative societies, 35–36, 37, 55, 75, 84

Corporate ethnicity. *See* Ethnic groups, corporate groups of

Credit (financial): and boat people, 14, 36; and ethnic associations, 55, 85, 137; and firecracker associations, 95, 139; and local leaders, 120, 125, 134, 136, 142; and women, 59. *See also* Cooperative societies

Cultural differences: as basis for ethnic grouping, 2–3, 148–152; in Sai Kung, 90–117. *See also* Chinese; Ethnic groups

Cultural Revolution (1967), effects of, 34, 120–121, 125–126, 129–130, 132. *See also* China, People's Republic of

Decorated straps, 150. *See also* Patterned bands

D'Estrey, Comte Meyners, 10, 11

District office. *See* Government of Hong Kong

Double Five (Dragon Boat Festival), 97, 99, 130

Double Ten (October 10), 79, 144. *See also* Kuomintang

Dragon Boat Festival. *See* Double Five

East River (Anti-Japanese) Brigade, 31–32, 117n6, 125

Eberhard, Wolfram, 67, 106

Educational levels of ethnic groups in Sai Kung, 46n5. *See also* Schools

Elder and Younger Sister Association, 58, 97

Employment. *See* Wage Labor

Ethnic groups: boundaries of, 3, 15, 83, 111, 136, 148, 152–153; categories of, 4, 72, 152, 153; communities of, 4, 25, 142, 152, 153; corporate groups of, 4–5, 142, 145–146, 152–155; criteria for, 4, 5, 7–16, 69, 74–75, 152–153; cultural differences of, 3–4, 91–117, 148–152; dress of, 12, 67, 81–82, 104–111, 151; leaders of, 51, 104, 131–132, 151, 153, 154–155; phenotypes of, 2, 55, 67, 106, 116n5; as rhetorics, 5, 49, 87; as roles, 15, 69; social organization of, 3–4, 49–90, 152–156. *See also* Cultural differences; Language; Native place identity; Race; Social organization; Socioeconomic stratification

Federation of Fishermen's Cooperative Societies, 36, 70, 156

Fei Hsiao-Tung, 12

Feng shui, 17n5; and boat people, 13, 17n5; of Chaochow people, 85; used by Hakka, 78

Festivals: community, 99–103; domestic, 97–99, 150; fertility, 98, 99, 150. *See also* Double Five (Dragon Boat Festival); Double Ten; Field Festival; Hung Shing Festival; Hungry Ghost Festival; Kuan Yin Festival; Mid-Autumn Festival

Fictive kinship, 26, 83, 134

Field Festival, 98–99

Firecracker associations, 94–97; and boat people, 26; and Chaochow Association, 139; floral shrines in, 95, 96, 102; government policy toward, 155; local Hakka view of, 96; organizational basis for, 94–95; purposes of, 95–96

Fishermen's Credit Cooperative Society, 36

Fishing techniques and economic stratification, 73, 89n5

Fish Marketing Organization, 36–37

Fish production, 14, 29, 36–38, 41

Footbinding, 51, 121, 124, 150

"Four classes" (of Imperial China): conflicts with socioeconomic stratification, 15, 17n4; and unclassified people, 13

Freedman, Maurice, 8, 30, 47n9, 63, 115n1, 116n2, 145, 148, 150, 152, 154

Fresh Fish Merchant's Association, 36, 156

Fukien. *See* Hokkien boat people

Gaai-seuhng-yahn (C) ("street-borne persons"), 69

Gambling, 16, 41–42, 59, 78, 127. *See also* Mahjong

Genealogies, written, 6n1, 23, 24–25, 67, 153

Government of Hong Kong: and control of Sai Kung associations, 34, 94, 126, 129–131, 140, 152, 155–157; and control of Sai Kung market economy, 35–38, 44; and resistance of Sai Kung people to, 54, 78, 126. *See also* Riots

Great Leap Forward (1958–1960). *See* China, People's Republic of

Hai-lufeng, 11, 48n11, 72, 139, 143, 147n1. *See also* Hokkien boat people; Hokkien immigrants; "Hoklo"; Waichow Hakka; Waichow Hokkien

Hairdressing, 104, 105, 106–107, 117n6. *See also* Ethnic groups, dress of

Hakka language, 8, 111; dialect, 10, 17n3; importance of, 118, 129, 131, 132; infiltrated by Cantonese sounds, 112-113; to validate identity, 145

Hakka people: agricultural adaptation of, 8, 21-22, 54, 150; ancestor rites of, 92-93, 94, 115n1, 119; and Cantonese people, 10, 25, 61, 62-63, 132, 149; Field Festival of, 98-99; genealogies of, 24-25; "global traits" of, 150-151; historical origins of, 2, 8, 10, 16n2, 49-50; and Hokkien people, 10, 25, 77-78, 132; immigrants, 38-39, 60, 71, 118-119, 138; intermarriage, 54, 63-66, 68, 132; marketing strategy of, 136-137, 149; merchant families, 118-119, 126-132; and the Native Fellowship Association, 34; and the Rural Committee, 32; in Sai Kung market, 29, 38, 39, 41, 44, 78, 118; self-image, 2, 50-51, 60-61, 88; settlement in Sai Kung, 21, 22, 24-25; sojourners, 44; stereotypes, 49-51, 137; terms for, 49-50, 62, 67, 88n2. See also Chan Yat-Kuan; Chin Fuk-Loi, Hakka women

Hakka women: agricultural work of, 15, 54, 57; contrasted with non-Hakka women, 51-52; ethnic dress of, 104-105, 106, 107; "Productive labor" of, 56-59; role in village society, 51-59, 150; as sojourners, 54; wage labor of, 15, 43-44, 52

Hang Hau (market), 21

Hats: bowl-shaped, 105, 110-111, 117n8; calico-fringed, 105, 109-110, 116n8, 150-151; conical, 106, 110; to distinguish ethnic groups, 109, 150-151

Harvest Moon, 97. See also Mid-Autumn Festival

Hashimoto, Mantaro J., 10

Hayes, James, 45n1, 45n3, 46n6, 46n7, 46n8, 48n9

Heavenly Things Festival, 98

Ho Chung village, 103; Cantonese leadership in, 31, 47n9, 139-140, 147n2; Cantonese settlement of, 21, 22-23; factories in, 43, 103; Hokkien tenants in, 35, 85, 86, 89n4, 100, 102; marriage network of, 64; ta chiao, sponsored by, 103

Hokkien boat people, 89n4; ancestor rites of, 82; boats of, 74, 76; and Chaochow people, 76-79, 151; devotion to patron saints, 80-82; dress of women, 105-106, 107, 110; ethnic stratification of, 75, 151; fishing techniques and economic

status of, 75, 89n5; and Hakka, 77-78; organization of, 78-79, 89n4; reliance on fictive kinship, 83; settlement in Sai Kung, 73-79; stereotypes of, 80; terms for, 72-73; and Waichow people, 76-77; women, 81-82, 105-106, 107, 115

Hokkien immigrants, 2, 10-11, 72-73, 89n4; terms for, 72-73. See also Chaochow people; Hai-lufeng; Hokkien boat people; Hokkien language; "Hoklo"; Waichow Hakka; Waichow Hokkien

Hokkien language, 2, 10, 11, 113-114

"Hoklo," 72; boat people as, 72, 75-76, 77, 151; Chaochow as, 85-86, 102, 134, 135, 143; Chaochow, term rejected, 73, 76, 139; hat style, 110; Hokkien speakers as, 72, 88, 113-114; Waichow as, 87

Hong Kong. See Government of Hong Kong

Hong Kong Festival, 130-131

Hsin hui (county), 71, 121, 122, 125

Hsu, Francis, 1, 2

Hung Shing Festival, 94-95, 96, 99

Hungry Ghost Festival, 94-95, 96, 97, 99; distinguished from Hakka Field Festival, 98; distinguishes between Chaochow and Waichow, 85, 87, 99-103, 151

Icons. See Ancestor rites, Cantonese boat people; Firecracker associations, floral shrines in

Immigrants, 12; and community festivals, 99; economic influence on Sai Kung, 29, 38-39, 44, 133; and fictive kinship, 83; and firecracker associations, 94-95; local Hakka and Cantonese against, 61, 62-63; political influence of, 32, 34, 48n10, 129; settlement in Sai Kung, 35, 71-72; women, 44. See also Cantonese immigrants; Hakka, immigrants; Hokkien immigrants; Waichow Hokkien people

Imperial Chinese government, 13, 17n6, 30, 47n9

Income: fishing, 70, 89n5; overseas remittances, 42; rent, 38; vegetable farming, 38; wage labor, 43, 55, 80

Independence: of Chaochow Association, 85, 88, 102, 137; of Hakka, 88; local-level concept of, 19, 34, 47n9

Industrial development, Sai Kung, 41, 42-44. See also Urbanization

Japanese occupation: communist-led resistance to, 22, 31, 125; effects on Sai Kung, 14, 26, 30, 124, 127
Jewelry: boat people identified with, 107–109; distinguisher of ethnic groups, 105–106, 117n7; vendors of, 28, 41, 59, 108–109. See also Ethnic groups, dress of
Johnson, Elizabeth, 52, 56, 116n4
Johnson, Graham, 48n10

Kaifong ("neighborhood") Association: elections, 32, 61, 130, 131; firecracker association, 96, 143; leadership of, 128–129, 133, 137, 139–140; local festivals, 99, 102, 130; organization of, 32–34
Kaifong Survey of stores, 38–42
Ka-siu-lao (H) ("house-floating fellows"), 69
Kau Sai (Island): fishermen's cooperative societies at, 36; Hung Shing temple festival of, 94–95, 96
Kinship ties, 26, 44. See also Affinal relations; Agnatic relations; Fictive kinship; Matrilateral relations
Kowloon. See Kowloon Walled City; Sai Kung Market, trade with Kowloon
Kowloon Walled City, 30, 41, 47n9, 121
Kuan Kung (temple deity), 47n8
Kuan Yin Festival, 95, 99
Kuomintang (Nationalist Party): against the East River Brigade, 32, 125; in Sai Kung, 71, 79, 129, 139, 144, 147n2, 156. See also Sun Yat-Sen Memorial Association

Labor. See Occupations; Rice cultivation; Vegetable farming; Wage labor
Language: attitudes toward, 7–8; bilingual competence and leadership, 154–155; ethnic group distinguished by, 5, 7–11, 111–114; Imperial attitude toward, 12–13. See also Cantonese language; Chaochow, dialects of; Hakka language; Hokkien language; "Hoklo"; Speech groups; "Tanka"; Waichow Hakka; Waichow Hokkien
Leach, Edmund, 3, 104
Lehman, F. K., 3, 114
Li Hung-Fuk: immigrant in Sai Kung, 134–135; leader of Chaochow Association, 140, 141, 142, 146, 147n3; relations with Hakka, 132, 134, 146, 147n3; spokesman for Chaochow identity, 84, 89n4, 143

Lineage organization: compounds, 45n4; and marriage networks, 63; in Sai Kung, 23–24, 93, 126–127; studies of, 8. See also Ancestor halls; Genealogies
Liu Yüeh (Six-way Alliance), 47n9
Lo Hsiang-Lin, 16n2, 45n3, 50
Loewen, James, 136
Lufeng. See Hai-lufeng
Lung Shuen Wan (Island): fishermen's cooperative societies at, 36; Tin Hau Temple of, 46n8, 95, 97

Mahjong, 39, 58, 144. See also Gambling
Marriage: Cantonese and Hakka, 63–66, 121, 128; Cantonese and Waichow, 87; distance, 63; and ethnic affiliation, 3, 54, 63, 66, 132; Hakka and Chaochow, 144–145; land and boat people, 63, 68, 120, 124; networks, 64, 65
Matrilateral relations, 25, 63
Meihsien (county), 8, 11
Mid-Autumn Festival, 77, 142. See also Harvest Moon
Min (ethnic group), 10, 16n1

Native Fellowship Association (of Sai Kung): Chaochow memberships in, 61, 130, 133, 146; factionalism in, 34, 61, 128, 129, 131; founding of, 34; local identity, 61, 137, 156. See also Rural Committee, and Native Fellowship Association
Native place identity: as basis for ethnic grouping, 7, 11–12, 16, 60, 153; boat people's lack of, 67, 72; and Hokkien immigrants, 72–73, 89n4; of recent immigrants, 71; Sai Kung villagers, incorporation of, 61
New Territories, 29, 30–31
New Territories Congress of Rural Committee Chairmen, 45n3. See also Rural Consultative Council
New Year celebration, 38, 97
Nichiren sect (Japanese Buddhism), 80–81

Occupations: and differences in men's dress, 104; and ethnic grouping, 12–16, 69, 74–75, 77, 152–153; and firecracker associations, 94; as indicator of social status, 13–16; and phenotype, 106
October First, 79, 144
Opium, 22, 41
Paiyüeh. See Yüeh (ethnic group)
Pak Kong (village): Cantonese settlement of, 21, 22, 23; immigrant tenants in, 35,

89n4; *ta chiao* site, 103; Tin Hau temple, 47n8
Pao chia, 48n9
Paper shops, 40, 119
Pasternak, Burton, 115n1, 116n1, 149
Patterned bands, 105, 116n4. *See also* Decorated straps
Phenotypes. *See* Ethnic groups, phenotypes of
Piton, Charles, 2, 51, 115n1, 117n6
Police: during riots (of 1967), 126, 129; and government surveillance of associations, 33 (chart), 156; increased personal security in Sai Kung, 22, 45n4, 53
Population (of Sai Kung), 32; of boat people, 26, 35, 46n5, 68–69, 70; of immigrants, 35, 38–39, 71–72, 84, 86, 89n4; of local land people, 21, 22–23, 28, 35, 38–39, 45n2, 46n5; of Sai Kung sojourners, 43
Pork, production of, 35, 36, 41, 54
Potatoes, production of, 10, 21, 43, 57
Pratt, Jean, 52, 57, 63
Procommunist organizations, 33, 112, 156. *See also* Communist elements
Public Security Advancement Association, 33, 129, 141, 146
"Punti" ("local folk"), 12, 60, 61–62, 85, 98; boat people as, 61, 74–75; Hakka as, 60–61; hat style, 110; immigrants as, 71. *See also* Cantonese people

Race, 2, 7, 106. *See also* Ethnic groups, phenotypes of
Refugee aid and political factions, 77, 79, 139, 147n2
Remittances, overseas, 30, 42–43, 47n8, 57. *See also* Sojourning
Rice cultivation: Cantonese and Hakka compared, 8, 21–22; compared to vegetable farming, 16, 54–55; and conflict between Sai Kung and Tai Po Cantonese, 29, 30; and fertility rites, 98; and Hakka women, 57–58; and lack of water, 19–20, 54, 55; relative status of, 15; and size of village population, 45n2; by village women, 43, 54–55, 57. *See also* Water supply
Rice supply: conflict between Japanese and East River Brigade, 31, 124; importation of, 35; and political factions, 79
Riots (of 1967): causes of, 54, 126; effects on boat population, 14, 26; effects on local associations, 59, 129, 140; government responses to, 129, 130, 140
Rural (Affairs) Committee: boat people

and, 71, 77, 86; elective office in, 61–62; establishment of, 32, 33, 125; function of, 47n9; Hakka-Cantonese rivalry in, 32, 34, 139–140, 147n2; Hakka control of, 130; leadership of, 128, 129, 131, 139–141, 147n2; and Native Fellowship Association, 34, 128, 129, 131, 142, 156; reconstitution, 129–130, 131; transformed into Struggle Committee, 33, 129, 140, 156
Rural Consultative Council, 33. *See also* New Territories Congress of Rural Committee Chairmen

"Sa," 62–63, 111, 113
Sai Kung market: changing ethnic composition of, 28, 35, 38–39, 44, 68, 71–72, 89n4, 118; emergence of, 35–38; organization of, 35–38; shops in, 28, 38–42, 133; as sociocultural system, 3, 4, 19, 25, 35, 46n8, 63, 111, 150–151; trade with Hong Kong Island, 3, 21, 26–27; trade with Kowloon, 28, 29, 34, 41, 43, 47n9, 52, 84; trade with Paoan (China), 27, 28, 29, 38, 40, 109, 118, 127; untraditional periodic market, 29, 46n7; versus Tai Po market, 28–29, 110, 116n4, 150–151
Sai Kung Native Place Association. *See* Native Fellowship Association (of Sai Kung)
Schools: for children of boat people, 36; ethnic interaction in, 113; taught in Cantonese, 66, 112, 113. *See also* Educational levels of ethnic groups in Sai Kung
Schurman, Franz, 45n1
Secret society, 29, 31, 41–42, 59, 129, 144
Self-Administration Association (of Sai Kung), 31, 32
Seui-seuhng-yahn (C) ("water-borne persons"), 69–70, 73–74
Sha Kok Mei (village): Cantonese settlement in, 21, 22; and firecracker association, 96–97; immigrants in, 24, 35, 84, 89n4; lack of *ta chiao,* 103; landholding compared to Hakka village, 21–22; marriage network of, 63–66, 64; temple patronage of, 47n8, 97
Skinner, G. William, 19, 46n7, 63, 155
Social organization, 152; ethnic groupings as, 3–5, 152–157
Socioeconomic stratification: of Cantonese boat people and land people, 70; within Cantonese boat community, 38, 68, 74, 90n5; of Cantonese and Hok-

kien boat people, 74–75, 79; of Chaochow and Hokkien boat people, 115, 151; of Chaochow and Waichow, 77, 87; distinguished by dress, 104; distinguished by phenotype, 67, 106; and ethnic grouping, 61, 151; and hypergamy, 63, 65, 68, 132; relation to self-image, 88; within Sai Kung lineage organizations, 92

Sojourning: effects on village women, 53–54, 57–58; immigrants, take advantage of, 44, 133; organization of, 41, 128; means of livelihood, 27, 29–30, 41, 42–43. See also Remittances

Speech group: and Hokkien boat people's identity, 72; and nature of Hakka identity, 10. See also Language

"Spirit Place," 101; of Chaochow Association, 100, 102, 139; of Hokkien boat people and Chaochow, 115

Stereotypes: changes in, 50, 68–71, 88; as a function of social organization, 49, 51, 67, 85–88, 137

Struggle Committee (of Sai Kung), 33, 34, 129

Sun Yat-Sen Memorial Association (of Sai Kung), 33, 71, 128, 156

Surname: and ancestor tablets, 92, 93, 94, 116n2; and Chinese identity, 2, 91, 153; firecracker association, based on, 94; Hokkien boat people's community, organized on the basis of, 72, 89n4

Ta chiao ("rite of cosmic renewal"), analyzed, 99, 100, 103

Tai Mong Tsai (village): ancestor halls of, 93; immigrants in, 89n4; landholdings, 21; marriage network of, 63–65, 65; settlement of, 24

Tai Po market: dominated by Cantonese, 23; and Hokkien boat people, 78, 82, 89n4. See also Sai Kung market, versus Tai Po market; Tang lineage

Tan ("egg"), 17n6. See also "Tanka"

Tang lineage (of Tai Po market), 30, 45n3, 47n9

"Tanka" ("egg folk"): derogatory meaning of, 2, 66–67; hat style of, 111; term for boat people, 69, 73, 74, 106

Temple tablets, 28. See also Tin Hau Temple

Teochiu. See Chaochow people

Tin Hau Temple, 46n8, 97; as center for Hakka identity, 25; Chan Yat-Kuan's management of, 126; Hokkien boat people's devotion to, 81, 83; reconstruc-

tion of, 30, 46n8, 126; temple tablets as social registry, 68, 118, 120, 121. See also Temple tablets

Tin Hau Temple feast days: celebrated at different temples, 97, 99; celebrated by firecracker associations, 95; Chaochow participation in, 102, 115, 139; and Chin Fuk-Loi's management of, 130; secret society participation in, 59

Tou chung (measure of rice paddy land), xix

Truck farming. See Vegetable farming

Tsuen Wan (township), compared to Sai Kung, 48n10, 52, 56

Tsung Tsin Association (Ch'ung Cheng Association), 45n3, 50

Urbanization: agricultural water supply affected, 20; ancestor rites affected, 93–94; Chaochow identified with, 84, 141; and employment opportunities, 29, 42; and ethnic group organization, 3, 4, 152; and local Hakka opposition, 78; sense of time affected by, 107–108. See also Industrial development, Sai Kung

Vegetable farming: compared to rice cultivation, 15–16, 55; as livelihood, 15, 54; relative status of, 15–16

Vegetable marketing, in Sai Kung, 40, 41, 144, 145

Village representatives, 15, 32, 58

Villagers, status of, 15

Villages: Hakka and Cantonese compared, 45n4; as social units, 19, 25, 153

Wage labor: conscripted by Japanese, 31; construction, 30, 43–44; cottage industry, 29, 43; urban and overseas, 29, 31, 42–43. See also Hakka women, wage labor of

Waichow Hakka: and East River Brigade, 31; native place of, 11, 147n1; in Sai Kung society, an ethnic category, 71, 118; and Sun Yat-Sen Memorial Association, 71; women's hat identification, 109, 151

Waichow Hokkien people, 11, 89n4, 146n1; Chaochow people affinities with, 86, 114; Chaochow people conflict with, 86, 139, 145; distinguished from related groups, 72–73, 85; Fellowship Association of, 77, 89n4, 138; and Hokkien boat people, 77, 79; Hungry Ghost Festival, 99, 100, 102, 115; native place of, 11, 146n1; settlement in Sai

Kung, 39, 86–87. *See also* Hai-lufeng;
  Hokkien immigrants; "Hoklo";
  Immigrants
Ward, Barbara, 2, 14, 38, 69, 90n5, 93,
  116n5
Water supply: land classification based
  on, 21; and land use, 19–21, 44; and
  local protests against government, 54.
  See also Rice cultivation
"Water-borne person" *(seui-seuhng-
  yahn)*, 61
Watson, James L., 8, 53, 127, 128
Willmott, W. E., 155
Wolf, Margery, 51, 56, 57, 88n1

Women: dialects preserved by, 112, 113;
  ethnic dress of, 12, 104–111; ethnic
  group culture expressed, 115, 117n6,
  151; and husband's ethnic claims, 132;
  labor of, 36, 41, 42, 43–44, 54, 55–56;
  organization of, 36, 58–59, 97

Yang, C. K., 8, 14, 16, 45n2, 51
Yang, Paul, 17n3
Yao (ethnic group), 13, 17n6
Yent'ien commune, 38
Young, John, 83
Yüeh (alliance), 30, 47n9
Yüeh (ethnic group), 8, 16n1, 67

Index preparation by Carol E. Bandre, Linda S. Barb, Martha Chantiny, Sri H. Dahana, Patti Lei Hironaka, Ruth H. Horie, Ann E. Jacobs, Robert Kajiwara, Kat Kan, Terese Leber, Jean O'Brien Lowery, G. F. Lukos, and Miriam M. Takahashi, with special thanks to Professor Sarah K. Vann of the Graduate School of Library Studies, University of Hawaii at Manoa.

Fred Blake, Assistant Professor of Anthropology at the University of Hawaii, has served as a Peace Corps Volunteer in the U.S. Trust Territory of the Pacific and has lived in rural Hong Kong where he conducted his dissertation fieldwork.

Generally his research endeavors toward the study of how people identify their interests and create values in the formation and dissolution of social groupings.

He received an M.A. from Washington University at St. Louis and his Ph.D. from the University of Illinois at Champaign-Urbana. Currently his research focuses on family interaction among the Americans of Chinese descent.

Asian Studies at Hawaii

No. 1   *Bibliography of English Language Sources on Human Ecology, Eastern Malaysia and Brunei.* Compiled by Conrad P. Cotter with the assistance of Shiro Saito. September 1965. Two parts. (Available only from Paragon Book Gallery, New York.)

No. 2   *Economic Factors in Southeast Asian Social Change.* Edited by Robert Van Niel. May 1968. Out of print.

No. 3   *East Asian Occasional Papers (1).* Edited by Harry J. Lamley. May 1969.

No. 4   *East Asian Occasional Papers (2).* Edited by Harry J. Lamley. July 1970.

No. 5   *A Survey of Historical Source Materials in Java and Manila.* Robert Van Niel. February 1971.

No. 6   *Educational Theory in the People's Republic of China: The Report of Ch'ien Chung-Jui.* Translated by John N. Hawkins. May 1971. Out of print.

No. 7   *Hai Jui Dismissed from Office.* Wu Han. Translated by C. C. Huang. June 1972.

No. 8   *Aspects of Vietnamese History.* Edited by Walter F. Vella. March 1973.

No. 9   *Southeast Asian Literatures in Translation: A Preliminary Bibliography.* Philip N. Jenner. March 1973.

No. 10   *Textiles of the Indonesian Archipelago.* Garrett and Bronwen Solyom. October 1973. Out of print.

No. 11   *British Policy and the Nationalist Movement in Burma, 1917–1937.* Albert D. Moscotti. February 1974.

No. 12   *Aspects of Bengali History and Society.* Edited by Rachel Van M. Baumer. December 1975.

No. 13   *Nanyang Perspective: Chinese Students in Multiracial Singapore.* Andrew W. Lind. June 1974.

No. 14   *Political Change in the Philippines: Studies of Local Politics preceding Martial Law.* Edited by Benedict J. Kerkvliet. November 1974.

No. 15   *Essays on South India.* Edited by Burton Stein. February 1976.

No. 16   *The* Caurāsī Pad *of Śrī Hit Harivaṁś.* Charles S. J. White. 1977.

No. 17   *An American Teacher in Early Meiji Japan.* Edward R. Beauchamp. June 1976.

No. 18   *Buddhist and Taoist Studies I.* Edited by Michael Saso and David W. Chappell. 1977.

No. 19   *Sumatran Contributions to the Development of Indonesian Literature, 1920–1942.* Alberta Joy Freidus. 1977.

No. 20   *Insulinde: Selected Translations from Dutch Writers of Three Centuries on the Indonesian Archipelago.* Edited by Cornelia N. Moore, 1978.

No. 21   *Regents, Reformers, and Revolutionaries: Indonesian Voices of Colonial Days, Selected Historical Readings, 1899–1949.* Translated, edited, and annotated by Greta O. Wilson, 1978.

No. 22   *The Politics of Inequality: Competition and Control in an Indian Village.* Miriam Sharma. October 1978.

No. 23   *Brokers of Morality: Thai Ethnic Adaptation in a Rural Malaysian Setting.* Louis Golomb. February 1979.

No. 24   *Tales of Japanese Justice.* Ihara Saikaku. Translated by Thomas M. Kondo and Alfred H. Marks. January 1980.

No. 25   *Mandarins, Gunboats, and Power Politics: Owen Nickerson Denny and the International Rivalries in Korea.* Robert R. Swartout, Jr. March 1980.

No. 26   *Nichiren: Selected Writings.* Laurel Rasplica Rodd. 1980.

No. 27   *Ethnic Groups and Social Change in a Chinese Market Town.* C. Fred Blake. 1980.

Orders for Asian Studies at Hawaii publications should be directed to The University Press of Hawaii, 2840 Kolowalu Street, Honolulu, Hawaii 96822. Present standing orders will continue to be filled without special notification.

DATE DUE

GAYLORD			PRINTED IN U.S.A.